Current practices in software development

A guide to successful systems

by DAVID KING

foreword by David Katch

YOURDON PRESS

Current practices in software development

A guide to successful systems

Current practices in software development

A guide to successful systems

by DAVID KING

foreword by David Katch

Yourdon Press
1501 Broadway
New York, New York 10036

Library of Congress Cataloging in Publication Data

King, David, 1940-
Current practices in software development.

Bibliography; p.
Includes index.
1. Programming (Electronic computers) 2. System design. 3. Software maintenance. I. Title.
QA76.6.K565 1984 001.64'2 83-27401
ISBN 0-917072-29-4

Printed in the United States of America

Library of Congress Catalog Number 83-27401

ISBN: 0-917072-29-4

This book was set in Times Roman by YOURDON Press, 1501 Broadway
New York, N.Y., using a PDP-11/70 running under the UNIX® operating system.*

---

*UNIX is a registered trademark of Bell Laboratories.

Dedication

First and foremost, I dedicate this book to my wife, Roslyn, partly for her forbearance through years of my saying, "I must write a book on that subject!" and then for her endurance, with love and understanding, as I gave birth to this volume.

Also, I dedicate this book to all my colleagues, past and present, who have given me inspiration for the many ideas contained within these pages. They know who they are in these organizations: IBM United Kingdom, Elliott Automation, Simpact Systems, and Security Pacific National Bank.

More recently, I feel obliged with pleasure to thank the staff members of Yourdon Press for their great assistance, advice, and coercion. They helped greatly to shape my early, less organized draft into its current, structured shape.

Contents

Preface

I believe that I first became curious about computers in the early 1950s when I was reading a short, bad science fiction novel. In this long-forgotten text, the mysterious mechanical marvel of the computer, speaking with the simulated voice of Bing Crosby, was the semi-deity of a future civilization. The hero of the story, as part of a common theme, destroyed the electronic dictator by asking it illogical questions, which caused its vacuum tubes to become incandescent and the machine itself to finally explode in a series of pyrotechnic death-throes.

So, this was my introduction to the world of computers and data processing. In the intervening three decades, computers have changed dramatically. Except for a few military installations, vacuum tubes are very difficult to locate, and an overloaded computer behaves very much like a computer that is switched off. These days, it tends to be the programmers who behave pyrotechnically when the computer is overloaded. Although computer components are drastically different, the public perception of the now ubiquitous computer has not really changed a great deal from those early days.

After graduating with a degree in electronic engineering, I started to practice my chosen profession. Designing circuits and soldering transistors together in push-pull configurations to form flip-flop control amplifiers became my life for a while. In those days, we engineers did not just design our circuits, we built them, laborious component by laborious connection.

As I produced my own engineering reports of the design processes involved and of the performance of those electronic marvels, I began to realize that documentation was a problem in the industry. Quite what an understatement that was I was to realize years later. Rapidly, I perceived (I *was* quick when I was young!) that my interest in and aptitude for technical documentation was unusual for an engineer. So I became a sort of engineering free agent and moved rapidly into the new profession of engineering technical writing. Even more rapidly, I perceived that while engineers only *resisted* documenting their work, computer professionals considered documentation to be the responsibility of some lower subspecies of life with which they, the programmers, really did not need to communicate. Clearly, my early career path was set.

For several years, I wrote all levels of documentation, from publicity brochures to design descriptions, for many and various computer-based commercial and military systems. I recognized that my technical author colleagues and I often ended up being more conversant with the hardware and software than were the original designers and the current maintainers. In fact, many times we were ourselves intimately involved with the original design activities as technical advisers to the design team.

As a result of managing the total creation and production of the hardware and software documentation for a major European airline's computerized reservation system, I became a teleprocessing specialist with the great god IBM in England. I soon progressed from the position of applications programmer to senior systems analyst. Several projects and countries later, I realized that even within the white-hot, technologically revolutionary design laboratories of Big Blue, the software development life cycle in use at that time needed to evolve further before reaching a satisfactory steady state. Having since left those hallowed halls, I've found that the overall software development process industry-wide is definitely in need of some radical surgery.

The data processing profession already has experienced enormous changes in its short life, but the growth in DP applications over the last three decades will seem like a snail's pace compared with the meteoric growth that has just started. The data processing industry is genuinely at a major decision point. DP system development in the commercial world seems poised between a research-oriented academic pursuit and a rigorous, well-defined engineering discipline. Both must coexist in order for the DP profession to survive and mature. As we move into the Information Age, it becomes extremely important to take a good look at DP's current position. Only by learning from past mistakes and successes can we ensure that this Information Age breeds a profession that not only survives but commands respect as well.

I believe that this profession will survive, and I also believe that right now it is at least as exciting as it was when then Lieutenant Grace Hopper discovered that first real "bug." Many techniques and tools are now available to enable DP professionals to improve their productivity and the quality of their products by several orders of magnitude. These include top-down development, structured design and programming, prototyping, and application generators, among others, all described in this book. Are we going to take advantage of some of the new ways of rapidly developing maintenance-free systems that are now available or are we going to merely support the systems that are already installed? An optimist, I believe that the data processing profession has shown that new opportunities can be exploited to their fullest extent. By applying engineering disciplines and well-organized procedural concepts to the DP profession, the rewards promised by the computer revolution can be achieved. This book presents an overview of how systems can be developed in organizations today. It does not attempt to provide a detailed blow-by-blow account of how to use any of the esoteric system analysis, design, and development methodologies that are currently being presented as panaceas for all of data processing's ills. But what it does present is a distillation of my more than twenty years' experience with DP systems.

This book is my attempt to summarize, categorize, and suggest some currently available practices, tools, and techniques that if applied in a coordinated and integrated fashion throughout the system development life cycle, could revolutionize the way that systems are developed and implemented. This revolution could not only improve the standards within and improve the external image of the DP profession, but could position the DP industry to provide a massive boost to our national and international productivity and help provide a better future for all of us. This is an objective worth striving for.

December 1983 D.K.
La Canada, California

Foreword

Over the past fifteen years, the field of software application development has progressed very slowly, but steadily, from an art form to a semidisciplined approach. This approach embraces the notion that one can build consistently better systems using a phased system life cycle for development. Concurrent with this progression has been a shift in DP budgets from mostly hardware to mostly people costs. As a result, many installation managers have been forced to embrace the system life cycle as a basis for more effective utilization of their development resources. This same shift in budgetary expenditures has also provided an impetus for discovering new and better methods and techniques that can be utilized within each phase, for finding more cost-effective and less time-consuming life cycles, and for achieving greater degrees of development automation. And, it is the very high and ever-increasing cost of system development that has given rise to a multibillion dollar industry in application packages. Even though there now is a choice in many instances to build or buy a system, the need to build one's own system will continue.

Today's computer age has brought with it a plethora of books and publications, far more than any of us are capable of scanning, leave alone reading and absorbing. While some of them are worthy of shelf space, many others are merely rehashes of outdated methods. Many authors push their own causes and solutions, albeit some of them are very deserving of one's consideration. Unfortunately, only a few provide a proper perspective for management action. But just as there is no universal medication for the many illnesses in our world, there is no one way to do it right in DP application development. Any DP manager who wishes to do it right must first understand the proper framework that will get him there. Only then can one begin to select properly from the available set of choices. *Current Practices in Software Development* provides such a framework. David King offers an excellent perspective on a proper development framework and on the tools and techniques currently in widespread use (as well as to those emerging on the horizon) to cope with the current state-of-the-art in DP technology and future directions.

To build a house, one first requires a proper foundation, if it is not to crumble and collapse over time. To build software applications or even purchase those built by others, it must be done with a proper foundation in place, one that will support the structure placed upon it. As someone who has developed a system life cycle methodology, I have been able to strengthen my own framework of understanding through David King's perspective. I expect that many managers will find it as informative as I did.

August 1983
Atherton, California

David Katch
Author, SDM/70

Current practices in software development

A guide to successful systems

1

Introduction

If you can keep your head whilst all those around you are losing theirs, you don't really understand the problem.

— with apologies to Rudyard Kipling

1.1 A framework for development

From the early days of data processing in the 1960s until today, countless tools and techniques have been offered as *the* way to develop maintenance-free DP systems. Unfortunately, as it turned out, many of the so-called improved tools and techniques have been used to develop systems that have consumed more and more of organizations' DP resources to maintain. Why has this happened? The reasons are discussed below, but perhaps the key reason is the lack of a proper framework to unify and control when and how each system development technique is applied.

The system development life cycle (SDLC) is an excellent example of such a framework, and it has received a great deal of attention in recent years. Unfortunately, in many organizations, the SDLC is just another set of initials bandied about to describe a process that is often not clearly understood. Quite simply, an SDLC offers a way for DP and user management to monitor, control, and understand what is going on during that vast, unexplored period of system development beginning with the first glint in a user's eye and culminating with the final triumphant installation of the new, all singing, all dancing SYSTEM.

Developing a large data processing system is not a simple activity, as it consists of many subtasks that are complex in themselves, with many dependencies forcing linear and nonlinear relationships between them. And so the theme of all SDLCs is generally the same: Subdivide the development process into a series of smaller, simpler tasks.

Although the number of detailed activities required in the SDLC varies from one SDLC to another, they all share certain characteristics. The standard SDLC assumes a series of sequential phases or stages. Each stage produces a documentary end product that provides the starting point for the next stage. This concept is a giant leap forward from the traditional "mongolian horde" style of system development, in which all of the available resources are devoted immediately in a mad scramble to get the system installed as quickly as possible.

Although many data processing organizations still do not use an SDLC, the number that do subscribe to one is growing rapidly, even exponentially as the successful experiences with SDLCs increase. The increase in use stems from two major benefits provided to system developers. First, it gives management much needed control over DP projects by making estimation possible. How often have we been guilty of saying that the system is "ninety percent finished" again and again at widely different times? The SDLC allows management to make reasonably accurate and consistent estimates of the total effort for final system implementation at the start of development and to revise the estimates throughout the life cycle.

The second benefit of the SDLC is that it allows system developers to overcome a major challenge — namely, to deal with large, highly complex systems. Many computerized systems today are far too complex for any one human mind to comprehend fully. Therefore, it is clearly impractical to try to develop and implement such systems in one fell swoop. The major objective of the SDLC is to break down the complete system life cycle into "chunks." Hence, by applying this divide-and-conquer strategy, we realize that this enormous activity becomes manageable.

1.2 Purpose of this book

My goal in this book is to recommend a practical system development life cycle and specific techniques, both structured and otherwise, that support the life cycle. To prepare for the discussion of the SDLC, I trace in Chapter 2 the origins of the structured techniques and review the work of the pioneers in the field. Chapters 3 and 4 discuss the various techniques involved in designing and implementing today's computer systems. Clearly, some set of standard procedures is desirable to help control system development, but the set must be flexible enough for the highly variable needs of different systems and different development techniques. I compare the two main structured design approaches — functional decomposition and data structured design — and suggest a set of design methods that are flexible enough to be applicable across several SDLC stages. Chapter 4 presents the rules for coding the structured designs and discusses the use of the infamous GOTO.

With that background, Chapter 5 traces the SDLC's evolution and suggests commercially available SDLC packages. This chapter also recommends seven basic stages of the life cycle. Chapters 6 through 12 then explore in detail the activities of the SDLC, with sections on objectives, people involved, tools and techniques, and documentation for each stage. The related topics of management structures, chief programming teams, egoless programming, project libraries, and walkthroughs are discussed in Chapters 13, 14, and 15, in terms of enhancing the SDLC's effectiveness.

Chapter 16 considers the changes required to this basic SDLC to meet future needs. In organizations that use state-of-the-art techniques (such as interactive development tools, application generators, and prototyping), this set of stages is regarded as the traditional SDLC and as not being flexible enough to handle today's sophisticated development techniques. Sadly, however, most DP organizations have not yet successfully installed even this so-called traditional SDLC, and they continue to find their way through the system development jungle by seat-of-the-pants navigation.

Finally, Chapter 17 considers how the various DP professions will change in the future. A practical selection of the currently available structured techniques is listed in the Appendices, and the Bibliography provides additional sources of information.

1.3 The current DP situation

Before I begin to describe a greatly optimized system development process, I need first to explain how the current far-from-optimal processes evolved and why they continue to be used. As stated above, organizations are increasingly devoting most of their DP resources to maintaining existing systems. This section discusses some of the reasons for this increase and why it is so important.

For the purposes of this text, I define program and system maintenance to include all those changes made to a program or system after it has been installed. Of course, this means that all corrections and enhancements, whether user-oriented or market-driven, must be included under the name of maintenance. Additionally, in our increasingly regulated society, changes required by state and federal regulations must be given space under the maintenance umbrella. Because of the vast plethora of maintenance tasks, many organizations today prefer the term production support. This, of course, sounds better than maintenance. After all, who wants to be known as a maintenance programmer?

If we apply the above definition of maintenance to real situations, we see that many large DP organizations are expending more than seventy-five percent of their people resources on this type of work. As a result, the backlog of new programs and systems required grows year by year and the end users become more and more dissatisfied with the speed of service from the DP development group.

Let's take a hypothetical case to illustrate how this can happen. The Acme Road Runner Traps, Inc., decides to computerize all of its operations. It hires two hot-shot programmers and sets a production schedule of two new systems per year. Each system requires one programmer for one year to develop it, and one-quarter of a programmer forever after to maintain it. After the first year, two new systems have been developed, and for the second year, one-half of one programmer will be required to maintain the two new systems. Now, management has a choice: It can hire one more programmer to maintain the new systems, or it can reduce the new development resources by one-half of a programmer and wait until four systems are developed before hiring the additional programmer. In real life, the latter course is usually chosen. If we analyze this policy over a few years, the results presented in Table 1-1 emerge.

In Table 1-1, the percentage of required maintenance effort grows to seventy percent of the development effort in a ten-year period. The graph in Figure 1-1 illustrates the point even more dramatically. These figures are somewhat simplistic, but they are based on my direct and observed experience with both large and small DP projects over a twenty-year period. However, real-life situations can be much worse.

Table 1-1
The Ten-Year Development-to-Maintenance Ratio

By the End of	Year 1	Year 2	Year 3	Year 4	Year 5	Year 6	Year 7	Year 8	Year 9	Year 10
Total New Systems	2.0	3.5	4.75	6.75	8.25	10.25	11.75	13.00	14.75	16.25
New System Development Staff	2.0	1.5	1.25	2.0	1.5	2.0	1.5	1.25	1.75	1.5
Maintenance Staff	0.0	0.5	0.75	1.0	1.5	2.0	2.5	2.75	3.25	3.5
Total DP Staff	2.0	2.0	2.0	3.0	3.0	4.0	4.0	4.0	5.0	5.0
Maintenance Percentage of Total	0.0	25.0	37.5	33.0	50.0	50.0	62.5	68.75	65.0	70.0

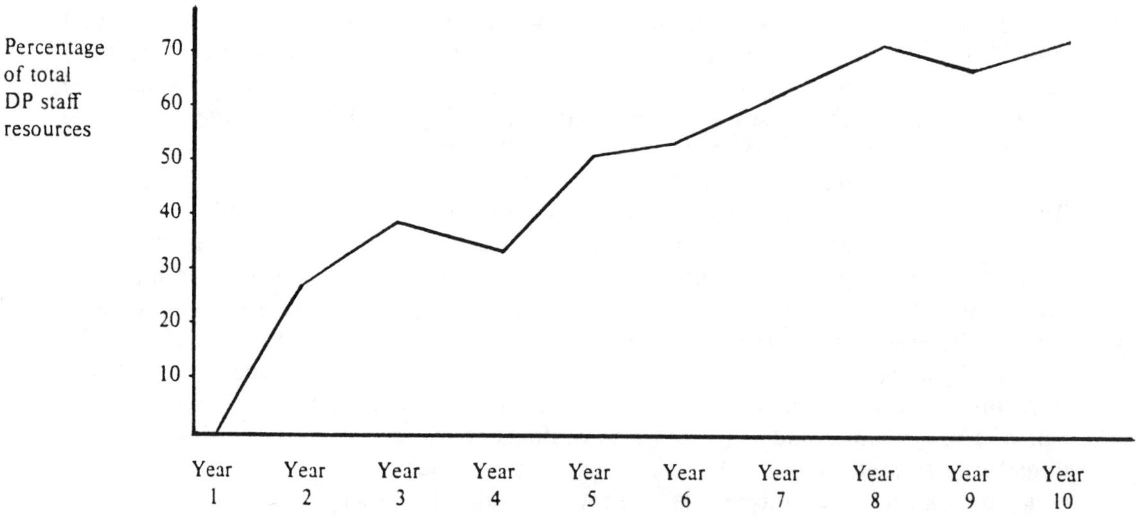

Figure 1-1. Growth of maintenance effort as a percentage of the total DP staff resources available.

As our world becomes increasingly automated and as demands for new systems increase, we DP professionals will have to make a decision. Either we will have to accept the current situation, with maintenance requirements eventually reaching one hundred percent of the available resources, or we must find a radically new way of developing maintenance-free systems. If we choose the second option, we first must understand the reasons for our maintenance-ridden systems.

Why do so many systems require so much maintenance? There is no one answer, but the following four factors certainly have an effect: premature installation of systems, lack of user involvement in system development, inconsistent design practices, and absence of documentation. These factors are discussed in the following subsections.

1.3.1 Premature installation of systems

One valid criticism is that we in data processing often put our prototypes into production. Our business makes it easy for us to do that, since there are no *apparent* differences between the product developed in the test environment and the product put into production. However, appearances can be deceiving, because substantial changes are still usually needed to the product following testing before a prototype is ready for full-scale production. Typically, performance tolerances must be widened, recovery procedures added, and many other practical additions made. These changes to the system thus result in additional maintenance costs.

1.3.2 Lack of user involvement in system development

A second reason for the ever-increasing maintenance costs is the lack of communication between users and data processing professionals. This results from excluding users from the system development process. A claim that is often made by otherwise intelligent DP experts is that the users don't know what they want. Few statements can be guaranteed to raise quite so much anger. As the end users are usually paying for the system in terms of development, operational, and maintenance costs, it is ludicrous for the DP staff to maintain that these same users are not aware of their own needs. The users may well need assistance to express these needs in data processing terms, but it is the responsibility of the *true* DP professional to educate users about the power of the computer. A simple one-for-one translation of manual tasks directly into computer programs is seldom the most effective way to automate a system. Only an ongoing dialogue between the system developers and the system users will ensure an effective system design and implementation.

The lack of communication between user and developer is not solely the fault of data processing people, however. Many system users behave in an arrogant and noncommunicative fashion and make unrealistic demands on the DP development group. In addition, the users often cut off the communication lines at the end of the Requirements Definition phase of development. Then, at installation time, the users receive a system that may be a complete surprise in terms of its performance, accuracy, quality, or other factors.

Figure 1-2 shows the classic situation in which the users and DP professionals often behave as if they live in separate buildings, even if they do not. Little communication occurs until the finished system is available. Then, it is as if the system is mailed to the user through some remote and impersonal transmittal service, like the U.S. Post Office.

From the maintenance percentages in Table 1-1, we realize that the user and the system developer have no choice but to communicate with each other *throughout* the life cycle of the developing product, as I recommend throughout this book. Specifically, in Chapters 5 and 13, I offer suggestions for management and team structures that guarantee user involvement, if not control, of the process. Then the result is, as the well-known motel chain says, "No surprises!" and the usual stream of user-requested changes received immediately after implementation is avoided, thus reducing the maintenance burden.

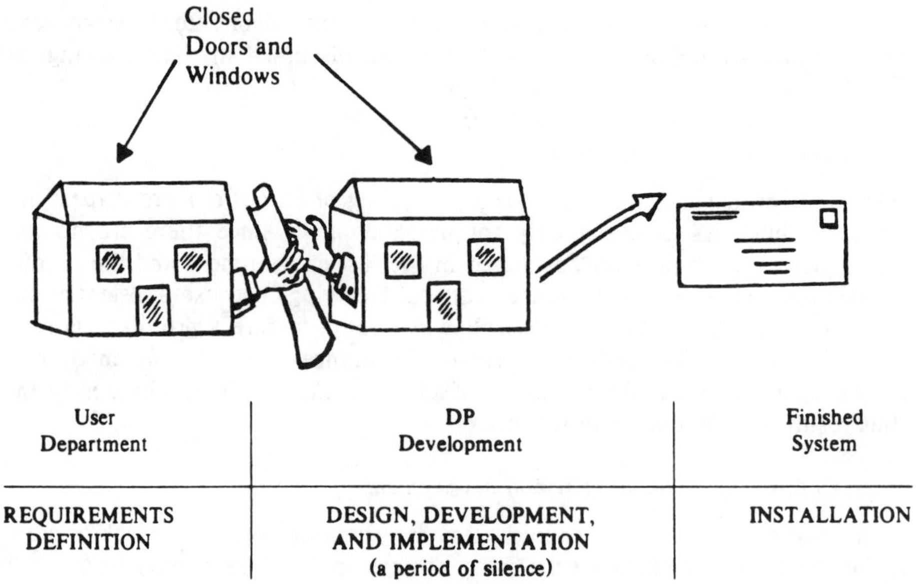

Figure 1-2. The hand-off from the users to data processing during system development.

1.3.3 Inconsistent design practices

Software design is probably the only engineering discipline that has such a vast array of different techniques and tools for doing the same job. Also, it is probably the only discipline that experiences such wide disagreement as to the specific application and integrity of these techniques and tools. Added to this controversy, the protagonists of one tool or technique vigorously refute the validity of any other tools; worse, a majority of DP practitioners seem to be unaware of the existence of *any* new tools or techniques. There are at least two major negative results of all this. One result is that often no two programs or systems, even within the same organization, use the same design technique or tool, so the wheel is invented over and over again. The poor maintenance programmer in such an organization must learn a new design philosophy and technique for each program that he maintains.

A second result is that the field of inventing design techniques and tools is wide open to the charlatan, the amateur, and, what is sometimes even worse, the pure academician. The products of such a situation are design techniques and tools that are easy to use but totally inaccurate and, conversely, techniques and tools that are valid and highly accurate but totally impractical.

What *is* required for successful system design, development, and implementation is an integrated set of tools and techniques that is effective throughout the complete system development life cycle, that is compatible, and that produces systems that are understandable to the users as well as to designers, coders, implementers, testers, and operators. Additionally, these techniques and tools must produce documentation that enables all of these groups to use, understand, change, and correct the systems quickly and efficiently — in other words, documentation that enables them to maintain the system effectively.

The data processing professional has played a large and important part in sending frail craft a billion miles out to the icy wastes of Saturn's rings and in receiving remarkably clear television images of pieces of frozen rock only a few miles in diameter, orbiting silently around the gaseous giant. If data processing professionals can help to achieve such a monumental task as this, then the task of organizing ourselves to produce understandable, easily maintained commercial systems should be simple.

1.3.4 Absence of documentation

Most programmers dislike documentation; they dislike producing it, reading it, or changing it. But documentation is the only effective means that programmers have to explain their efforts to someone else. Programming languages, even those that are advertised as self-documenting, are woefully inadequate in expressing what is really happening in the program or system. So, until a genuinely automated method comes along (which may be soon), additional documentation must be written to explain those esoteric entities known as computer programs. As programmers are well known for not documenting anything, many systems are installed whose only documentation consists of a completely out-of-date specification, a few operators' run sheets, and a great deal of very buggy code — not the sort of documentation that helps to provide effective maintenance. Without good documentation, programs are difficult to maintain. Despite "real" programmers' claims, the code is seldom obvious. Each of the design methods and tools recommended in this book will help to enforce good program and system documentation.

1.4 Summary

In this first chapter, I have described the maintenance problems that are besetting the still young data processing industry, and I have thereby laid the groundwork for the book's theme: that systems can indeed be developed to be more maintenance-free by using a rigorous system development life cycle and by applying several specific techniques within that life cycle framework. Therefore, the remaining chapters concentrate on my personal ideas of a practical life cycle and a description of the use of various structured and other techniques that support that life cycle.

2

The History of the Structured Revolution

The vast majority of human beings dislike and even actually dread all notions with which they are not familiar. . . . Hence, it comes about that at their first appearance innovators have . . . always been derided as fools and madmen.

— Aldous Huxley

During the 1940s and 1950s, an Englishman named Alan Turing provided the budding computer industry with invaluable foresight and invention, and his computing machine designs were successfully implemented into some of the earliest computers. During World War II, the Allied Forces used the computers designed by Turing to gain a decided edge over their enemies in the esoteric but vital realm of cryptography. Turing continued his work in England after World War II but tragically, only a few years after the cessation of hostilities, he died under mysterious circumstances, apparently by his own hand. One of Turing's more important concepts was that a limited set of only two or three basic constructs was required to build a logical computing machine. The same constructs later became well known as the basic building blocks of structured programming.

During the 1960s, the computer became more and more a part of our lives. This was due as much as anything to the wholesale exploitation of William Shockley's invention of the transistor in 1947. But the big jump from vacuum tubes to transistors between the mid-1950s and the mid-1960s was only the prelude for the enormously powerful, laboratory-grown circuitry used today. By 1970, the transistor in computer circuits had largely been replaced by various types of integrated circuits.

Computer hardware was not the only area to receive a technological jolt in the 1960s, however. Software development also changed dramatically. Of course, any methodology for programming was an improvement over the seat-of-the-pants type of programming that was common then. The superprogrammer of the 1960s was that person who could make the lights blink fastest on the system console. Mere mortals stood in awe as this superbeing changed the contents of the computer's internal storage with a flick of an IBM reference card. His creations extended the concept of the black-box type of program to unprecedented limits; not only was it difficult to see the internal details of the program, but even when these details were exposed and explained thoroughly, the program's exact workings were still obscured by the convoluted logic and the heavily optimized code. Naturally, the only available documentation for these superprograms was in the form of source listings and a few cryptic comments. Since these programs were understood only by their creators, only their creators could effectively maintain them. Unfortunately, the superprogrammers tended to be mobile and often were not around to maintain or fix the programs when needed.

In 1962, two Italian mathematicians, C. Böhm and G. Jacopini, demonstrated a mathematical proof of the validity of Turing's concepts [6]. Two years later, Böhm suggested in a paper for the *ICC Bulletin* a programming language that needed only Turing's basic constructs — sequence, selection, and iteration [5]. The structured revolution had started, albeit slowly. Böhm and Jacopini's work first reached a larger American audience in 1966 when their 1962 paper was published in the prestigious *Communications of the ACM* [7], but it was still a highly mathematical paper that even today proves to be too much for most programmers to absorb.

In 1965, a Dutch software engineer named Edsger Dijkstra presented a paper at a major international computing conference held in Amsterdam [12]. His paper described, in easy-to-understand language, how programming could be simplified to a few basic rules. In 1968, he more directly stated the concepts of his earlier paper in a letter to the *ACM* entitled "Go To Statement Considered Harmful" [13]. This letter caused an immediate increase in momentum of the embryonic structured movement, for his statements could be interpreted as saying that GOTOs can and should be eliminated and that only the three types of constructs are needed to build a program — the simple sequence construct; the alternative, conditional, or selection construct; and the repetition or iteration construct.

This interpretation was the one that most programmers found acceptable because it was the simplest. They believed they could go "structured" merely by eliminating GOTOs and by coding only sequences, selections, and iterations in their programs. Thus, off went the superprogrammers, armed with their three constructs and their GOTO exterminators, ready to show the world some perfect, structured programs. There were small improvements in clarity in some cases. In many situations, however, the programs simply got longer and neater but no better; and the programmers became dangerously complacent, believing that since their programs were structured, they were now perfect.

Dijkstra's work, however, went deeper than most of the popular paraphrases of it. While he did indeed decry the undisciplined use of GOTOs and stated that only a few basic constructs were required to develop any program, Dijkstra emphasized time and again that one should have a very clear idea of the problem before attempting to formulate the solution. In his inimitable style, Dijkstra implied that many programmers actually enjoy the academic challenges of wrestling with poorly formulated problems rather than forcing clear problem definitions at the start and hence rapidly generating solutions. This is an accusation that still could justifiably be aimed at many so-called software engineers: These lovers of esoterica seem to derive a great deal of intellectual satisfaction out of not quite understanding what they are doing.

Up to the end of the 1960s, most of the publications and presentations on the new structured ideas were aimed at and accepted by much of the academic community, even though the ideas themselves were often formulated by well-respected DP practitioners. The average journeyman programmer had not even heard of Dijkstra, Böhm, Jacopini, Turing, or any of the other structured pioneers, much less put their ideas into practice. What was needed for those in industry to accept and practice the structured techniques was a practical example that successfully used the new techniques.

In 1972, such an example was reported in the *IBM Systems Journal* [1]. Terry Baker, of IBM's Federal Systems Division (FSD), became the leader of a project to develop an on-line information storage and retrieval system for The New York Times Company after the original IBM project team had fallen far behind schedule and the Times had threatened to cancel the project. The superstars from FSD moved in, en masse, with Terry Baker as their leader to rescue the project. The sinking project was re-floated and turned into a success, as documented in many different publications.

In the Times project, Baker and his disciples applied the techniques of structured programming, but they added a critical ingredient to the recipe for success: techniques used by project management to control the nebulous activity known as system development. The new organizational methods were based on the chief programmer team concept offered by IBM's Harlan Mills in an internal report [26]. What's more, these techniques all seemed to encourage higher productivity from the project participants. Baker's team was a super team in every sense, and it has been suggested that improved results would be achieved by a team of that caliber whatever the methods and tools used. Basically, there were four new concepts used in the successful development of the New York Times system: chief programmer teams, program production library, top-down programming, and structured programming.

Chief programmer teams replaced the traditional idea of having a pool of similarly talented programmer/analysts who performed all tasks equally with the new idea of using a team of skilled individuals, each of whom is trained in a separate area and performs a specific task. A chief programmer team has been likened to a surgical team wherein each team member has a specific function requiring specific skills. The chief programmer himself is a project leader who manages the technical activities of the team. In Chapter 13, I describe the functions of the team's various members.

The *program production library* was an attempt to centralize the clerical aspects of the system development activities so as to relieve the programmers of these duties. All routine procedures for entering code, recording changes, keeping track of different pieces of the system, and so on, were automated as far as possible and the responsibility for these tasks was handed over to a program librarian.

Top-down programming reversed the traditional sequence of implementation activities by forcing coding to start at the least detailed level of the system hierarchy, or at the "top." In the early 1970s, most systems were *designed* from the top down by gradually adding detail to the initial general design statements until the design was complete. Then the systems were *implemented* from the bottom up by waves of programmers, furiously coding all of the detail first and then joining the details to complete the system. The New York Times project did both design and implementation from the top down.

Structured programming rules followed in the New York Times project were based on the papers of Böhm and Jacopini and of Dijkstra. Only three constructs were allowed: sequence, if-then-else, and do-while. GOTOs were definitely frowned upon.

As a result of the reports from the New York Times project, almost overnight, every commercial programmer wanted to learn to write structured programs and to become a chief programmer, just like Baker. Managers insisted that programming resources be organized into chief programmer teams; they tried desperately to come up with a correct job description for program librarians; and many system programmers worked feverishly to build a program production library for the librarian.

A social upheaval in data processing was in progress, as many corporations tried to introduce every new technique at once. For a few years, everything connected with data processing became "structured": structured project management, structured human resources, structured testing, structured walkthroughs, structured programming, and so on, ad nauseam. Fortunes were made and lost in the training and consulting arenas as the enthusiasm for all things structured waxed and waned. Although it seemed obvious that the structured techniques *should* have worked, unhappily, in most cases, they simply did not provide the hoped-for improvements. Productivity did not appear to improve at all, and significant resources were apparently lost forever in the bottomless pit of structured education, as programmers were constantly being trained in the new, ever-changing techniques.

Not having serried ranks of superstars like those of Baker, those who tried to impose the new techniques succeeded only in alienating programmers and DP management alike. Other failures occurred because an individual technique was implemented with the expectation of its being a panacea for all of DP's problems. Unfortunately, it often turned out to be only an expensive placebo. A compatible, complete set of techniques that could be applied across the whole development life cycle was still needed.

All this turmoil was going on at a time when the requirements for new business applications of the computer were growing at an alarmingly accelerating pace. Increased programmer productivity was necessary simply as a matter of survival for the DP industry. The pressure to improve productivity and the failure to achieve that goal caused many of the structured techniques to rapidly fall into disrepute. The structured revolution started to falter almost before its first unsteady step had been taken.

Despite all of the improved programming techniques (IPTs in IBM-ese) being presented by IBM and others, it was painfully apparent that bad systems were still being written and were absorbing multitudes of programmers into the maintenance black hole. Up to this point, some techniques did offer improvements in organizational methods and coding practices; and, indeed, organizing programmers into teams, "egoless" or otherwise, did seem to enhance management control.* Some program librarians definitely helped to remove some of the repetitious clerical work for the programmers, and the structured programming rules made programs easier to read and understand. Yet, even the top-down development procedures, with all of the associated control techniques, did not seem to produce correct solutions. Dijkstra's earlier implications — that programmers gain intellectual satisfaction from being confused — appeared to be even more valid.

If I may use a frequently employed analogy, the data processing situation was like being presented with all of the necessary, correct components in order to build a house but having the necessary tools and plans withheld. Then, the builder is forced to construct the house brick by brick, only able to *imagine* the final, completed building, and is forced to implement design errors fully in order to realize their effect or even their existence. Only a near-genius or an extremely fortunate designer could hope to implement an even partially correct product under such circumstances.

Clearly, there was a large gap in the spectrum of structured methodologies: There was no effective method for *designing* programs and systems. The actual shape or

---

*An *egoless* programming team is composed of programmers, who all regard their code as a team product and not a personal possession. Therefore, the defensiveness a solo programmer often feels toward his work is removed. This concept is discussed in Chapter 13.

design of individual programs resulted from the intuition of the individual designers or programmers. From the early 1960s on, much of the controversy over program and system design has focused on how to decide upon this program or system structure, with the combatants falling into essentially two camps: functional decomposition, which bases the design structure on the functional structure; and data structured design, which, as its name implies, uses the logical structure of the data as the basis.

Functional decomposition assumes that a system can be easily split into its main functions, forming a hierarchy of functions. This functional hierarchy forms the basic design structure (see Figure 2-1).

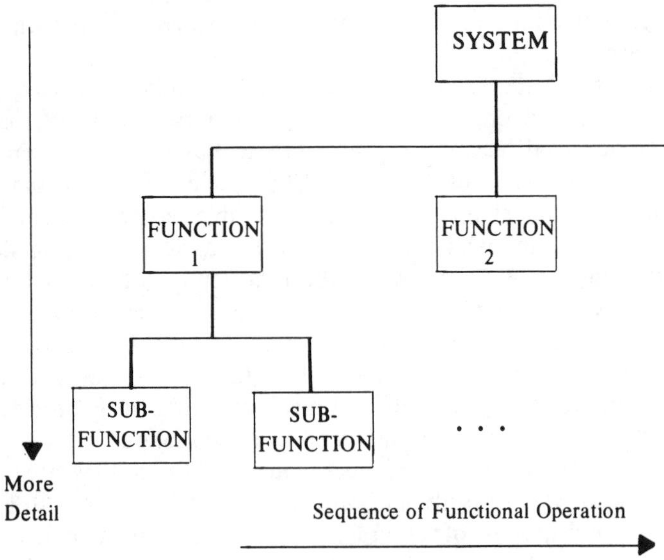

Figure 2-1. A functionally decomposed hierarchy.

In 1974, three leaders in the structured revolution linked closely with functional decomposition — Wayne Stevens, Glen Myers, and Larry Constantine — attempted to provide the missing design methods. Their landmark article in the *IBM Systems Journal,* entitled "Structured Design" [35], was important not only for the design concepts that it introduced, but also for the first widely published use of the phrase structured design. Although no startlingly revolutionary techniques were introduced, the article discussed a methodology for measuring the "goodness" of a design, including the new concepts of cohesion and coupling applied to the structure charts.* If these measurement techniques worked as the authors claimed, they offered a method to progressively check the quality of a design as it developed. The authors casually suggested that good programs might consist of greater than five lines and fewer than one hundred lines of code; they also mentioned, almost as if it were an afterthought, the use of data flow diagrams† as precursors to the more traditional hierarchical structure charts (see Figures 2-2 and 2-3).

---

*The structure chart is one of the primary graphic tools of structured design; it shows the structural, or hierarchical, aspects of a system rather than the procedural aspects. Section 3.1.1 defines the terms cohesion and coupling.

†Data flow diagrams, graphic tools to show the transformation of data in a system, are described in detail in Section 3.1.2.

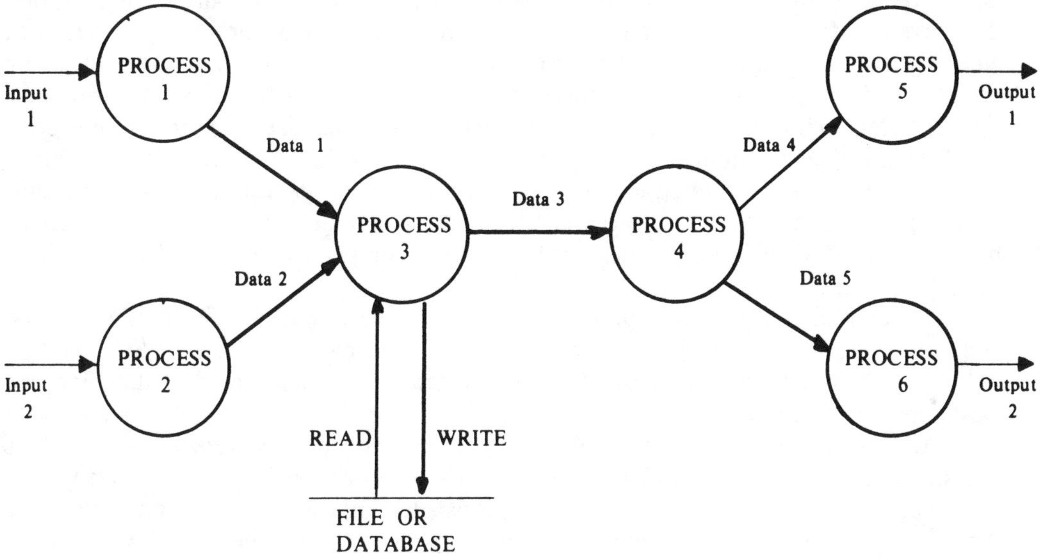

Figure 2-2. An abstract data flow diagram.

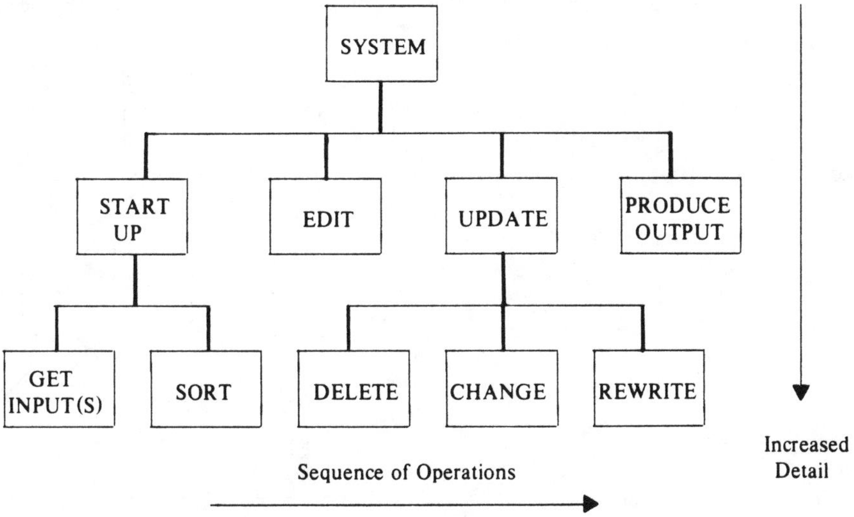

Figure 2-3. A hierarchical structure chart.

The separate techniques described in "Structured Design" did not together constitute a wholly workable or reliable methodology to develop systems. Nevertheless, each technique was picked up and carried forward on the ever-widening structured wavefront that was now rolling inexorably through the data processing industry.

A number of organizations, including IBM, further developed the ideas into papers, articles, books, programmed learning workbooks, and full-fledged, marketable, training courses. Yourdon, Inc., is by far the most widely known of these organizations. Its founder, Edward Yourdon, married the structured design techniques from the Stevens, Myers, and Constantine article with the best of Baker's methods from the New York Times project. Since the mid-1970s, his company has put together an impressive and comprehensive set of training courses and documentation. With the addition of minispecifications (minispecs), data flow diagrams, data dictionary, and structured walkthroughs, among other tools, a practical and effective set of development techniques has been marketed aggressively throughout the data processing community. More than that, Yourdon has received the highest accolade of all: His operation has been faithfully copied many times over by other companies, large and small, in the same business.

Another important development of the early 1970s was the Structured Analysis and Design Technique (SADT®), a package developed by Doug Ross of SofTech, Inc. [32, 52]. This methodology, treated fully in Chapter 3, is another data flow approach closely related to Yourdon's.

All of the early structured analysis and design techniques were an outgrowth of Dijkstra's structured programming rules, Baker's organizational techniques used in the New York Times project, and Myers' functional decomposition design philosophy. In the mid-1970s, however, two books on program design challenged this functional approach: *Logical Construction of Programs* by Jean-Dominique Warnier of France in 1974 [36] and *Principles of Program Design* by Michael Jackson of England in 1975 [19]. Both of these books proposed that the structure of the data being processed, rather than the flow of data through a system, is the key to the "shape" or the structure of the program or system. Jackson's technique utilizes structure charts to depict the input and output data and then merges data structures to form the program structure (see Figure 2-4).

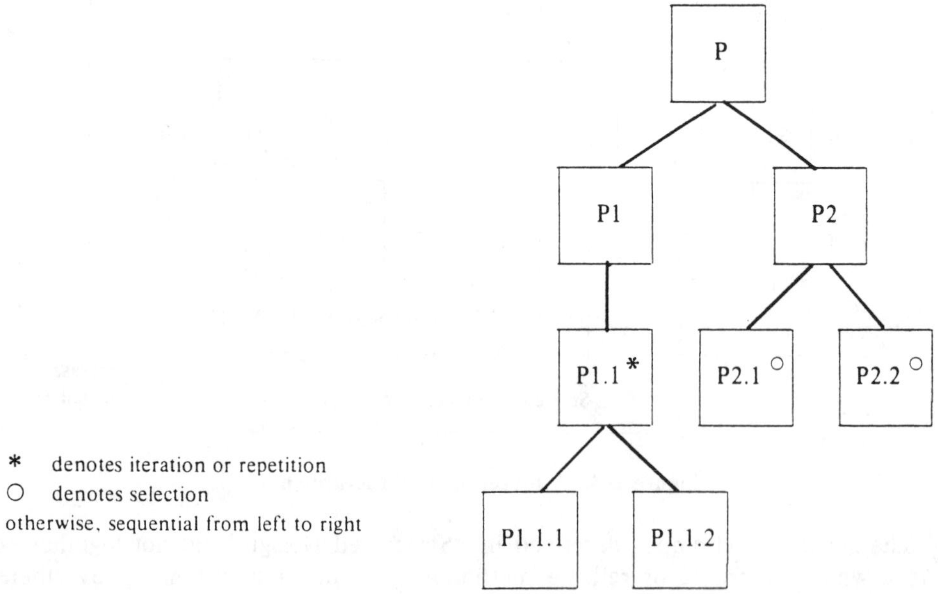

Figure 2-4. A Jackson diagram.

As shown in Figure 2-4, a superimposed notation is used to denote sequences, selections, or iterations (Dijkstra's three constructs), and exactly the same notation is used to represent data and program structures. The Jackson technique is an extremely rigorous methodology for designing programs and systems and is acknowledged as providing a valuable new insight into the real nature of programming.

Warnier's methodology is slightly less rigorous and complete than Jackson's and it uses a different, more narrative-type notation (see Figure 2-5). Because of the left-to-right narrative style of diagramming, however, the Warnier technique is sometimes more palatable to management and non-DP users of the programs and systems.

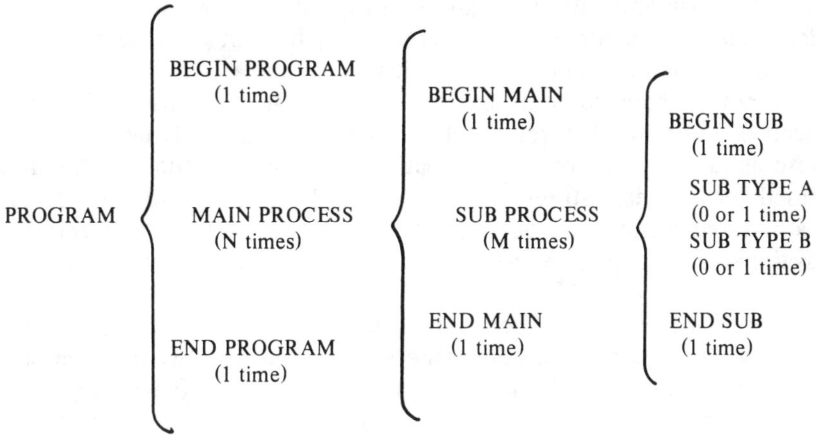

Figure 2-5. A Warnier diagram.

Ken Orr, an American software engineer and DP consultant, has worked with the French engineer to develop the original Warnier technique into a package of rules and more rigorous diagrams called Warnier-Orr diagrams [29]. Superficially, the Warnier-Orr diagrams are identical to the Warnier diagrams. Orr has also added software aids to help automate the production of Warnier-Orr diagrams, an innovation that makes the Warnier-Orr methodology a significant contender for becoming the most popular DP design methodology of the 1980s.

Both the Jackson and the Warnier-Orr techniques represent a significant step forward in implementing a step-by-step process of program design by combining the concepts of structured programming and the principle that the shape of the data to be processed determines the shape of the program. For several years, there was a public debate between the adherents of functional design and data structured design. The Myers/Yourdon/SofTech camp insisted that theirs was the only correct way and, of course, the Jackson/Warnier-Orr disciples said the same thing about their methods.

In the latter half of the 1970s, the "functionals" and the "data structureds" began to admit the merits of each other's philosophies and to integrate them into their own. Aspects of both types of methodologies apparently are required within the system development life cycle, and different circumstances require different emphases on the various design techniques available. Chapters 3 and 4 discuss this issue in more detail.

Structured analysis generally uses some of the structured design techniques, such as data flow diagrams and in some cases structure charts, to help provide a picture of the users' requirements of the system in the form of a system specification. If done well, this picture naturally leads into the system design activities.

Structured Systems Analysis: Tools & Techniques, by Chris Gane and Trish Sarson, appeared in 1977 [17]. Since publication, this book has been enthusiastically accepted by the DP community as a practical extension of the data flow-based techniques into the Requirements Definition phase of system development. An important addition to the structured analysis and design techniques is the system data dictionary. While others had earlier discussed and even recommended this concept, Gane and Sarson were the first to present it in a clear and easy-to-understand manner. Further works on structured analysis have appeared since 1977: Notably, Tom DeMarco's *Structured Analysis and System Specification* [11] highlighted the separation between logical and physical representations, and Orr's *Structured Requirements Definition* [30] extends the use of Warnier-Orr diagrams into the analysis and specification activities.

An ideal, eclectic structured design methodology has not yet appeared, but the situation seems to be much less confused than it was in the early 1970s. Structured programming may not yet have come of age, but it is at least out of its childhood and into early adolescence. As noted before, structured design is still evolving and seems to be headed toward an amalgam of, or even an option between, the data structured- and the data flow-based techniques. Structured analysis is, I believe, earlier in its evolution than other structured techniques, but the extensive use of data flow diagrams coupled with data dictionary techniques seems to hold great promise for future analysis activities.

Many names, papers, and books prominent in the growth of the structured methods have not been mentioned here; otherwise, this chapter would have been inordinately long. Rather than simply develop a list, I have given the reader a flavor for what has occurred in these tumultuous years, and I give additional citations in the Bibliography. I apologize to all those thousands of contributors to the structured revolution whom I have not mentioned and without whose efforts we would not be where we are today.

3

Structured Design

It must be remembered that there is nothing more difficult to plan, more doubtful of success, nor more dangerous to manage than the creation of a new system, for the initiator has the enmity of all who would profit by the preservation of the old institution and merely lukewarm defenders in those who gain by the new one.

— Machiavelli

What is this process called design? The 1975 edition of the *International Webster's New Encyclopedic Dictionary* includes the following definition:

> **design**, *v.* to make drawings, preliminary sketches or plans; to plan and fashion the form and structure of an object, decorative scheme or work of art; to have intentions or purposes.

Although this definition may be straightforward enough, something more is needed. To ensure that the design process becomes more than just an entertaining intellectual exercise, the designer must possess a great deal of prior knowledge and related experience.

A delightful description of the design process in general, not specifically related to data processing but certainly germane to the subject, was offered by Chris Jones [21]. He made two important points: One is that design must be iterative; that is, the design process is not a simple sequence of events. Some parts of the process need to be repeated an indefinite number of times until a satisfactory result is obtained. Jones's second point is that design cannot be successful unless it is firmly based upon some previously proved truths about the general class of objects to be designed. These truths are those characteristics that are present and consistent for each separate object within a given class.

If we presume that we do have a reasonably good understanding of what design should be, what is "structured design"? This question has been posed innumerable times ever since the phrase was coined, twenty or more years ago. Since I have not yet seen a good definition of structured design, the following represents my thoughts on the subject: Structured design is a logical, step-by-step, iterative process of defining the structure and substructure of a new entity to the point at which, given the necessary physical resources, the defined structure or design can be implemented.

An overall outline of the new entity's structure, which is usually in graphic and narrative form, is the product of the initial steps of the design process. This early structural outline is developed in progressively more detail until the design is completed. Iteration within the process must be encouraged to permit correction of design errors. In the context of data processing, the entity whose structure is to be defined is normally a program or a system.

One obvious inference from the above definition is that the initial structural outline is critical to the eventual successful completion of the design. The initial shape or general structure of the entity to be designed exerts an often unwarranted influence over the final detailed shape of the entity. Human nature being what it is, once the initial structure is developed (even if it is hopelessly wrong), it is likely to be slavishly followed as the model for further development, despite its inaccuracy. Therefore, it is of overwhelming importance for the preliminary design to be as accurate as possible. This, of course, is much easier to talk or write about than it is to achieve.

Since the early 1960s, much of the controversy over program and system design methods has focused on how to decide upon this early, critical view of the program or system structure. Most of the primeval dust stirred up by the leviathans of the structured revolution has now settled, and two main approaches to structured design have survived. These two approaches are known generically as functional decomposition and data structured design. The history of their development has been covered in Chapter 2, so in this chapter I will only concentrate on a description of the methods themselves and how they can be applied.

3.1 Functional decomposition

Data processing systems and many of their programs tend to be rather complex. A major objective of the system design process must be to decompose the system into less complex pieces that are easier to design. Consequently, functional decomposition could be considered a designer's version of the divide-and-conquer concept. Top-down development is generally considered to be the correct way of doing things, partially because the top-down process is a natural process and partially because this method has achieved improved results. Functional decomposition certainly subscribes to that philosophy. In addition, modularity has long been an aim of DP system designers, and functional decomposition provides some very useful procedures and guidelines for attaining modularity in design. (Modularity is simply the accepted terminology for decomposition into small, uncomplicated components, each of which carries out a specific system function.)

Functional decomposition can be characterized by Dijkstra's description of a series of "levels" of computing machines and languages [14]. Let us imagine that we have a powerful high-level programming language and its associated machine available. We could then write a simple report-writing program as follows:

```
START
  PRODUCE REPORT
STOP
```

These three statements would form the first, or highest, level of our design. The next level is produced by decomposing these statements into lower-level, more specific programming statements. The purpose of this "stepwise refinement" process is to produce a set of statements that can be translated directly, one-for-one, into the target programming language.

```
START
OPEN FILES, DATABASES, . . .
INITIALIZE COUNTERS
WRITE REPORT HEADING
FOR EACH PAGE
    WRITE PAGE HEADING
    WRITE LINES
WRITE REPORT TRAILER
CLOSE FILES, DATABASES, . . .
STOP
```

Now the second level of design is complete. If one of today's high-level, user-friendly languages is being used, this step may be as far as the coder needs to go for the translation process. However, since it is still relatively unusual for such a high-level language to be used, some further decomposition is normally required. Clearly, since the steps defined in the first level are expanded into the subsequent lower levels, it is crucial that the first level be correct.

Each high-level statement represents a module or segment of coding that, when implemented, will carry out a specific system function or related set of functions. For instance, the simple report writing program described above can be represented as a structure chart, as shown in Figure 3-1. The program structure at this point in its development consists of eleven modules: one at level 0, three at level 1, and seven at level 2.

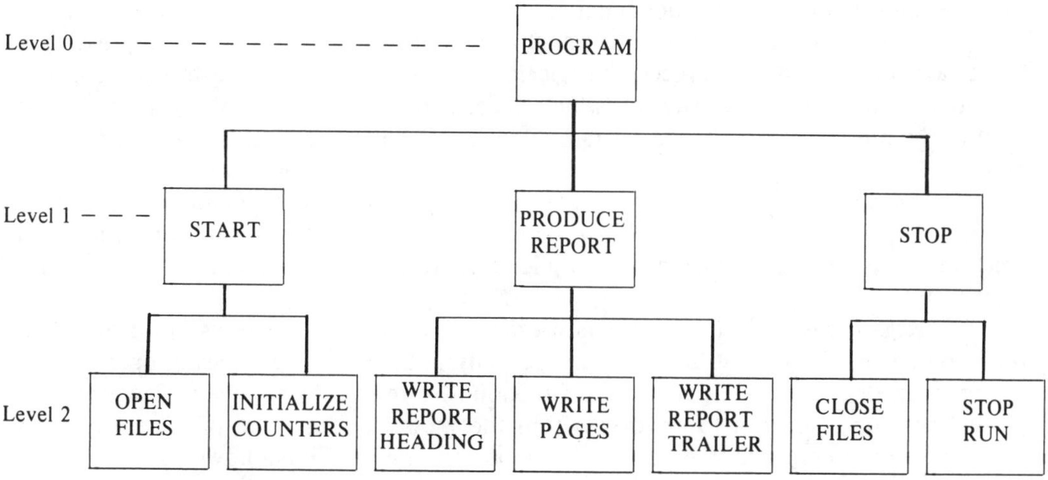

Figure 3-1. Structure chart showing decomposition to level 2.

How can we tell that this is a good decomposition? Are the modules good modules? And what does "good" mean anyhow? The following paragraphs describe some guidelines for the decomposition process.

3.1.1 Metrics for measuring design quality

Stevens, Myers, and Constantine, three of the leading players in the structured sagas, developed a series of inexact metrics for assessing the "goodness" of a structured design as illustrated by a structure chart [35]. Their work was further refined by Yourdon and Constantine [42]. The metrics included two measurements of important characteristics of a hierarchical program and system structure: *cohesion* and *coupling*. Cohesion is a description or measure of the internal strength and consistency of a module; this consistency should be as high as possible in order for a module to be considered good. (Consistency here means that all of the activities in a module should be functionally related, as far as possible.) Coupling, on the other hand, is a measure of the dependence of one module upon the others; it is kept as low as possible in a good design. Although the definitions and measures of both cohesion and coupling remain vague and subjective, I'll try to be specific in my explanation of these metrics in the next few paragraphs. Coupling and cohesion apply only to hierarchical structure charts, including Jackson diagrams, and do not apply to any other design techniques.

3.1.1.1 Cohesion

Cohesion is often referred to as the "glue" that holds a module together. Stevens, Myers, and Constantine defined seven types of cohesion, ranked from most desirable to least desirable. In order of goodness, starting with the best, these types of cohesion are defined as follows:

Functional cohesion (best) is the most desirable type of cohesion; it occurs when every action in the module contributes directly to performing one single function. Often, in this type of module, a single input is transformed into a single output. A simple example is the square root function.

Sequential cohesion (good) is demonstrated when the module simply represents a "gateway" in the system's process. Typically, a sequentially cohesive module consists of two or more activities, each of which accepts data from the activity preceding it (within the module), modifies the data, and passes it on to the next activity (within the module).

Communicational cohesion (moderate to good) occurs when functions that operate on common data are grouped within a module. Examples of such modular functions are "Read input record and eliminate duplicate characters" and "Compute solution and print results."

Procedural cohesion (moderate) is present when several functions are grouped in one module simply because they are procedurally linked in the processing operation of the program or system. The individual functions are related by the flow of control that passes from one function to another within the module. This type of cohesion often occurs when the program or system is developed from a traditional flowchart.

Temporal cohesion (moderate to poor) occurs when functions are grouped within a module merely because they occur at the same time. Initialization routines are often combined in one module simply because they are all carried out close to the start of the program. Several functionally cohesive modules can be created from one such temporally cohesive module by isolating the individual initialization routines and creating a separate module from each one. These modules are then much more easily maintained and modified when necessary.

Logical cohesion (poor) is achieved when several separate modules that perform almost the same function are combined into one module. This type of cohesion is often the most tempting for the system designer to succumb to. A single module, modified dynamically by a series of switches, could replace all of those different modules. How elegant and efficient! This single, switch-driven module is a typical example of logical cohesiveness, but it is efficient only in its use of space. Execution time will increase while the system examines all those switches. In terms of maintenance, this module will present many problems. The original programmer will probably be the only one who knows what the module truly does and even that knowledge will be lost after the first modification. A much improved design and the implementation strategy that it implies result from the originally defined set of separate, yet similar, modules.

Coincidental cohesion (worst) is often the result of an accident or blind panic by the designer. In a coincidentally cohesive module, there is no discernible relationship between any of the functions contained in the module. Arbitrarily drawing boundaries around pieces of a flowchart in order to make conveniently sized modules often produces coincidental cohesion.

A definition of the type or types of cohesion that a module exhibits will not provide the designer with an exact measure of its goodness. However, the designer can establish the relative quality of modules within a system and, if necessary, make changes to improve individual module quality and overall system quality while still in the design stage.

3.1.1.2 Coupling

Coupling is a measure of the degree of connection between modules. Clearly, there must be *some* connections – if not, the unconnected modules would belong to different systems. Nevertheless, the amount of coupling should be minimized between any two modules in a program or system. In general, if the modules are functionally cohesive, the coupling is low. As with cohesion, the level of coupling can vary. There are three types of coupling, as follows:

Data coupling (best) is the most desirable form of coupling, wherein one module passes data to another as part of an invocation or as a return of control. The fewer pieces of data passed between the two modules, the better the design will be able to withstand change.

Control coupling (moderate to poor) is present when a module must pass a condition flag to another module, either up or down the system hierarchy, so that the operation of the recipient module is dependent upon the value of the flag. Although sometimes necessary, this type of coupling should be minimized, since it often signals the presence of logical cohesion in related modules. As explained above, logical cohesion is undesirable and should be avoided.

External, content, or pathological coupling (worst) occurs when one module refers to the internal contents of another module. The first module may extract some data from the second module, change data inside it, branch to an internal statement within the second module, or even branch to a third module depending upon the contents of data in the second module. Figure 3-2 demonstrates an example of this least desirable type of coupling.

A major problem with pathological coupling and the main reason to avoid its use is that one module can be modified without anyone's realizing that the modification has a dramatic effect upon the other pathologically connected module. In order to avoid the situation shown in Figure 3-2, the value of RECTYPE must be passed up the hierarchy to PROGRAM and then fed as input to OUTPUT, which will in turn pass the information to WRITE.

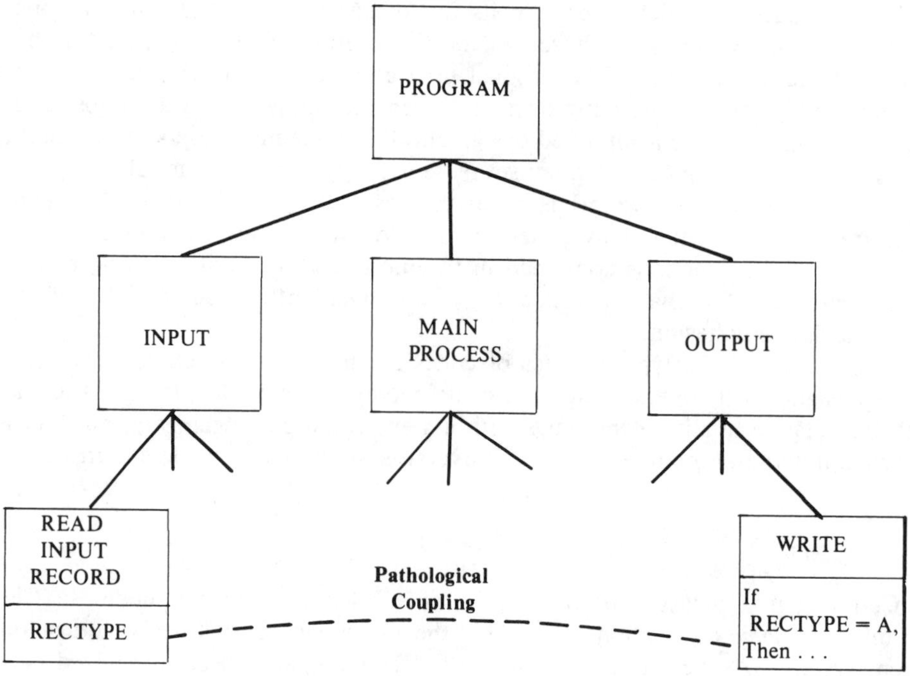

Figure 3-2. Example of pathological coupling.

A summary of the types of cohesion and coupling and their relative goodness is shown in Table 3-1. Any one module may exhibit several types of cohesion and may be coupled to other modules in different ways. The designer should keep the level of cohesion as high (functional) as possible and the intermodule coupling as low as possible. In general, high cohesion and low coupling occur together.

Table 3-1
Summary of Types of Cohesion and Coupling

LEVEL	COHESION	COUPLING	LEVEL
High (best) ↕ Low (worst)	• Functional • Sequential • Communicational • Procedural • Temporal • Logical • Coincidental	• Data • Control • External, content, pathological	Low (best) ↕ High (worst)

3.1.1.3 Other metrics

Coupling and cohesion are not the only metrics available for measuring the quality of a design, although they are the most well documented and the most quantifiable, relatively speaking. Other, less exact metrics or characteristics of functionally decomposed system structures are *complexity* and *correctness.*

Complexity is a subjective characteristic at best, but less complexity is generally considered to be better than more complexity. One program is more complex than another if it contains more possible logical paths and more separate logical functions, and if it processes more discrete inputs and outputs than the other program. A complex module can usually be rendered less complex by dividing it into its subcomponents.

Correctness of a program would seem to be quantifiable, but in practice it is almost impossible to prove. A small industry of "program provers" has sprung up with little real impact yet on commercial programming. At this time, the closest we can come to gauging program correctness is to produce one that exactly meets its specifications.

All of these metrics of quality are after-the-fact measurements. A program or system structure must first be developed before the metrics can be applied, and that structure is heavily influenced by how the designer views the program or system. Consequently, the decomposition of the program or system into modules is based upon the designer's interpretation of what the major program or system functions are; that is, the decomposition may be based on function, on time sequence, or on separate transformations of data. By far the most effective basis for decomposition is that of data transformations.

3.1.2 Decomposition by data transformations

Traditionally, systems have been decomposed based upon a time-ordered sequence of major functions. The trend today seems to be more toward a decomposition based upon major data transformations within the system. A favored technique is the use of a "bubble" chart or a data flow diagram (DFD), as shown in Figure 3-3. Although the use of DFDs is more favored in system analysis, they also can be used as a basis for the design activities.

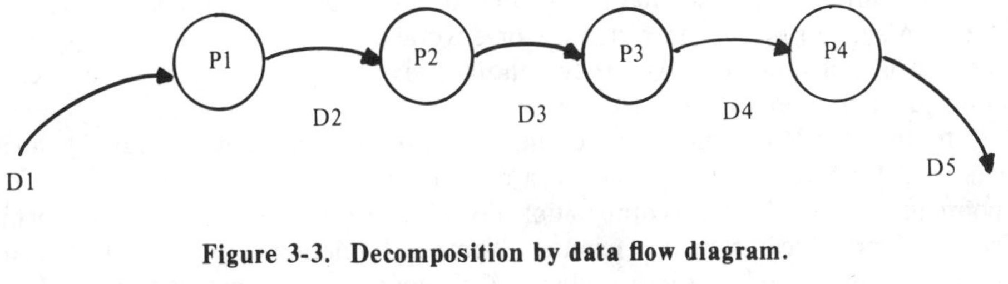

Figure 3-3. Decomposition by data flow diagram.

Figure 3-3 depicts a system that has as input some data designated as D1 and as output data designated as D5. Between the submission of D1 and production of D5, four separate data transformations P1, P2, P3, and P4 are defined. For example, P1 transforms input data D1 into data D2.

This DFD represents only an overview of the system. In fact, a DFD as simple as Figure 3-3 is unusual in that the bubbles often have more than one data flow entering and leaving them. Each of these transformation bubbles probably can be decomposed into a DFD. This process can be repeated and more detailed diagrams successively developed until the system is fully represented by a leveled set of DFDs. At the lowest level, each DFD's bubbles represent elementary data transformations, which means that it is not useful to perform any further decomposition.

Figure 3-4 shows how the simple system in Figure 3-3 can be further decomposed. Data transformations P1 and P3 have been decomposed further, while P2 and P4 have been deemed elementary enough. Obviously, each program design team should have a DP-oriented Sherlock Holmes aboard to determine if a bubble is elementary. (Perhaps Holmes's celebrated pipe was a bubble pipe, after all?) But there are a few, admittedly loose, criteria to guide the decomposition process. For instance, a bubble is elementary if it can be described in a minispec of half a page, or if it has only one input and one output.

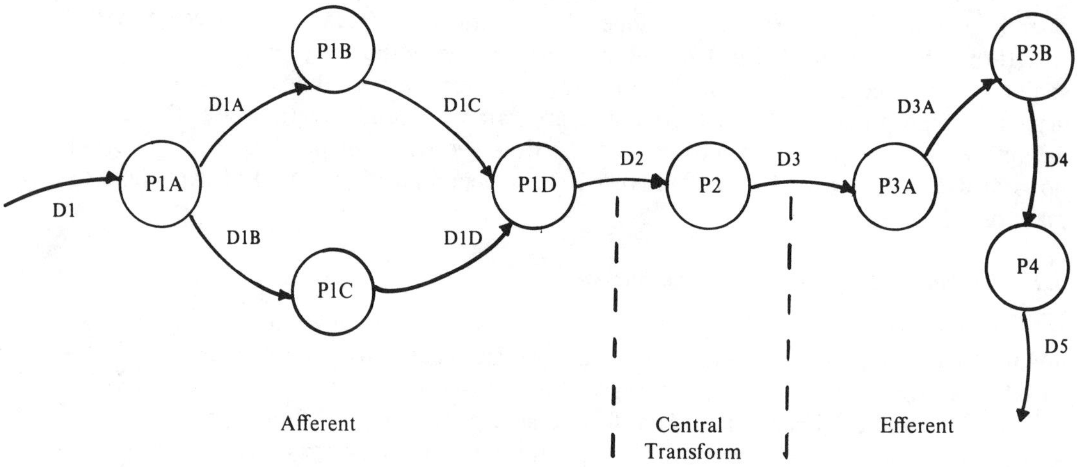

Figure 3-4. Further decomposition of a DFD.

One major problem with using DFDs in design is the difficulty in showing temporal relationships. It is clear that P1D should occur before P2, but does P1B happen before P1C? Also, is P3A carried out once or several times? Are there occasions when D1A or D1B is not created? Are they mutually exclusive? We cannot answer these questions just from looking at the DFD.

If temporal relationships are denoted on a DFD, the diagram rapidly becomes complex and loses its ability to provide a clear overview of the system. Therefore, at this point in the functional decomposition design process, the designer transforms the DFDs into hierarchical structure charts. Temporal relationships are much easier to represent accurately on a structure chart. Consequently, the program code, which is temporally sequential, is easier to generate from the chart. The set of lowest-level, or working-level, DFDs is usually transformed into structure charts. In order to carry out this transformation, the designers must decide which bubbles are the central transform in the data flow diagram. Meilir Page-Jones provides an excellent definition of the central transform: "the portion(s) of a data flow diagram or structure chart that remains when the afferent and efferent streams have been removed; the major data-transforming functions of a system."* Essentially, in a DFD that flows from left to right, all data transforms to the left of the central transform are termed *afferent* or input-related, and all data transforms to the right are called *efferent* or output-related.

Sometimes, the selection of the central transform is obvious and easy; other times, it is not. In difficult cases, the designer must exercise his own experience and judgment. Generally, the more logical the DFD is, the easier the decision will be. The logical DFD is uncluttered with the confusing physical information. The physical DFD, however, can only be implemented in one way because the physical implementation has been already decided and included in the diagram.

In Figure 3-4, I made the arbitrary decision, exercising *my* experience and judgment, that P2 is the central transform. To form the equivalent structure chart, the designer must, in his imagination, "pick up" the DFD by the central transform and let the afferent bubbles dangle on the left and the efferent ones hang on the right. (At this point, the reader should be awed by the rigorous scientific approach of this technique.) The resulting diagram is shown in Figure 3-5.

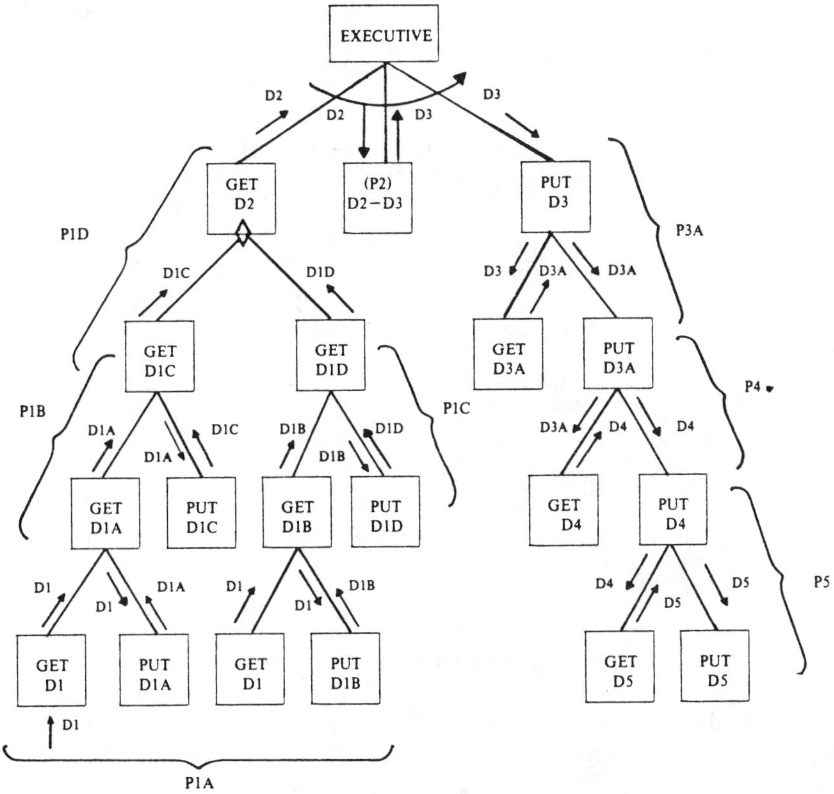

Figure 3-5. Transformation of a data flow diagram into a structure chart.

*M. Page-Jones, *The Practical Guide to Structured Systems Design* (New York: Yourdon Press, 1980), p. 338.

In Figure 3-5, one component in the structure is drawn to represent the central transform P2, and there is a GET module for P2's input D2, and a PUT module for P2's output D3. These three components form sequential parts of the overall controlling component, which represents the complete program or the complete system and which is called EXECUTIVE in this example. On the afferent, or input, side of the DFD, each triad of input/transform/output is translated into a triangular structure, as shown in Figure 3-6. Similarly, the efferent, or output, side of the DFD is translated into a triangular structure, as shown in Figure 3-7.

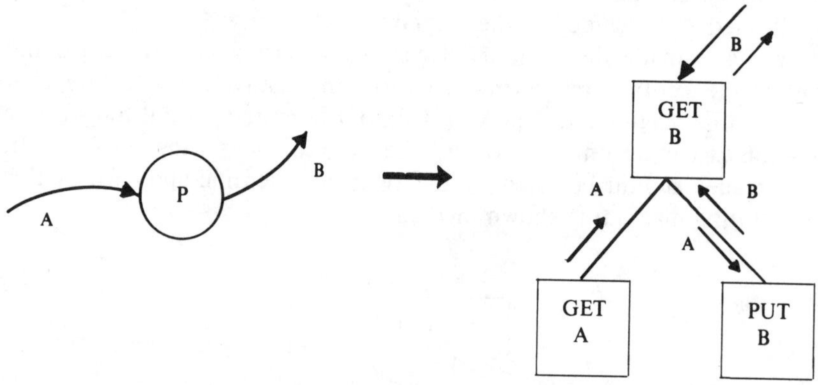

Figure 3-6. Transformation of afferent data flow.

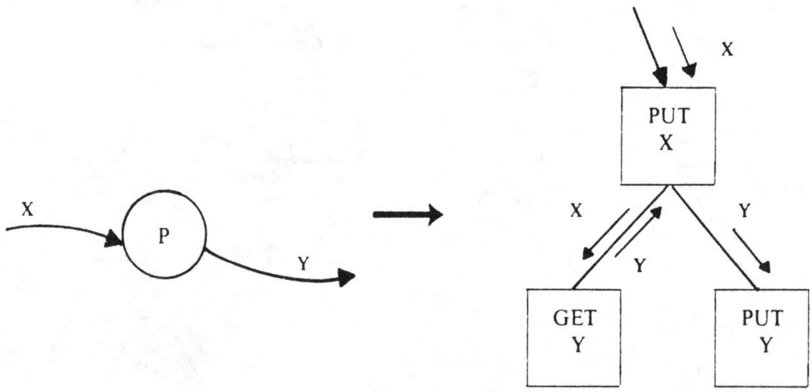

Figure 3-7. Transformation of efferent data flow.

In Figure 3-5, the inputs and outputs of one data transform overlap the inputs and outputs of other transforms. Similarly, the structure triangles representing the data transforms also overlap. The directions of the flow of the various pieces of data can still be seen in the structure chart by following the arrows and data item names D1 through D5.

When a data transform has more than one input, the designer must decide if these inputs occur in a chronological order, if they occur simultaneously, or if they are mutually exclusive alternatives. In Figure 3-4, transform PID has two inputs, which are represented as mutually exclusive alternatives in Figure 3-5. The diamond notation in the GET D2 module indicates either a GET D1C or a GET D1D action each time it is called. Without this selection construct, the normal left-to-right sequence of operation within each component is assumed.

Multiple outputs from a single transform can be treated in a similar fashion. If a repetitive or iterative process must be indicated on the structure chart, then a curved or semicircular arrow is used, as shown beneath the EXECUTIVE component in Figure 3-5. In this case, the arrow implies that the complete process implemented by this design structure is iterative.*

Many popular methodologies are based on the foregoing description of the functional decomposition type of analysis and design. In fact, to my knowledge, this approach is the only complete, formalized system analysis and design methodology. Most of the methods follow the pattern of developing DFDs and structure charts and then implementing the program (coding and testing). Additional documentation in the form of highly formatted, English-language statements — known variously as minispecs, structured English, or pseudocode — is used to describe the internal functions of the components of the designed program or system. The need for such a documentation tool proves that data flows and structure charts alone are not enough to fully describe the system.

3.1.3 Commercially available methods

The three best-known commercial presentations of functional decomposition for requirements definition are these: structured analysis and design of Yourdon; Improved System Technology (IST) of Gane and Sarson (a product of McDonnell Douglas Automation); and Structured Analysis and Design Technique (SADT) of SofTech.

3.1.3.1 Yourdon's structured analysis and design

The Yourdon brand of structured analysis and design follows the procedures outlined above. Yourdon, Inc., of New York, in collaboration with Constantine among others, is responsible for a great deal of the development of the functional decomposition-based structured analysis and design techniques and has contributed enormously to the state-of-the-art of software engineering. Yourdon has integrated the techniques of DFDs, structure charts, and minispecs, among other tools, into a system development life cycle, which is illustrated in Figure 3-8.

In the figure, the life cycle itself is depicted as a data flow diagram. Major stage deliverables are denoted by the data flows between each bubble. DFDs are used in the analysis stage to generate the structured specification, which describes in detail the logical and physical functions that the new system must perform. Minispecs also form an integral part of this deliverable.

---

*More detailed explanations of the transformation process from DFD to structure chart are provided in Yourdon and Constantine's *Structured Design* [42], and in Gane and Sarson's *Structured Systems Analysis: Tools & Techniques* [17].

Following the analysis stage, structure charts, more minispecs, and the final program code, along with the user manual, form the documentation of the new structured system. A system data dictionary serves as a formal repository of all information about the system. The Yourdon life cycle is detailed in *Managing the System Life Cycle* [41].*

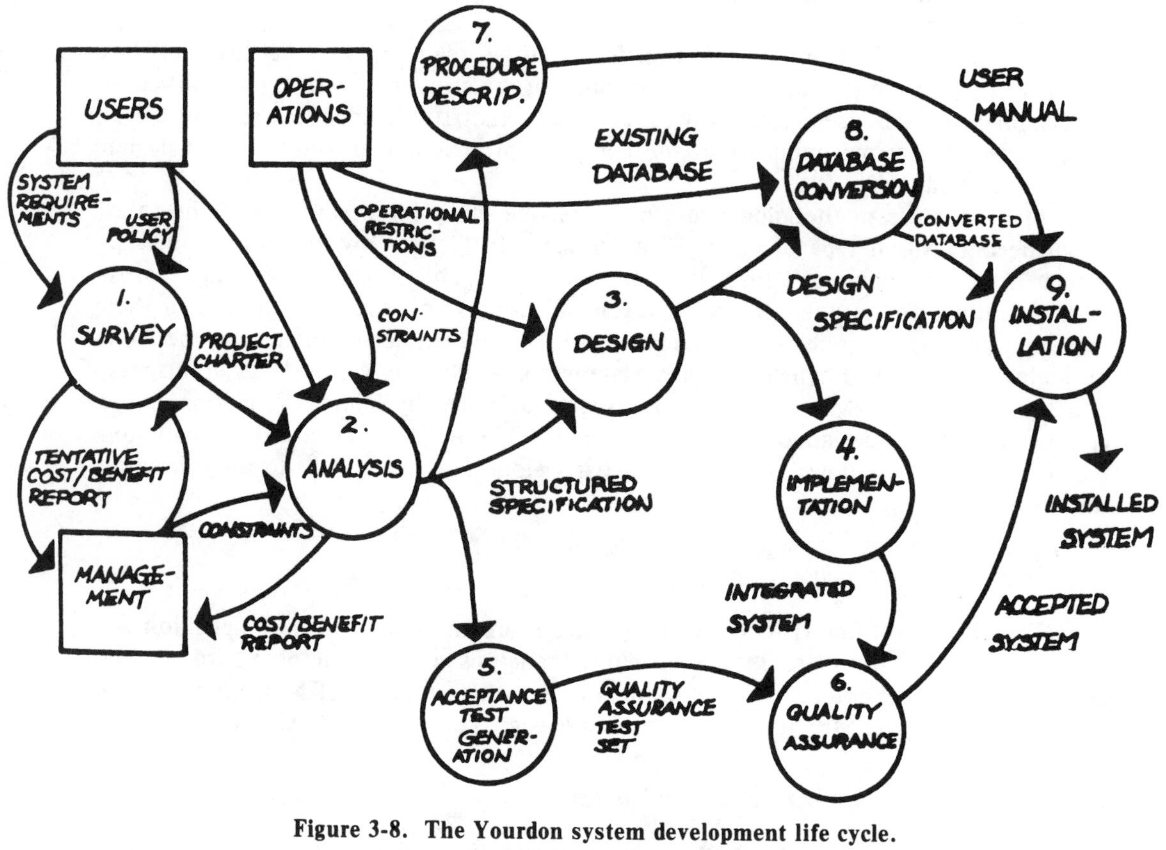

Figure 3-8. The Yourdon system development life cycle.

3.1.3.2 Gane and Sarson's Improved System Technology

Gane and Sarson offer their own version of the functional design methodology, which they call Improved System Technology or simply IST. Essentially, IST is very similar to Yourdon's version of structured analysis; both use data flow diagrams, structure charts, minispecs, and a system data dictionary. The major difference is in the shape and orderliness of the DFDs (see Figure 3-9). It is a cosmetic difference only, but this style of presentation seems to have gained a great deal of popularity.† Part of the popularity is probably because Gane and Sarson's method is simplified: It uses less

---

*From E. Yourdon's *Managing the System Life Cycle* (New York: Yourdon Press, 1982), p. 43. Copyright © 1982 by Yourdon, Inc. Reprinted by permission.

†Gane and Sarson's book, *Structured Systems Analysis: Tools & Techniques* [17], is a clearly presented, detailed version of their methodology. Improved System Technology, Inc., has been acquired by McDonnell Douglas Automation (McAuto) of St. Louis, Mo.

leveling of DFDs, with more bubbles per diagram. Unlike the Yourdon methodology, however, it provides no detailed procedure for logicalization of the *current* system.

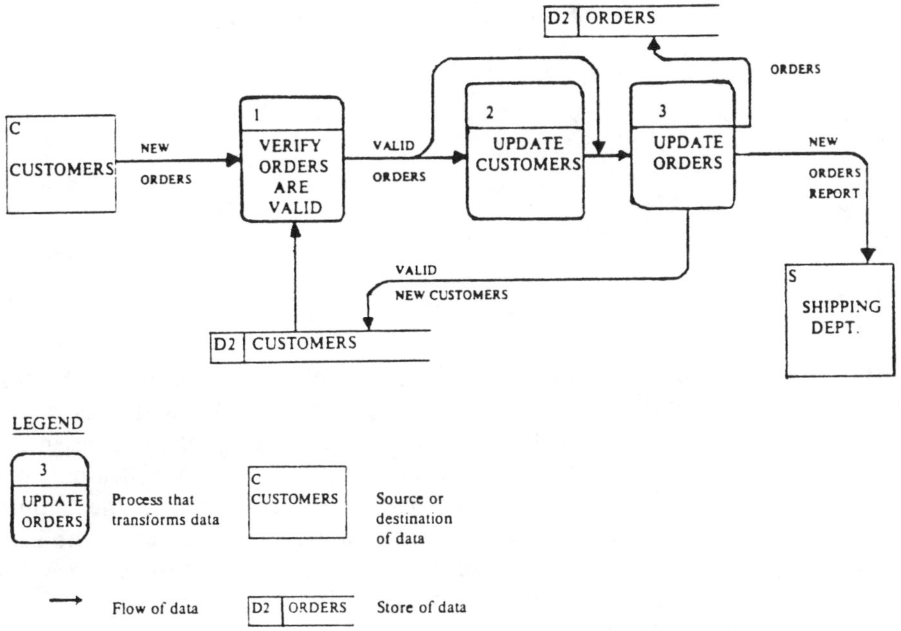

Figure 3-9. A sample IST data flow diagram.

3.1.3.3 SofTech's Structured Analysis and Design Technique

Structured Analysis and Design Technique is a proprietary product of SofTech, Inc., of Waltham, Mass. [32, 52]. It is a powerful but simple diagrammatic technique that can be used to analyze and functionally decompose system problems. SADT is based upon the principles of functional decomposition but uses its own unique notation. This methodology consists of techniques for performing both system analysis and system design, including a process for applying these techniques in requirements definition and system development.

Figure 3-10 shows the basic components of all SADT diagrams. The box represents either an activity or a data item. If the box is an activity, the inputs and outputs are data items, and the diagrams made up of these units are similar in content to data flow diagrams. If the diagramming unit represents a data item, the inputs and outputs are activities. Boxes representing data items do not appear in a diagram that contains boxes representing activities, and vice versa. Therefore, two separate types of diagrams are used in SADT: an activity model in which the boxes represent activities, and a data model in which the boxes represent data items.

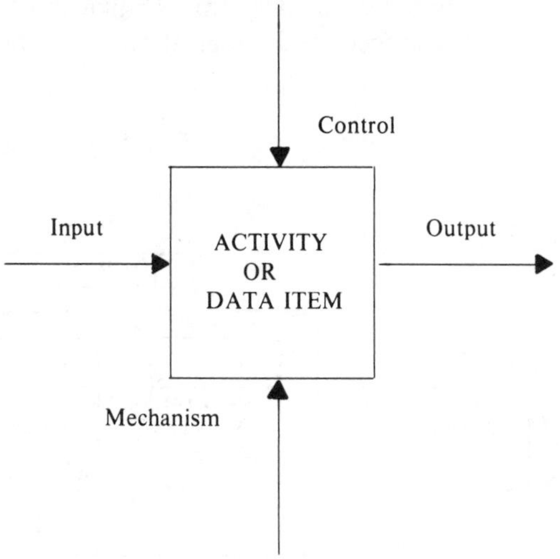

Figure 3-10. The basic SADT diagramming unit.

SADT uses two other connectors in addition to inputs and outputs. The first is the "mechanism" connector, which enters at the bottom of the box. It is used mainly with activity boxes and denotes how the activity could be implemented using an external mechanism. Examples of these mechanisms are sorters, data validators, queue handlers, and occasionally human operators. The second connector is the "control" connector, which enters at the top of the box. It too is normally associated with activity boxes and is a special type of input. A control input is not one that is processed or transformed, but rather is a piece of data such as a switch value that controls the type or degree of activity within the box.

There is the argument that controls and mechanisms simply add unnecessary complications to the activity model and that they are really only special types of inputs. This argument seems valid to me.

In practice, a high-level activity model of the proposed system is produced during the analysis stage. Figure 3-11 is a simple example. In the design stage, each activity is decomposed into a more detailed activity model. This procedure is repeated several times, with each member of the design team being asked to critique the activity model at each iteration.

Eventually, a sufficiently detailed activity model of the proposed system is produced and agreed upon by the design team. At this point in the design process, a complete data model of the system is generated, using the same notation and iterative procedure previously employed to create the activity model. With both models of the system complete, they can be compared with each other for consistency, and any discrepancies must then be resolved. The final activity model must contain enough detail such that the activities are so well defined that they can be programmed directly in the programming language to be used.

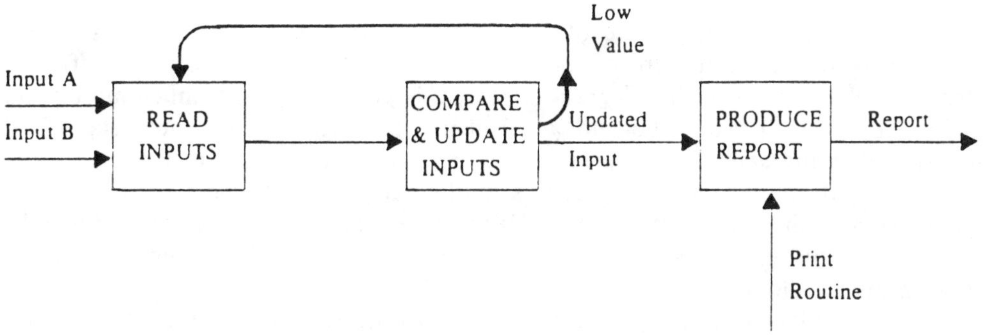

Figure 3-11. High-level activity diagram.

Although SADT offers a procedural and a disciplined approach to structured design, it lacks criteria for assessing the quality of the resulting design and therefore depends significantly upon intuition and experience. But in environments where it has been used comprehensively, improved results over those attained using traditional non-methods have been achieved.

Functional decomposition, especially à la Yourdon and Constantine, is the most widely used structured design technique in the United States' DP industry. However, even this level of popularity and usage has not prevented its users from feeling somewhat abandoned when it comes to procedures for actually designing the specific programs in a system. Even the most fervent admirers of the functional decomposition approach admit that accurate, consistent results are only obtained when experienced, talented systems designers are responsible for the design activities. Even then, a considerable amount of intuition is still required to arrive at the first one or two levels of the data flow diagrams. Nevertheless, the use of these diagrams, the derived structure charts, and other tools of structured design is an enormous step forward from the traditional, seat-of-the-pants methods used in the BS era.*

The technique of DFDs is also used in structured system analysis. A fairly widely held opinion, which I also believe, is that system analysis is not yet an activity that easily succumbs to any procedural methods such as those described above, because the process of system analysis often tends to be a subjective and disorganized activity. I believe that applying structured techniques to such an activity is a waste of time. Nevertheless, many adherents of Yourdon, IST, SADT, and other methods maintain that they are conducting system analysis when they use these methods. My own feeling is that if there is enough detail known about the new system to develop a detailed DFD, the analysis has been completed and the design activities have begun.

However, a strong argument for the use of DFDs to perform structured analysis is that they can be used to help define the problem. If this means that DFDs can be used to further define a general problem or requirement in greater detail, then indeed, DFDs can be defined as an analysis technique. I feel that the major part of system analysis is

*BS stands for Before Structured, of course.

spent in arriving at the general statement of system requirements. What follows is simply detailed requirements definition.

3.2 Data structured design

Data structured design, the other major structured design approach, is based on the premise that the structure of the program or system should be derived from the structure of the data that the program or system is processing. It is much more popular in Europe, where it had its beginnings, than it is currently in the United States. DSD was started in the early 1970s by Jackson of England and Warnier of France. There is little formal documentation of Jackson's methodology, and his book *Principles of Program Design* is the only complete text [19]. Other textual material consists mainly of course notes and examples provided by the various vendors of training courses in the Jackson methodology.

The Warnier methodology is better known as the Warnier-Orr methodology in the United States because of the many practical enhancements made to the basic method by Orr [29, 30]. Both the Jackson and Warnier methodologies provide a strict notation for describing data that can be translated into a program or system description.

3.2.1 Jackson design methodology

Jackson maintains, as does Warnier, that the correct structure of a program is based upon the logical structure of the data that the program is designed to process. The logical structure of the data is defined as the minimal structure that the required program needs to recognize without any of the physical requirements that may be superimposed upon the data by the environment or by other programs. Therefore, the first and major step of the Jackson methodology is to draw the logical structure of the program's input and output data. Jackson uses hierarchical structures to represent data, and he restricts these structures to contain only Dijkstra's three basic structured programming constructs: sequence, selection, and iteration. In this way, exactly the same notation can be used for data and for programs or processes. Figure 3-12 shows the basic notation of Jackson constructs.*

The sequence construct consists of one or more subcomponents, each of which occurs once and in a strict order, shown as left to right in the notation. In Figure 3-12, FILE is an example of the sequence construct composed of BEGINNING, MIDDLE, and END, in that order. SWITCH is a selection that is either ON or OFF or BROKEN each time it is encountered. A selected part is denoted by a circle in the top right-hand corner of the box. No special order of the selected parts is implied by the left-to-right sequence. Neither a sequence nor a selection composed of only one part each is used in this methodology, since a sequence of one part is trivial and a selection of only one part is wrong.

The RECORD component in Figure 3-12 is an example of the iteration construct and it consists of zero or more FIELDS. The "iterated" or repeated part is denoted by the asterisk in the top right-hand corner of the box.

---

*Lest I mislead you, this activity is also carried out in structured analysis and design in order to build the system data dictionary. SADT attempts with less success the same consistency of notation.

In these diagrams, note that the upper-level components FILE, SWITCH, and RECORD are, respectively, the sequence, selection, and iteration components. The lower-level components BEGINNING, MIDDLE, END, ON, OFF, BROKEN, and FIELD are considered for the moment to be elementary because they are not decomposed any further. Of course, depending upon their internal construction, they each could be decomposed into a sequence-, selection-, or iteration-type of structure.

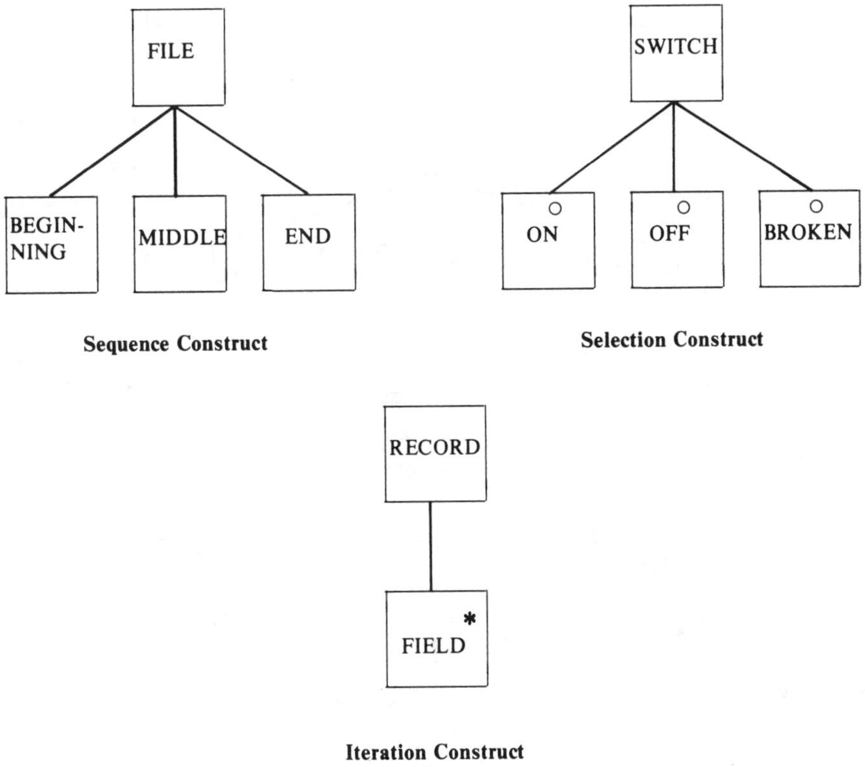

Figure 3-12. Jackson design structural notation.

The three basic constructs can be combined to define the logical structure of a data file, a database, a stream of transactions, or a physical report. Figure 3-13 illustrates how the notation could be used to depict a sales report. This sales report is essentially a list of orders sorted by salesman within region. Each order is either a complete or an incomplete order. Any one salesman's list of orders is preceded by the salesman's name and followed by the total value of his sales. Each group of one region's orders and salesmen is preceded by the regional name and followed by the total sales value for that region. There is a special report header at the beginning of the report itself, and a complete sales total is provided as the last record on the report.

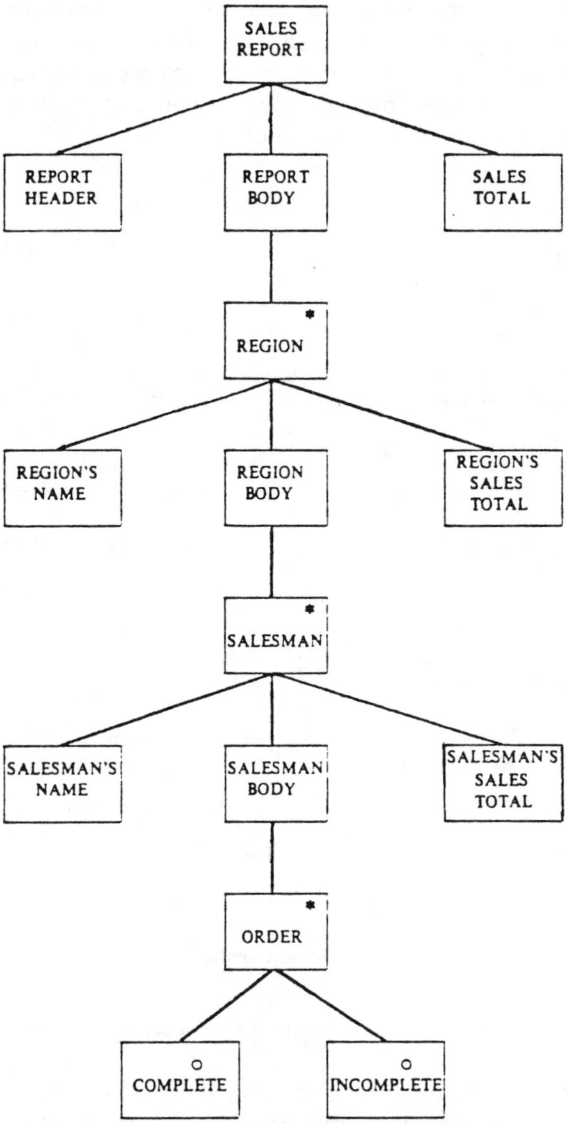

Figure 3-13. Example of a Jackson data structure.

The Jackson methodology for program design is highly procedural and involves the following five steps:

1. *Draw the data structure.* Using the notation described, the designer depicts the input and output data for the program as a series of hierarchical structures. End users and designers review and amend the structure diagrams until both groups are satisfied that the correct logical relationships are represented.

2. *Identify correspondences between the data structures.* The designer identifies processing relationships or "correspondences" between components of the input and output data structures. These correspondences indicate one-for-one processing relationships between the data structures and form the basis for the generation of the program structure. Figure 3-14 shows this step for a simple summarizing report program.

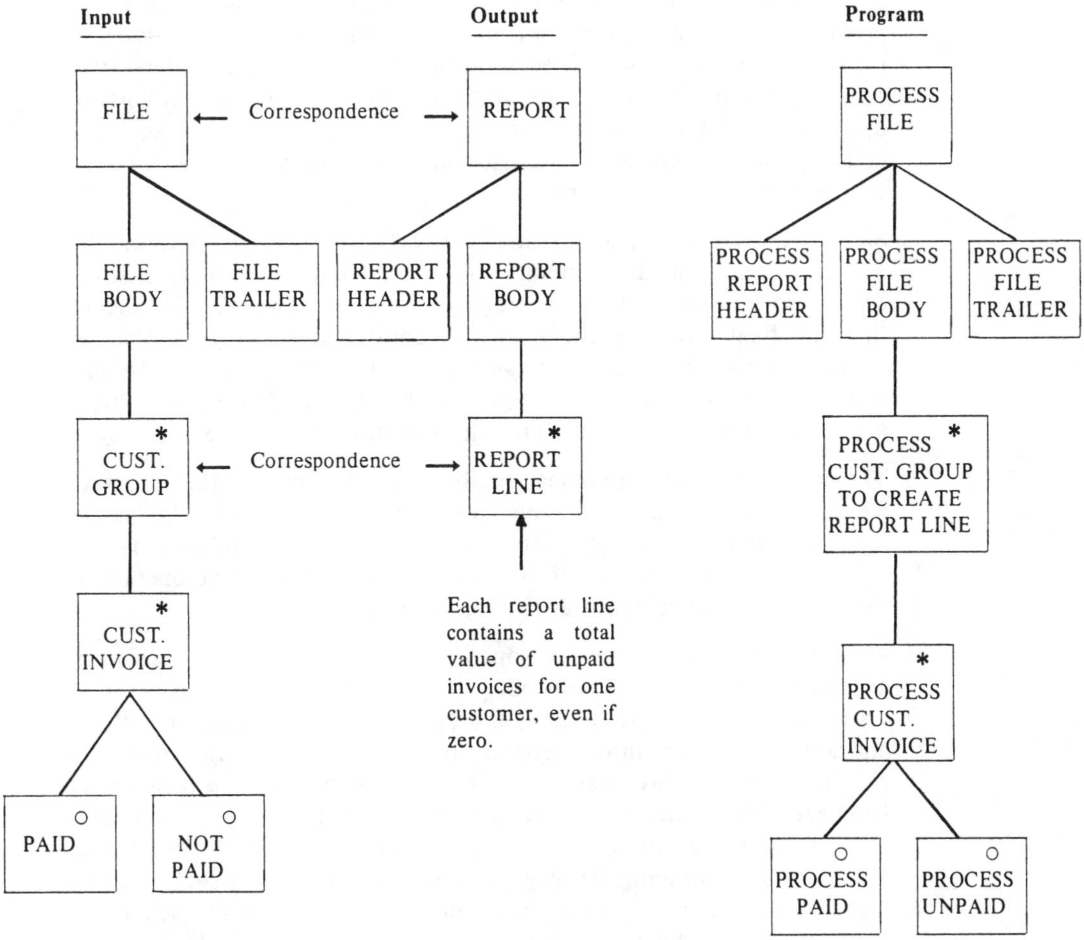

Figure 3-14. Example of a Jackson program structure diagram from input and output data structures.

3. *Form the program structure.* Use the corresponding data components to form single program structure components. Then, add processing components for the remaining, noncorresponding data components to the program structure in the same relative hierarchical positions as they occupied in the data structures. In the resulting program structure, there must be a program component to process each data com-

ponent, although one program component may process several data components in some cases.

For example, in Figure 3-14, data component REPORT BODY doesn't appear in the program structure because it is contained in PROCESS FILE BODY. Additionally, as in the data structures, each program structure component must be either a sequence, a selection, an iteration, or an elementary component. Figure 3-14 shows the creation of a program structure according to these rules.

4. *List and allocate the executable operations.* Since the program structure provides the static, or the control, part of the program, the designer must generate the dynamic, action-oriented part. The Jackson methodology provides a set of rules and a checklist for creating this list of operations and for allocating the items on the list to the correct parts of the program structure. The list and its allocations for the previous example are shown in Figure 3-15.

   Since executable operations are always sequential in nature, the designer usually needs to modify the original program structure in order to preserve the structural integrity. In plainer English, this means that the final structure must still be composed of only correct sequences, selections, iterations, and elementary components. To this end, the components PROCESS CUST. GROUP BODY and PROCESS INVOICE BODY have been added to the program structure in Figure 3-15.

   The operations are intended to be independent of the program language but, in practice, the designer must consider the target language when allocating operations. The general guideline is the lower the level of language to be used, the more executable operations there will be to allocate for any one program.

5. *Write schematic logic.* The Jackson methodology has its own version of structured English or pseudocode. It is called schematic logic and it provides a means of translating the program structure, along with its allocated operations, into a program narrative. The program narrative can then be readily translated into any procedural programming language. Many argue that this step of the methodology is unnecessary, insisting that the program structure can be translated directly into the target programming language without the intervening step of creating schematic logic. This is true, but remember that the schematic logic version of the program is portable, and therefore can be easily translated into a new version of the language or even into a different language when necessary. The program code cannot be changed so easily. A second benefit is that the schematic logic can be regarded as a kind of "super-comment," providing an almost English-language version of the program that can be easily understood by the DP professional and layman alike.

List of Operations

1. STOP
2. OPEN FILES
3. CLOSE FILES
4. WRITE REPORT HEADER
5. WRITE REPORT LINE
6. ADD AMOUNT TO CUST. TOTAL
7. READ FILE RECORD
8. SET CUST. TOTAL TO ZERO
9. STORE CUST. ID

Program Structure

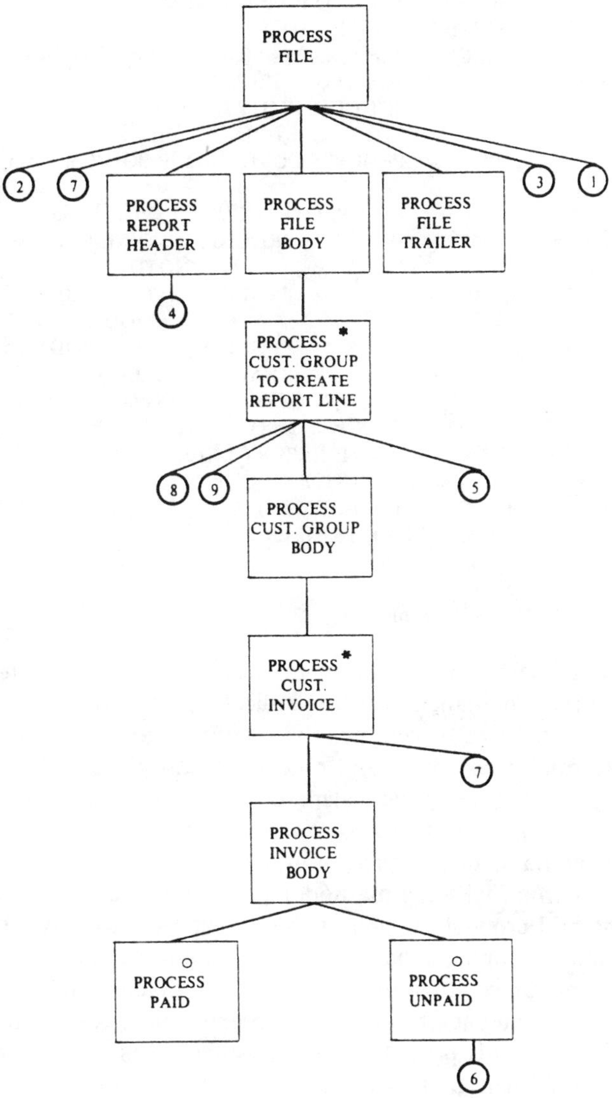

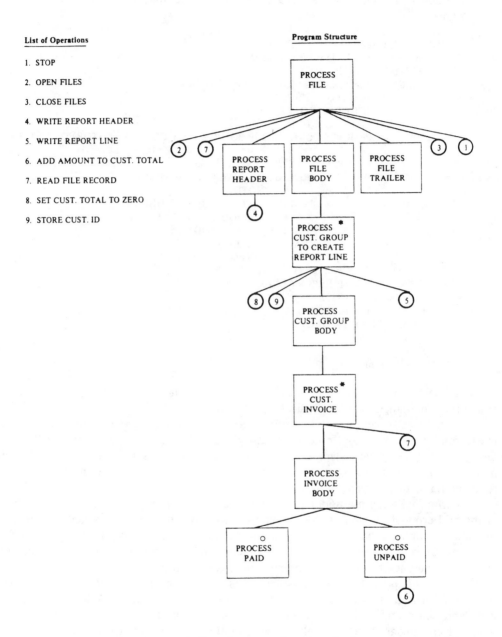

Figure 3-15. Listing and allocating operations to a Jackson program structure.

The schematic logic for the program structure example in Figure 3-15 is as follows:

```
PROCESS FILE seq
    OPEN FILES, READ FILE RECORD
    WRITE REPORT HEADER
    PROCESS FILE BODY iter until TRAILER RECORD
        PROCESS CUST. GROUP seq
            SET CUST. TOTAL TO ZERO
            STORE CUST. ID
            PROCESS CUST. GROUP BODY iter until CUST. ID ≮ STORED CUST. ID
                                           or TRAILER RECORD
                PROCESS CUST. INVOICE seq
                    PROCESS INVOICE BODY sel (PAID)
                        (DO NOTHING)
                    PROCESS INVOICE BODY or (UNPAID)
                        (ADD AMOUNT TO CUST. TOTAL)
                    PROCESS INVOICE BODY end
                    READ FILE RECORD
                PROCESS CUST. INVOICE end
            PROCESS CUST. GROUP BODY end
            WRITE REPORT LINE
        PROCESS CUST. GROUP end
    PROCESS FILE BODY end
    PROCESS FILE TRAILER
    CLOSE FILES
    STOP
PROCESS FILE end
```

The levels of indention in the schematic logic match the levels of the program structure. The italicized words indicate the beginning of the various constructs.

Irrespective of whether the schematic logic step is used, the Jackson methodology is extremely procedural and repeatable and gives highly reliable results in the Program Design and Development stage of the system development life cycle.* With his techniques, Jackson has provided the DP profession with valuable new insights into the fundamental nature of programming.

Within Jackson's methodology are many checklists and tests to ensure the validity of the end product of each of the five steps. Additionally, there are specific techniques to handle complex situations, including structure clash resolution for noncorresponding data structures, program inversion for efficient implementation of multiple concurrent programs, and backtracking for unpredictable error situations.

Use of this procedural methodology does create considerably more program documentation than traditional methods. Data structures, program structures, operations lists, and schematic logic all are produced for each program. As the programs are modified and updated, so must the documentation be changed accordingly. Many DP professionals consider this to be a disadvantage of Jackson's and others' structured design methodologies, but of course, one of the major characteristics that distinguishes

---

*Although Jackson's original method was aimed specifically at program design, a considerable body of work extends the technique into the area of system design [20, 30]. Much of this work consists of merging the system analysis ideas of entities and relationships with the reduction of data structures into third normal form and Jackson's structure clash resolution techniques.

a method from no method is documentation. Full acceptance of the structured design methods may well depend upon the availability of effective automated documentation production and updating tools.

Designers for Exxon in Florham Park, N.J., have partially automated the Jackson documentation. In their PST (Program Structured Technology) software developed internally, they can produce Jackson program structures using their computer terminals. The program structures, when completed on the screens, are transmitted automatically to a preprocessor, which creates the requisite PL/I code.

Jackson's company, Michael Jackson Systems, Ltd., of London, England, has developed a preprocessor called JSP-COBOL, which accepts schematic logic-type text as input. This preprocessor then produces COBOL text, program structure diagrams, and other outputs.

3.2.2 Warnier-Orr methodology

The Warnier-Orr methodology is the most popular data structured approach in the United States, mainly due to the work of Orr [29, 30]. Its approach is similar to Jackson's but it differs in that data and program structures are represented by different notation (brackets).

In a Warnier-Orr diagram, the same basic structures of sequence, selection, and iteration can be represented. In Figure 3-16, which shows the Warnier-Orr notation used to describe a simple sales report, each bracket represents a sequence of entities from top to bottom. In addition, the entities SALE, AREA, SALESMAN, and ORDER are all repeated or iterated items. Each entity on the diagram can occur the number of times indicated within the parentheses under the entity name. The COMMISSION entity at the order level of the structure is a selection or alternative construct. This is denoted as shown by placing COMMISSION and NO COMMISSION in the structure, each of which can occur 0 or 1 time (the line above a word means "not").

A disadvantage of the Warnier-Orr methodology is that it relies too heavily on the assumption that the logical structures of the input and output data are similar. Although this is often the case, the Warnier-Orr technique falls somewhat short of completeness when the structures are very different. The Jackson methodology, by contrast, forces total consideration of the differences and implements their resolution into the design of the resulting program. In assuming that the logical structures of the input and output data are similar, the Warnier-Orr methodology tends to be output-driven. This means that the logical structure of the output data is used as the basis for the program structure in most cases.

The technique used to develop programs from the Warnier-Orr data structures is similar to the five steps of the Jackson methodology:

1. Produce a Warnier-Orr diagram of logical output files.
2. Produce a Warnier-Orr diagram of logical input files.
3. Generate a list of logical operations/functions.
4. Generate a list of executable operations and allocate them to the list of logical operations/functions.
5. Code and test.

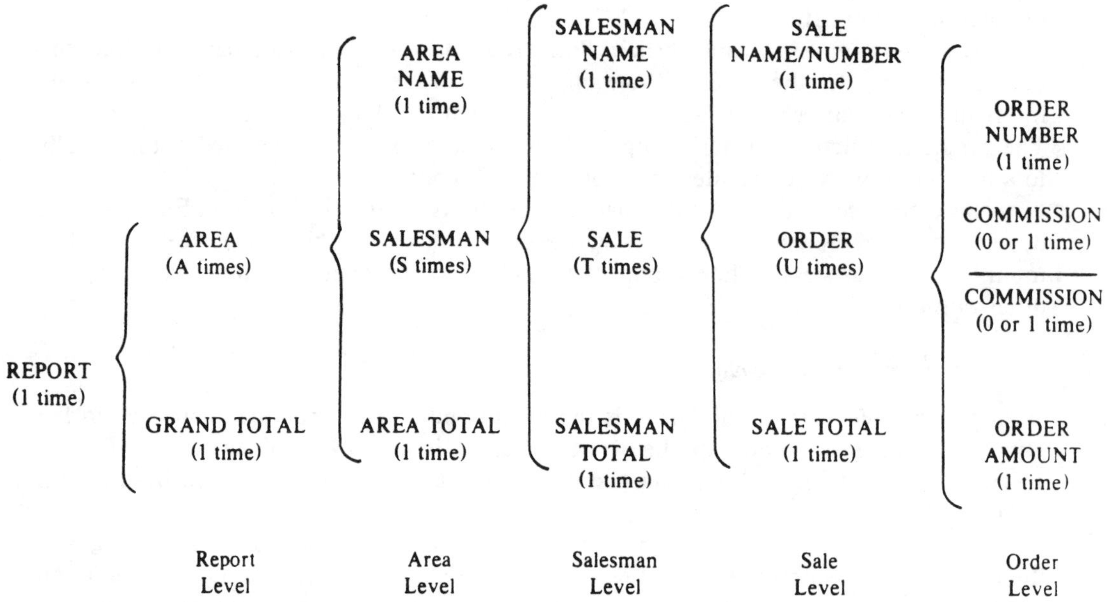

Figure 3-16. A Warnier-Orr data structure.

Although similar to the Jackson procedure, the Warnier-Orr method is not quite so rigorous and procedural. Probably because of this lack of rigor, it has found more favor with DP professionals than has the Jackson methodology and it has been used more at the system design level. Also, the Warnier-Orr notation seems to be more user-friendly than the Jackson structures, and the bracket diagrams are certainly more readily translatable into program narratives.

3.3 A recommended set of design methodologies and techniques

With the plethora of suggested structured analysis and design techniques, it is difficult, and sometimes impossible, for the poor program or system designer to easily choose the right one. I feel there is no single correct choice, and I recommend a framework of compatible techniques applied with some flexibility over the System Specification, System Design, and Program Design and Development stages. In the Requirements Definition stage, I do not recommend using any of these tools unless the users and developers are familiar with them.

Specifically, at the System Specification stage, the Yourdon style data flow diagrams are a useful tool for system definition and for communication between users and the data processing staff. As specification moves into design, DFDs are still valuable tools and I prefer the superficially more organized IST approach. The Yourdon style of DFDs could be simply translated into the IST type if desired. Of course, the original DFDs could be used as the basis for producing the structure charts. The final product of the System Design stage should be a set of clear, hierarchical structure charts and minispecs, with each structure chart component or module representing an easily programmable function.

In order to design the individual programs effectively, the Jackson and Warnier-Orr methodologies seem to be a significant improvement over the functional decomposition techniques. My personal preference is for the Jackson methodology because of its procedurality and completeness.

Figure 3-17 summarizes this recommended subset of structured design techniques. As the figure illustrates, there is some overlap, but this is necessary to allow for differing circumstances in the types of systems being developed, the expertise of the design staff and their familiarity with the methodologies, and existing design standards within the organization.

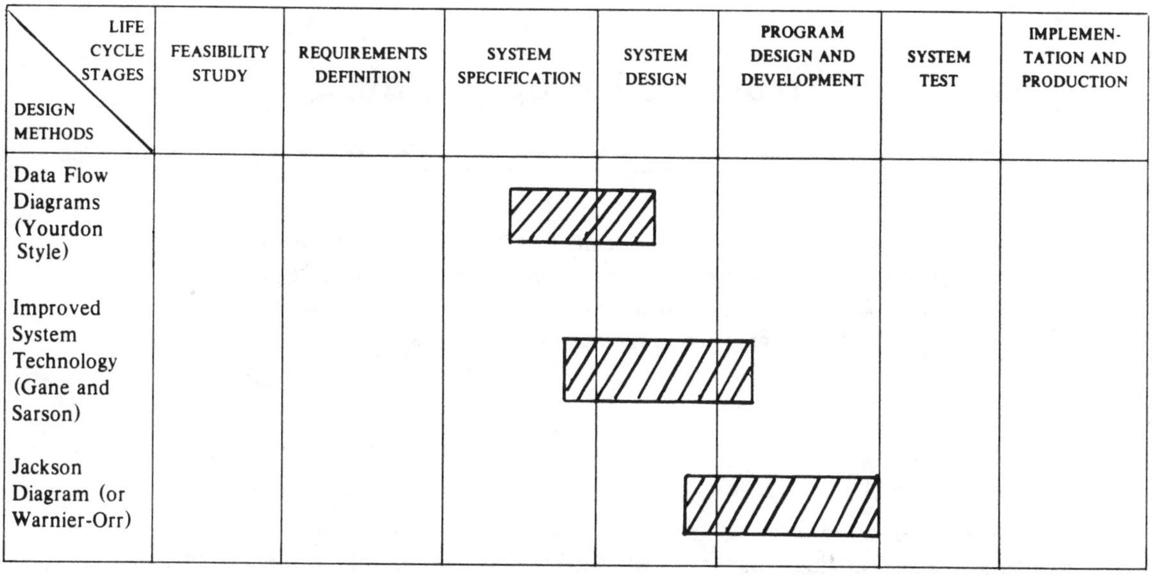

LIFE CYCLE STAGES
DESIGN METHODS
FEASIBILITY STUDY
REQUIREMENTS DEFINITION
SYSTEM SPECIFICATION
SYSTEM DESIGN
PROGRAM DESIGN AND DEVELOPMENT
SYSTEM TEST
IMPLEMENTATION AND PRODUCTION
Data Flow Diagrams (Yourdon Style)
Improved System Technology (Gane and Sarson)
Jackson Diagram (or Warnier-Orr)

Figure 3-17. A practical set of design methodologies in the system life cycle.

3.4 Summary

In this chapter, I have not mentioned all of the structured analysis and design techniques available, merely the most used and the most successful so far. One notable omission is that of Dijkstra's Programming Calculus [14, 18]. I feel that this particular method, although it carries great promise, is not yet in a usable state.

Any of the structured analysis and design methodologies discussed could be effectively installed in any data processing organization, and the resulting change in system developers' thought processes alone would be beneficial. A benevolently dictatorial imposition of a subset of techniques such as those recommended in the previous section could reap enormous rewards — but not immediately. There is a significant learning curve and a variable gestation period for applying the techniques successfully. However, the benefits of doing so include eminently more maintainable programs and systems, DP development staff members who are much more easily transferable between projects, and, best of all, installed systems that the user understands and likes. These benefits are definitely worth the substantial effort.

4

Structured Programming

Any programmer who fails to comply with the standard naming, formatting or commenting conventions should be shot. If it so happens that it is inconvenient to shoot him, then he is to be politely requested to recode his program in adherence to the above standards.

— Michael J. Spier

4.1 Definitions

Structured programming, as it is conventionally understood, should be truly named structured coding, for that is what it is: applying the rules, formats, procedures, and standards for producing structured code that precisely represents the previously developed structured design of a program or a system. More importantly, nontechnical-language comments must accompany the code to explain it to the programming expert and layman alike.

Perhaps Spier's quotation can be more kindly stated as in one of Chumra and Ledgard's famous programming proverbs [9]:

Proverb No. 4 — *Think first, code later.*

In an ideal system development environment, the coding activity should be brief, because the thinking in the analysis and design activities will have already determined how the code should be written; ergo, this chapter will also be brief. If all of the development activities that precede the coding stage have been conducted according to the recommended structured methodologies, the programs will already have been designed in a structured manner. As we saw in Chapter 3, "designed in a structured manner" means that the programs in the new system are designed to maximize the cohesion and minimize the coupling of their internal modules. The detailed logic of each program module is described in pseudocode, schematic logic, or structured English. All that needs to be done now is to translate this semi-English into program code. As the venerable bard wrote, "Aye, there's the rub."

Although lines of pseudocode can be translated into program code, often on a one-for-one basis, most programming languages possess many options as to how this translation can be carried out. Since it has now been proved many times that most, if not all, programs can be implemented using only Dijkstra's three basic constructs, it also should be possible to restrict the number of different types of programming language statements used. This is one of the main thrusts of structured programming — to provide consistent rules for translating sequences, selections, and iterations into the popular programming languages.

4.2 Basic constructs

Each of the modern procedural programming languages provides for the creation of Dijkstra's three basic constructs — sequence, selection, and iteration. In fact, it would not be much of a programming language if it did not provide these basic facilities. In the high-level, user-friendly languages such as COBOL and PL/I, the basic constructs can be implemented directly, whereas in BAL, FORTRAN, and other low-level languages, they cannot. In any event, there always should be consistent standards for coding the three constructs. The generation of a sequence construct is of course trivial. Selections and iterations can be produced in COBOL and PL/I, as described in the next two sections.

4.2.1 COBOL constructs

To code a selection construct in COBOL, the programmer uses the standard IF-ELSE statement. For example,

```
IF SEX-CODE IS EQUAL TO 'M'
    ADD 1 TO TOTAL-MALES
ELSE
    ADD 1 TO TOTAL-FEMALES.
```

A CASE statement in COBOL and in many other languages can be used to implement more than two choices in a selection.

In order to generate an iteration in COBOL, the most commonly used translation is the PERFORM-UNTIL statement. A typical example is

```
PERFORM PROCESS-RECORD
    UNTIL EOF IS EQUAL TO 'E'.
```

This loop iteratively carries out the processing contained within a paragraph of logic identified by the name PROCESS-RECORD. The iteration stops when the "flag" EOF-FILE contains an 'E'. In standard COBOL, paragraphs such as PROCESS-RECORD must be written "out of line." That is, the detailed statements of paragraph PROCESS-RECORD cannot be written directly following the PERFORM statement but must be contained elsewhere, out of line from the main-line code. The PERFORM then effectively extends a branch to the detailed statements. When the processing within the paragraph is complete, the program branches back to recheck the EOF condition. This process is repeated until the required EOF condition to terminate the loop is encountered. The PERFORM-UNTIL type of loop has the capability of being carried out zero times. In this case, if EOF-FILE already contains an 'E', an "empty" file is encountered and no processing of records is carried out — which is just as well!

Although the PERFORM-UNTIL is the standard COBOL iteration construct, there are numerous other ways to implement an iteration in COBOL, many of them using other variations of PERFORM. Although their use should be limited as much as possible, some of the PERFORM variations are required under special circumstances. For instance, PERFORM-VARYING is used to terminate the iteration when a variable reaches a specified limit, approaching that limit by a series of fixed increments. PERFORM (paragraph name) N TIMES is self-explanatory. The PERFORM can also be used to execute blocks of code only once, but we are not concerned with that simple use here.

4.2.2 PL/I constructs

Like COBOL, the most common implementation of the selection construct in PL/I is the IF-THEN-ELSE statement. Typically, the statement is used as in this simple example:

```
IF BALANCE = 0
THEN
    PAYMENT = 0;
ELSE
    PAYMENT = SUM;
```

In PL/I, as in COBOL, a CASE statement easily implements a multiple selection.

Many options are available in PL/I to implement the iteration construct, but the most effective is the DO WHILE. This loop construct, like COBOL's PERFORM-UNTIL, allows the zero iteration and therefore is the most general type of iteration. A simple implementation of the DO WHILE is

```
DO WHILE (EOF = 'E');
    READ FILE(IN) INTO (INDATA);
    D = DOLLARS;
    P = PR + DOLLARS;
END;
```

In PL/I, the actions within the iteration are in-line, unlike in COBOL. This provides the advantage of revealing more clearly what is really happening in the program. As with COBOL, there are many other ways in PL/I to implement the iteration construct. For example,

```
DO UNTIL(A = B);
DO I = 1 TO N;
```

PL/I, in fact, is so rich in different ways to implement all the structures that defining local standards for their implementation is very important. Otherwise, every programmer will find a good reason for implementing the iterations and selections in a totally different manner from all other programmers. This may be personally satisfying, but it is not at all conducive to easily understanding and maintaining the programs.

4.3 The infamous GOTO

I call the GOTO statement infamous because of the controversy that it has provoked for at least two decades. Should we or shouldn't we use it? As soon as any program other than the most trivial begins to be coded, it becomes abundantly clear that branching constructs are not only needed, they are essential. The question then becomes, How should the GOTO be restricted? Clearly, total abstention from the forbidden delights of branching is not practical despite the many learned papers to the contrary, but branches should be limited to where they are absolutely necessary. Some acceptable uses of GOTOs are described below, followed by a section on unacceptable uses.

4.3.1 *Acceptable uses of GOTOs*

GOTOs may be used when a COBOL subroutine has multiple entry points and when one or more of those entry points is within a nested-IF construct. Because of the ancient COBOL compiling rules, the labels to identify the entry points cannot be placed within the nested-IF. In this case, the nested-IF must be coded using GOTOs instead of IF-ELSEs.

For example, in pseudocode, an IF-ELSE construct such as

```
IF RECORD IS EQUAL TO RECEIPT
    BAL = BAL - AMT
ELSE
    BAL = BAL + AMT.
```

becomes

```
ASEL.
    IF RECORD IS EQUAL TO PAYM
        GOTO AOR.
    BAL = BAL - AMT
    GOTO AEND.
AOR.
    BAL = BAL + AMT.
AEND.
```

(ASEL, AOR, and AEND are labels.)

Similarly, in PL/I and COBOL, the iteration construct can cause problems when in a subroutine. For example, in order to avoid the problem of an index variable changing values in a subroutine, the loop can be coded in PL/I as follows:

```
PROC:
          •
          •
        ALOOP: IF (.NOT EOF)
            THEN
              •
              •
              •
            GOTO ALOOP;
        LOOPEND:
          •
          •
END PROC;
```

(ALOOP and LOOPEND are labels.)

The above situations illustrating when GOTOs can be used are often more mandatory than merely acceptable. There are many other cases when it makes good sense to use the branch constructs; and at these times, the walkthrough concept in a team environment is useful to obtain a consensus (see Chapter 14).

Whenever the GOTO is used, legitimately or otherwise, the accompanying documentation must fully explain why the branch is there and how it is being utilized. As long as procedural programming languages are being used, GOTOs or their equivalents will probably be necessary. The fanatical supporters of GOTO-less programs would be wise to remember that every COBOL PERFORM and every PL/I DO WHILE contains hidden GOTOs and to eliminate them entirely would only result in very long programs.

4.3.2 Unacceptable uses of GOTOs

Of course, there are situations when using a GOTO is not wise. If implementation of the GOTO would cause a pathological coupling to occur between two modules, as described in Chapter 3, the GOTO should definitely not be used. A second example is the case of a programmer who has coded and stored much of the program and then finds a portion of code needs to be inserted at the start of the source listing. The new code must *not* be implemented using labels and GOTOs. With modern interactive text-editing tools and techniques, this use of the GOTO becomes totally unnecessary.

Remember, GOTOs are like calories: We cannot live without some GOTOs, but an excess of them used indiscriminately is harmful to the health of our programs.

4.4 Consistent formatting rules

In addition to limiting the types of program statement used, each local DP environment must decide upon a consistent physical layout structure for each set of coding instructions or statements that is defined as a program. For example, the COBOL language provides such a structure, with every COBOL program constructed in a sequence of four DIVISIONS as follows:

- The IDENTIFICATION DIVISION identifies and generally documents the program.
- The ENVIRONMENT DIVISION defines the target computer and the various input and output devices used by the program.
- The DATA DIVISION describes the files, records, and components of the records used and created by the program.
- The PROCEDURE DIVISION contains the actual COBOL instructions that implement the logical operations of the program.

In another example, PASCAL also demands a formal structure. For the sake of formatting consistency, every PASCAL program should consist of nine parts:

- BEGIN defines the start of program logic and operations.
- PROGRAM contains the identifier (name) of the program and any general parameters and characteristics.
- LABEL lists all labels used in the program.
- CONST defines any constants used on the program.
- TYPE defines any nonstandard data types used.
- VAR declares and defines all variables used in the program.
- PROCEDURE defines a programmer-specified procedure to be called from within the program. There is one procedure statement for each such procedure.
- FUNCTION defines a programmer-specified function to be called from within the program. There is one function statement for each such function.
- END signals the end of the program.

PROCEDURES and FUNCTIONS are internally called subroutines and therefore themselves have the structure of a complete program.

Many of the other popular programming languages currently in use are not constrained in the way that COBOL and PASCAL are. PL/I, for instance, is a powerful, almost completely free-form, and totally unrestrained language. Because PL/I is almost as powerful as Assembly language, because of its ability to manipulate data, and because it is easy to learn to use, it can quickly become a tool of the inexperienced programmer. However, this inexperience coupled with the power of PL/I becomes dangerous if not controlled.

If a formatted language such as PASCAL or COBOL is not being used, some formatting rules must be defined to consistently locate data declarations, standard procedures, general descriptive information, and other common factors. Hence, when the programs are being maintained or updated, the maintenance programmer will always know where to look for particular types of information. This ease of maintenance is one of the major benefits of structured programs. In the absence of a given format, the PASCAL structure is a practical model.

4.5 Comments

The English- or nontechnical-language comments that accompany the code must be an integral and essential part of the source code of any program. These comments are non-executable explanations of what the program is actually doing at each point in the code. In general, the higher level the programming language being used, the less detailed the comments need to be. However, a high-level procedural language that needs absolutely no comments has not yet appeared.

With a very low-level language such as BAL, one comment per line of code is recommended. This level of detail in the comments is not always necessary, but one comment per line is probably a good, practical guideline because of the highly cryptic nature of most BAL instructions. Even then, it may be necessary to add a paragraph of ordinary English occasionally to explain fully some particularly abstruse function.

The higher forms of life in programming languages such as COBOL, PL/I, PASCAL, and ADA, certainly do not need one explanatory comment per programming statement. However, the practice of inserting a line or two, or even a paragraph, of comments for each half-page or so of code to explain the coded functions is one to be encouraged, even enforced, as a documentation standard.

Most of the structured design techniques discussed in detail in Chapter 3 provide for the generation of a pseudocode version of the program prior to coding. As suggested before, this structured English version of the program should be entered into the source library as a kind of super-comment at the start of the program code itself.

4.6 Summary

Modern programming languages such as PASCAL, ALGOL, and ADA have been developed with the structured programming constructs in mind so that standardizing the implementation of sequences, selections, and iterations is easy, and hence all programs in these languages can be built with just those three constructs (plus a few controlled GOTOs).

In *all* programming languages, the use of GOTOs must be controlled, and standard implementations of all types of branching constructs must be agreed upon within the data processing organization. Once the rules and standards have been established, they must be monitored and enforced. If the team environment is set up in the DP development group, the walkthrough process is the ideal mechanism for such monitoring and enforcement. (The team concept is discussed in Chapter 13, and walkthroughs are described in Chapter 14.)

The near and mid-term future of DP application programming certainly belongs to the modern, structured languages. However, many programmers continue to believe that the only *real* programming language is the one they first learned — BAL in many cases. Slowly and painfully, these programming masochists are dying out. But, as the procedural languages become easier to use, simultaneously the nonprocedural, user-friendly languages will begin to take over. Today's high-level, structured languages will appear restrictive and clumsy compared with the human-language oriented, conversational program development techniques of the future. Structured programming will eventually prove to have been only a phase, albeit a very important phase, in the movement of DP program development from an esoteric black art to an efficient, ubiquitous business process.

5

The Traditional System Development Life Cycle

A perfect method should not only be an efficient one, as respects the accomplishments of the objects for which it is designed, but should in all its parts and processes manifest a certain unity and harmony.

— George Boole

5.1 Evolution of the SDLC

A system development life cycle that consists of sequential stages, each with a specific end product, is now generally accepted as an effective way to control the diverse activities necessary to develop a medium to large DP system. The idea of phased development of DP products arose from many different sources, but there were certainly two major influences. One significant influence was the structured revolution of the 1970s. As explained in Chapter 2, what has emerged from that revolution is a strategy called top-down implementation that breaks a system or a problem into its major functions, with each function being decomposed into its components.

The second major influence was the development of the Polaris submarine in the early 1950s. Leaders of the Polaris project recognized the need to define the vast activity in terms of many discrete, controllable steps. It was one of the first major military projects to use critical path analysis and the "balloons and strings" diagrams for scheduling and for planning resource expenditures.

A simple version of this technique uses "event diagrams" similar in appearance to data flow diagrams. In event diagrams, the bubbles represent events, or milestones, and the lines between bubbles represent activities. Each activity is identified by the *real time* and the *elapsed time:* Real time is the amount of time needed to complete the activity from start to finish, assuming no interruptions. Elapsed time, on the other hand, is the amount of time available to carry out the activity, usually a longer period than that for the corresponding real time. For example, the real time for an activity A may be three and a half days, and the elapsed time six days. This means that in the six-day period available, activity A can be started at any time up to the middle of the third day and still be finished in the time available (see Figure 5-1). The difference between the elapsed time and the real time is known as the *slack time.* Obviously, for an activity to be realistic, the slack time cannot be negative, but it can be zero!

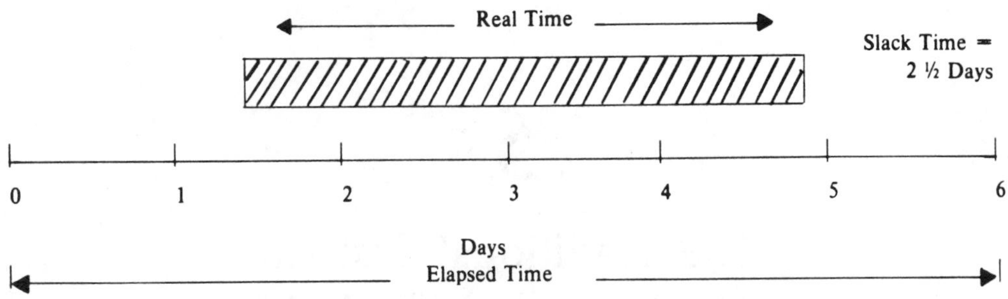

Figure 5-1. Real time versus elapsed time in an event diagram.

There are usually several paths through an event diagram. For example, there are four paths in the diagram in Figure 5-2. The path with the least amount of slack time is defined as the critical path, and consequently it is the one that contains the events and activities that should be concentrated on.

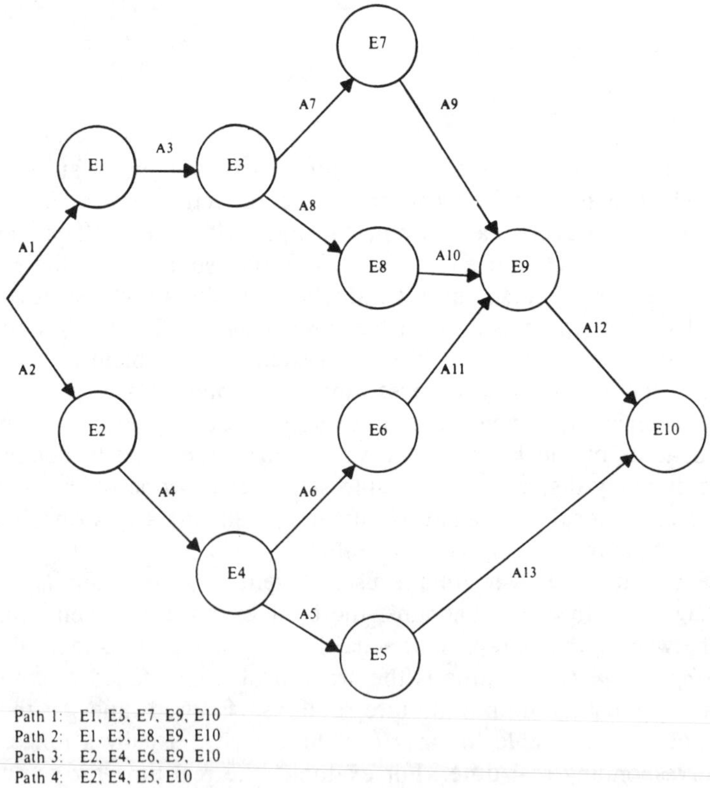

Figure 5-2. Critical path analysis.

To determine which of the four paths is the critical path in our example, add the amounts of slack time for the activities on each path. Table 5-1 lists the amounts of time for each of the thirteen activities in Figure 5-2. Path 1 has a total slack time of thirteen days, Path 2 fifteen days, Path 3 four days, and Path 4 eleven days. In this case, then, Path 3 is the critical path because it has the smallest margin for error and deserves the closest attention.

Table 5-1
Schedule for Activities A1 Through A13

	Time, in Days		
Activity	Real Time	Elapsed Time	Slack Time
A1	10	13	3
A2	12	12	0
A3	7	10	3
A4	8	9	1
A5	10	15	5
A6	3	4	1
A7	6	10	4
A8	5	7	2
A9	8	9	1
A10	10	15	5
A11	12	12	0
A12	10	12	2
A13	15	20	5

Both the success of the Polaris project from a scheduling and resource expenditure viewpoint and the improved results from applying the structured, top-down techniques pointed to one conclusion: that any large engineering development project was not simply an amorphous set of parallel tasks but consisted of a series of sequential phases, each of which produced its own discrete end product. Perhaps by focusing on these interim end products, the separate stages of development could be clearly delineated and a natural SDLC defined. The remainder of this chapter examines the many SDLCs available, their characteristics, and my own version of the traditional SDLC.

5.2 Variations on the SDLC theme

Many different versions of the SDLC are being marketed as products, taught as methodologies or philosophies, and used formally or otherwise in all types of organizations and on all types and sizes of projects. For example, Colin Bentley in *Computer Project Management* [2] defines eight major stages: problem definition, feasibility study, detailed analysis, design, development, site preparation, system load, and acceptance test. He also states that six general activities are essential for every stage: organization, planning, control, phase definition, tasks, and documentation.

There are many system development methodologies (SDMs), some of which are commercial packages. When a specific SDLC is marketed as a product, it normally takes the shape of a set of manuals and includes forms and checklists designed to monitor the activities in the various stages. In addition to a comprehensive set of generic task lists and generic descriptions of required end products, formats for the documentation products are also provided to guide the project manager through the maze of system development. The complete "Project Management" or "System Development" package is often a large, multi-volume set of manuals that can be intimidating at first glance. However, if used intelligently, this package can be extremely effective in organizing the myriad system development activities into a coherent whole.

Three of the most popular SDLC packages in use today in the United States are SPECTRUM, marketed by Spectrum International, of Los Angeles; SDM/70, marketed by Atlantic Management Systems, of Philadelphia; and PRIDE-ASDM, marketed by Milt Bryce Associates, of Cincinnati. All of these packages divide the complete system development effort into a number of sequential stages, with each stage producing an identifiable end product. PRIDE-ASDM is slightly different from the other two because it is fully integrated into a software package that includes several automated facilities and its own built-in system design method. This means that the users of PRIDE-ASDM have little choice in the design methods to be used. In contrast, SDM/70 and SPECTRUM are completely manual and forms-driven. They make no assumptions about design methods but simply provide a rigorous framework, based on phases and stages, onto which any compatible set of techniques can be superimposed. All of the techniques mentioned in this book are compatible with SDM/70 and SPECTRUM. All three packages have significant numbers of users outside of the United States, notably in Canada, Australia, and Western Europe.

Although there are other packages available, most of them were developed by individual organizations to meet a specific need and consequently are heavily tailored to a particular environment. IBM, for one, uses many such methodologies internally. For example, one in-house life cycle method will declare that fifteen discrete stages are necessary, and another will assert that three are sufficient. Nevertheless, all of these different methodologies have six important concepts in common: discrete stages, stage-limited commitment, sign-off of interim end products, in-stage reviews, generic task lists, and review boards or committees.

Discrete stages: The life cycle consists of a set of stages, each of which is distinguished by the activities performed and by a specific interim end product, usually in the form of documentation. This documentation serves as the input for the next stage.

Stage-limited commitment: At the end of each stage, a detailed commitment is granted to produce the next stage's end product only. Instead of trying to provide an accurate and detailed estimate of all of the SDLC stages at once, this concept requires that one of the activities in each stage must provide a detailed estimate of the next stage in terms of cost, time, manpower, and other resources to be expended. The estimate for all of the remaining stages (except for the very next stage) is given, but is for general guidance only and will become more accurate as more stages are completed. The stage-limited commitment, which is sometimes referred to as a "creeping commitment," is especially important for large projects with a rapidly changing environment that makes it almost impossible to develop an accurate long-term estimate. However, this type of commitment requires that the provider of funds for the project must accept that the estimate for the completion of the system will inevitably change with time and, as Murphy would undoubtedly confirm, will always increase in terms of time and resources to be expended.

Sign-off of interim end products: At the end of each stage, the interim end product is reviewed by all affected organizational functions, particularly those that will use the end product as a starting point to develop the end product of the next stage. Throughout the SDLC, the concept of feedback is important. The output documentation or end product from any stage must be compared with that of previous stages to ensure that a correct translation has been made. The general trend through the life cycle is a progressively more explicit, more detailed, more accurate, and more complete end product. In theory, at the end of each stage, the project manager can call for cancellation of the project because of the existence of one or more possibly critical situations. For example, the organization's business needs may have changed to the point at which the project is no longer cost-effective. A project may also be canceled if the cost estimate to complete the project exceeds a certain amount. In practice, however, cancellation of a project becomes progressively more difficult to justify as increasing amounts of resources are invested.

In-stage reviews: There are usually three or four significant points within each stage when sufficient results have been produced to have a "mini-review" of them. As a result, the final end-stage review is more of a formality because most problems and mistakes have been spotted early on and corrected prior to the end of the stage. The in-stage reviews can be carried out formally as walkthroughs or inspections or can be informal peer-group sessions. How they are carried out depends a great deal upon the management style of the project managers and upon the degree of rigor imposed by the methodology being used.

Generic task lists: No matter how different the systems being developed are and how different the end products for identical stages, there is one generic set of tasks to be carried out regardless of the methodology chosen. Therefore, in using one methodology to develop different systems, this set of generic tasks varies little, if at all, for any one stage from project to project. Since there is little variation in the set of generic tasks, product consistency is ensured and activities are not omitted, either through oversight or ignorance.

Recognition of a generic set of tasks is critical to the success of a system development methodology. Many objections to, and failures of, SDMs are because the users of a particular methodology focus on the formatted end products provided as examples in the manuals. Users perceive these examples as being necessary and sufficient end products for *all* systems to be developed using the methodology. This, of course, is looking at the SDM in a backward manner. The generic task lists for each stage are the driving force behind any good SDM, not the reverse.

Review boards or committees: Certain business functions are affected by the development and implementation of any significant DP system. Two functions that obviously are directly affected are the DP organization and the end users of the system. In addition, the organization's financial control function, usually known as the controller's department, is also affected because of the drain on corporate funds caused by the project development activities. Therefore, the review committee for each stage's end product should include members of each of these three departments to represent their specific interests. Representatives of DP operations also need to be involved if its members will work with the new system and if DP operations will be a separate organizational entity.

5.3 SDLC stages

With these six characteristics in mind, I now offer my own SDLC, which has seven stages: Feasibility Study, Requirements Definition, System Specification, System Design, Program Design and Development, System Test, and Implementation and Production. These seven stages are my own distillation of the practical SDMs that I have worked with and that I have seen working in various organizations; they are used for the detailed discussions in the book. I believe that these stages are always present in some form in all system development projects. Although the names may change and the boundaries between stages may differ, the set of contained tasks should remain constant.

The following sections briefly describe the purpose of, and the activities within, each of these stages. Chapters 6 through 12 are devoted to more detailed descriptions of the stages, and Chapter 16 deals with the changes needed to this basic SDLC for future DP and user requirements.

5.3.1 Feasibility Study

The objective of the first stage is to prove that the proposed system is practical. The Feasibility Study is carried out before the project has full financial approval, and it is of necessity usually one of the shortest and least expensive of all the stages. Involvement from the organizational triumvirate of financial controllers, end users, and DP developers is essential at this stage to ensure proper development and fast approval of the Feasibility Study.

Input to the Feasibility Study is often simply a one-page memo or a standard Project Request Form issued by a user organization describing the issue to be resolved. The end-stage document from the Feasibility Study contains at least the following:

- a brief description of the proposed system that includes a preliminary description of the project type such as batch or on-line, file or database (including probable hardware and software type, primary and secondary users, and so forth); some of these type descriptions will be little more than educated guesses and inevitably will be changed radically when better information is available later in the life cycle
- a cost-benefit analysis that includes a payback schedule and a gross estimate of the project costs
- a tentative schedule for completion of key end products

5.3.2 Requirements Definition

During Requirements Definition, the early description of the proposed system from the Feasibility Study is expanded into an accurate and complete set of user requirements. A detailed analysis of the existing equivalent system, manual or automated, is essential to ensure that the list of requirements is complete. This is not to say that the replacement system should be a duplicate of the current system; but the analysis of the current system must form a basis for the requirements of the new system, because the current system fulfills a current business need that must still be met by the new system. Therefore, the Requirements Definition document contains the following information or deliverables:

- an analysis of the current system
- a set of new system user requirements
- a summary of the proposed system

- estimates of the next stage and of the remainder of the project
- an index to all related material

Most of the information required for the above deliverables is obtained through direct interviews with current and future users of the system. These interviews supply information on user needs about such things as timing constraints, general performance expectations, and allowable tolerances in the accuracy of the information generated by the system; they should *not* specify types of hardware and software or any logical group of functions. The final output document resulting from these interviews should contain as little DP jargon as possible. Data flow diagrams can be used to represent the user requirements if the users and the developers are familiar and comfortable with this notation.

5.3.3 System Specification

The objective of the System Specification stage is to define a DP system that will fully meet the user requirements. That is, the user requirements from the previous stage are translated into data processing terms. When the end users are well acquainted with DP technology, including its capabilities and limitations, the System Specification will be a simple one-for-one translation of the Requirements Definition document into DP terms. Unfortunately, this is not normally the case. As a simple analogy, consider a set of requirements for an automobile and the resulting specifications by a knowledgeable auto designer:

Customer's Requirements	Automobile Specifications
Smooth ride	Highest quality shocks, four-wheel independent suspension
Clear-sounding radio	Four-speaker stereo AM/FM radio with minimum output of two watts per channel
Reliable, smooth braking under all weather conditions	In-board, non-fading, non-locking, hydraulic-powered, four-wheel disk brakes

To translate the requirements into DP terms, the developers start by defining the system data requirements in the system data dictionary, which exists at least in outline form from the previous stage's activities. If a corporate or global data dictionary already exists, the relevant extracts from it are incorporated into the system data dictionary. Any general database requirements are identified at this stage without being unnecessarily specific about the type of database to be used, and selection of a database management system may be started. If the organization has assigned a data administrator, now is the time for this person to get involved with the proposed system at an advisory level. The structured techniques and tools such as DFDs and structure charts can be applied in this stage. The system test plan is also begun in this stage.

5.3.4 System Design

The objective of the System Design stage is to produce a detailed, technical, logical definition of the final system, so that the final set of programs can be produced directly from that definition.* Therefore, the System Design document is a combination of both narrative description and diagrams that detail all the processing and data elements in the system and their relationships.

The structured design techniques are used fully in this stage to provide a top-down overall system structure, with every module or program identified and its inputs and outputs defined in as much detail as possible. (The final details may be left until the Program Design and Development stage.) All operational timing and physical constraints are identified during this stage, and a complete system flow diagram is developed based on that information. A recommendation is made as to which parts of the system should be developed from scratch and which parts should be purchased as complete packages. Development of the system test plan continues, so that the end users can provide their own test criteria in the next stage.

The System Design stage is the first major effort of the entire DP development organization. If a database administrator and a data administrator have not yet been assigned, this stage is the last chance to include them in any meaningful way in the project. A database administrator is needed if a database is to be used and if a database management system is to be selected. A data administrator is required if a corporate data dictionary exists for the organization. Both functions are involved in defining data conversion requirements in this stage. Conversion of data from old formats to new formats may require special one-time programs; their design requirements are detailed as part of this stage's end product. The end product of the System Design stage is, for the most part, a technical product and is the responsibility of the data processing members of the development team. By the end of this stage, the development team for the rest of the project is identified and assigned.

The following are the deliverables from this stage:

- a management summary of the proposed system
- a detailed system description
- system controls
- a revised cost-benefit analysis and payback schedule
- recommended design alternatives
- recommended program design techniques and programming standards
- a preliminary system test plan
- estimates of the next stage and of the remainder of the project
- an index to related material

---

*A logical description of a system tells *what* the system does; a physical description describes *how* the system does it.

5.3.5 Program Design and Development

This stage's objective is to produce the programs that compose the system, based on the specifications contained in the System Design document. Each program's specification, which was produced in the previous stage, is now given to the programming team. The activities carried out in this stage are those normally called programming, or what is regarded, according to popular programming folklore, as the *real* work. If the system design is of poor quality, the folklore has some merit. But if the System Design document is a high-quality, comprehensive product, the Program Design and Development stage will be the most procedural and straightforward stage so far.

Unfortunately, as most programmers know from their own experiences, the system design is often of poor quality and many parts of the system may need to be redesigned before the programming can start. Even if the system design is good, some additional design of the program and modules always is necessary. For instance, if the programming language to be used is a low-level one, the direct line-for-line translation of the program specification into code may not be possible. Then, further detailed design is necessary. Therefore, programmers need to know not only coding techniques, but also design methodologies at the program or module level.

At the same time the programs are being created, a great deal of both unit and integration testing is also being carried out. These tests are performed according to the preliminary system test plan developed in the previous stage. *Unit testing* ensures that each program or module meets its individual specifications. As each logical function of the system is coded, it is tested. Additionally, if top-down development techniques are being used, the system is tested from top to bottom as part of *integration testing.* Integration testing is the testing of logical groupings of programs or modules to ensure that the specifications of the logical functions are being met satisfactorily.

All programs, procedures, and documentation developed in this as well as in later stages must be such that the users can run the new system without any programmer assistance. The end product of this stage contains at least the following:

- detailed design (for each program)
- design diagrams (for each program)
- logic descriptions
- program documentation — narrative
- input/output data descriptions
- program source listings (including embedded comments)
- job control language (JCL) listings
- operator guide
- user guide
- results of unit tests for each program
- results of integration tests
- user training program and manuals
- operator training program and manuals
- system user guide (for the complete system)

- system operator guide (for the complete system)
- estimates of next stages (including the implementation schedule and conversion plan)
- system test plan
- index to related material

5.3.6 System Test

Although the System Test stage is designated to fully test the system against its original specification, both unit and integration testing should have been carried out during the previous stage, as described above. The system test plan also should have been created since all processing and data elements were defined in the System Design stage and since the users provided all of the detailed test criteria in the Program Development and Design stage. In addition, all required data conversion activities must be carried out before full system testing starts to provide a truly representative data environment. Therefore, at the start of the System Test stage, everything should be in place to carry out a comprehensive, user-directed test of the newly completed system.

There are, in fact, three types of testing required at this point in the SDLC. First, the system test (although a test of the user requirements) is typically conducted by the development team. After a satisfactory conclusion of this first major test, the test is often repeated, but with users actually controlling and carrying it out with the help of the DP operations staff. This second test is referred to as the users' acceptance test. Even though the users have control, this acceptance test is normally carried out in a test environment, rather than in a production environment. Finally, during this stage, a subset of the full acceptance test is carried out by the users and DP operations using the same procedures as in the actual production environment. A subset is normally required simply to save time. Satisfactory completion of all these tests results in the following deliverables:

- system test plan
- test results
- results at variance with the system test plan
- results of documentation tests
- implementation schedule and conversion plan
- index to related material

5.3.7 Implementation and Production

When all of the previous stages have been completed to the satisfaction of everyone involved, the system is then ready for implementation. With a simple replacement system, this implementation may well be short, sweet, and relatively painless. Normally, though, the implementation needs to be done carefully, slowly, and with built-in monitoring points. Additionally, some training of users and operators is usually required. Although a significant part of this training can be carried out in earlier stages, the actual running of the system in the production environment is always necessary as a final test.

Often, when a large, complex system that contains several critical functions is being implemented, both old and new systems are run in parallel for a certain period and their results are compared to ensure total compatibility and accuracy of the new system. Parallel running of the two systems also provides a valuable fall-back option if the new system proves to be a disaster during this period.

After the system is successfully implemented, it then settles into the production period of the life cycle. The production period should be the longest and most uneventful period, but unfortunately this is not often the case. An increasingly larger proportion of programming resources is being spent on changing, fixing, and enhancing systems already in production. The despair of many DP managers, this infamous maintenance burden is being eased by good design and development techniques and by the use of improved software packages.

The end of this stage is signaled by the need for a new system either because the requirements have changed significantly or because the system itself has become so patched that further changes would destroy it. Then, with a new Feasibility Study, the SDLC starts all over again.

5.4 Management of the SDLC

As can be seen from these brief descriptions of the SDLC stages, the character of the activities changes from stage to stage. Consequently, the skills and disciplines required, as well as the managerial responsibilities, also change. A skilled business system analyst who produces an excellent system specification may well be the completely wrong person to develop that specification into the corresponding system design. To manage the different people and activities needed at each stage, the natural solution may be a change in managers at certain points during the SDLC. Individual stages can have separate stage managers who are responsible specifically for completing that stage's end product and also for ensuring that the end product is acceptable to the Project Review Board. A critical member of this review board is the next stage manager, who obviously has a great incentive to ensure the acceptability of the end product being reviewed (see Table 5-2).

Table 5-2
Changing Managerial Responsibilities in the SDLC

STAGE	FEASIBILITY STUDY	REQUIREMENTS DEFINITION	SYSTEM SPECIFICATION	SYSTEM DESIGN	PROGRAM DESIGN AND DEVELOPMENT	SYSTEM TEST	IMPLEMENTATION AND PRODUCTION
Management Responsibility	Senior User	Senior User	Senior User	Senior DP Development Manager	Senior DP Development Manager	Senior User (with help from Senior DP)	User (with help from DP Operations and DP Development Manager)
Major Skills Required	business knowledge plus business system analysis		DP system analysis	DP system design	program design, coding, and testing	business analysis, design, and testing	production system testing and implementation techniques

Of course, one overall project manager is responsible for the complete life cycle and should come from the end-user organization. The end users view the proposed new system in a more business-oriented way, and they can rank different requirements and requested changes much more effectively than DP professionals. Also, the end users have much greater incentive for ensuring that the system is implemented on time, within budget, and according to the required specifications. After all, the end users are usually paying for the system. For these reasons, the project manager is chosen from the end-user function, particularly for large, expensive projects. Of course, such a user-oriented project manager needs to rely heavily on the DP members of the project team for technical advice in DP matters. Additionally, a DP development manager is appointed at the end of the Requirements Definition stage to manage the DP development resources for the project from that point on.

5.5 Implementation of the SDLC

Often, programmers and other DP professionals react adversely to the imposition of an SDLC methodology because of all of its procedural requirements, reviews, and checklists. Typical remarks are, "It's a paper mill," "Management wants too much control," and "It slows us down." These reactions are to be expected if the organizational environment prior to the introduction of the SDLC was unstructured, uncontrolled, and badly managed. Of course, the criticisms may well be completely justified if, for example, the SDLC methodology or package chosen does not suit the particular organization or does not allow effective use of available automated aids. Even if the chosen methodology is perfect, a clumsy and badly planned implementation will destroy any chance of its success.

Despite being at the leading edge of technology, DP professionals can be surprisingly resistant to new ideas. The SDLC package needs to be sold, just like any other package. Once sold, it must be treated like a software package and implemented just as carefully. All stages of the SDLC package — that is, the Feasibility Study, Requirements Definition, and every other stage — must be carried out to ensure its correct implementation. As with a software package, if the SDLC package fits the organization's system development requirements closely, few further design or other development activities are required to tailor it.

The SDLC cannot be implemented all at once, but it should be tried out in a "vanilla," unmodified version on a pilot project. This pilot implementation can demonstrate the usefulness of the chosen SDLC and also can indicate the modifications that are necessary to the package. The pilot project team must be fully trained in the life cycle concepts, in the SDLC methodology chosen, and in general project management theory. This team or cadre of SDLC experts must then become the missionaries within the organization, spreading the word through presentations and consultations with the next project designated to use the SDLC.

By contrast, user management typically reacts positively to the use of an SDLC by the programmers: "For the first time we know what is going on. We can now monitor and control how *our* money is being spent."

The poor DP manager is torn; he is between the proverbial rock and the hard place. His own staff may resent the imposition of the SDLC discipline, but his users may love the visibility and control that the methodology gives them. However, once DP managers fully realize the extent of the benefits for the DP staff, the SDLC concepts should start to become much more attractive to them.

If an SDLC methodology is to be successfully implemented, it is essential to train DP and user managers in the concepts of the methodology with emphasis on the benefits to *them* of using these revolutionary new techniques. If management can see and believe in the benefits, persuading the rest of the staff to use the methodology becomes much easier.

5.6 Tailoring the SDLC

After all this discussion of the SDLC, the question naturally arises, How large a system development project is necessary to use an SDLC effectively? Any system that requires more than six man-months of total effort to develop will probably benefit from the staged process. For smaller projects, it can be argued that the effort of managing the SDLC is greater than the total development effort. The break-even point will vary from organization to organization, depending upon the people available and the types of projects to be developed.

For borderline projects, the number of stages in the SDLC can be reduced dramatically. Several stages can be "concertina'd" into one to create an effective four-stage SDLC (see Table 5-3).

Table 5-3
A Shortened SDLC for Small Projects

REDUCED STAGES	FEASIBILITY STUDY	SYSTEM DEFINITION	SYSTEM DEVELOPMENT	IMPLEMENTATION AND PRODUCTION
COMBINED TRADITIONAL STAGES	Feasibility Study	Requirements Definition System Specification System Design	Program Design and Development System Test	Implementation and Production

Most commercial data processing systems being developed require the full SDLC, condensed or no, because all of the tasks listed in the full SDLC need to be at least considered, if not fully carried out. Scientific projects, on the other hand, can sometimes dispense with some of the more user-oriented stages because typically the users and the implementers are the same individuals or organization (see Table 5-4).

Table 5-4
An SDLC for a Scientific Project

REQUIREMENTS DEFINITION	SYSTEM DESIGN	PROGRAM DESIGN AND DEVELOPMENT	SYSTEM TEST AND IMPLEMENTATION

5.7 Summary

There are many other detailed methodologies and techniques available to the programmers, analysts, managers, and others involved in the life cycle activities. However, the use of an effective, relevant system development life cycle with clearly defined stages, stage end products, task lists, and checklists does more than any other technique to improve the productivity of the DP staff and raise the quality of the products. Once the SDLC is in place, it then becomes clear when in the life cycle many of the state-of-the-art automated software development aids can best be utilized. Without the life cycle framework, however, the development of large DP systems will still resemble the storming of an impregnable fortress by blind, unarmed foot soldiers. In fact, the foot soldiers will not even have time to search for any weapons; they will be too busy stumbling over each other and trying to knock down the ten-foot thick fortress walls with their bare hands.

6

Feasibility Study Stage

A bad beginning makes a bad ending.

— Euripides

6.1 Objectives

The main objective of the Feasibility Study is to provide a clear definition of the proposed system's practicality. This definition includes the estimated cost of the system and length of the project; the potential benefits, both tangible and intangible, of the proposed system; a cost-benefit analysis; a payback schedule; and the disadvantages of not developing the system. The enterprise is represented in this stage by a committee, a Project Review Board, which has the authority to approve or kill the project. The Board is composed of representatives from the three business functions affected by the new system: financial control, end users, and data processing.

It is important in this stage, as in all stages, to ensure the accuracy of the information produced, for inaccuracies discovered later are difficult to correct and detract from the integrity of the project team. To guarantee accuracy, at least one person from each of the three business functions represented by the Project Review Board should be involved in the Feasibility Study. These persons should be at a sufficiently high level in the organization in order to represent their functions adequately (see Section 6.2).

DP projects get started in different ways and for different reasons. Typically, however, the original request for the project comes from middle management in a user organization either because there is no current system, the current system is too slow, the current system has insufficient capacity, or the current system needs additional and modified functions because of changed business requirements. In these situations, the Feasibility Study should contain a complete cost-benefit analysis with well-supported statements of benefits. These benefits need to be more tangible than intangible, and a clear business need for the system demonstrated.

Unfortunately, in some organizations the Feasibility Study is used as an opportunity to develop pet theories and to promote pet projects. In these situations, the procedures and formalities of an effective review and approval process become extremely important. When the review and approval process is properly monitored, it prevents these pet theories and pet projects from being given undue importance and ensures that the proposed projects are indeed justified. If the project is requested directly by someone who has great influence in the organization, such as the President or Chairman of the Board, the Feasibility Study may be simply a formality. If the Project Review Board determines that the system is technically feasible (and the direct involvement of such a high-level personage is normally sufficient justification), the Feasibility Study may simply consist of a statement that says, "Yes, we'll do it." In this case, the pet project becomes the proposed project without the benefit of a proper Feasibility Study.

6.2 People involved

In order to produce a valid Feasibility Study, the persons involved should be knowledgeable about the organization's business and have sufficient organizational influence to be able to generate the needed data. This means a senior financial analyst or manager from the controller's department is involved, and a senior DP manager or senior analyst who has worked on a similar project also is a member. To represent the users, a senior manager or business analyst (preferably one who has experience with the current equivalent system) is appointed as the manager of this stage. The Feasibility Study manager often continues throughout the project as the project manager.

When multiple user departments are involved with a proposed system, the user representative chosen to work on the Feasibility Study has to represent every department adequately. In some cases, the user representative may be in the difficult situation of serving a dual role if, for instance, he represents the controller's department and the data processing organization. In such a situation, this role should be split into its two separate components of responsibility, with each assigned to individuals of equal status in the organizational hierarchy.

Much of the work to be done during the Feasibility Study is multidisciplinary and cuts across many organizational boundaries. For this reason, the people involved in this stage should have good oral and written communication skills. A project can falter severely, even at this early stage, because of clumsily formulated questions or a badly presented cost-benefit analysis that fails to deliver valid information. Since this analysis is at least partially based on the projections, participants need to know good estimating techniques.

In addition, they all should have some experience in business system analysis — how to analyze the needs and requirements of a business function and how to restate those requirements in a logical, accurate, systematic, nonredundant manner. Some knowledge of system analysis and system design techniques is most useful. If the structured techniques are to be employed, those persons involved in the Feasibility Study should understand data flow diagrams and structure charts, since they probably will be involved in the evaluation of the end products of later stages as well.

6.3 Activities

The tasks to be carried out during the Feasibility Study are primarily these:

- briefly analyze the required system and produce a written description of it

- investigate available types of the required system and develop a statement of the probable system type or types

- analyze the costs of developing similar systems
- produce a rough estimate of the new system development, including resource needs, production costs, and delivery schedules
- describe the potential tangible and intangible benefits of the new system and develop a payback schedule based on those benefits
- produce a detailed estimate of the costs and schedule for the Requirements Definition stage
- assign the project manager for the rest of the life cycle
- present the results of the above activities to top management and to the Project Review Board for approval to proceed to the next stage

Each activity is briefly discussed below.

The brief analysis of the required system includes a narrative description of the scope of the system and its users, and it offers a rough estimate of volumes of data and the frequencies of accesses, updates, and regenerations of data. Existing data and processes that are to be utilized are identified, and a list of the required new data and functions is produced.

Next, the DP and user representatives agree on the scope of the survey to be conducted of similar systems both inside and outside the organization. The information obtained from the survey forms the basis for making a preliminary decision on the type of system to be developed (for example, a batch, weekly update, on-line transaction-based, or database system). Once this basic set of data is gathered, up-to-date information can be added as it becomes available, so that the system type finally recommended in the System Specification stage will take maximum advantage of the available technology. For this reason, it is crucial for DP staff members to be familiar with state-of-the-art technology.

The costs of all previous similar systems developed within the organization are collected to form a basis for generating a preliminary estimate of the new project's development costs. This estimate then is expanded from a straight dollar figure to include manpower estimates and approximate schedules. At this point in the SDLC, it is often difficult to estimate accurately the costs of the rest of the project. However, in order for the Project Review Board to do its job at the end of the Feasibility Study, a gross estimate of the whole life cycle is essential.

Most good SDLC packages have detailed procedures for estimating project costs and schedules. If you lack an SDLC, the guidelines described in the next paragraphs could be used to start the estimating process.

One advantage of using the SDLC concept is that the stages themselves can be used as a basis to define standard percentages of resource usage and time expenditure. In Table 6-1, the numbers for resource and time expenditures are based on my own experience and on the experiences of many of my associates. These figures could be used as project estimates, or figures based on your own experience could be substituted.

Whichever set of numbers is used, a good first rough estimate of the total project resource requirements and schedules can now be determined, based on the cost and timing of the Feasibility Study itself. (This assumes that a full Feasibility Study has already been carried out.)

Table 6-1
Estimate of SDLC Costs and Schedules

	FEASIBILITY STUDY	REQUIREMENTS DEFINITION	SYSTEM SPECIFICATION	SYSTEM DESIGN	PROGRAM DESIGN AND DEVELOPMENT	SYSTEM TEST	IMPLEMENTATION AND PRODUCTION
Resource Expenditure* (percentage)	2	10	15	20	25	18	10
Time Usage (percentage)	10	15	15	20	30	5	5
Actual Time Example (months)	2	3	3	4	6	1	1

*includes manpower costs and all other costs associated with the project

Another type of estimate is based on the expected number of lines of code in the system. If the Feasibility Study provides a good estimate of the lines of code to be generated in the system, based on comparison with existing similar systems within or outside the organization, some estimating algorithms purport to produce a good life cycle estimate derived from this number. Barry Boehm, for instance, in *Software Engineering Economics* [4], offers this algorithm for developing an average system:*

$$\text{MAN-MONTHS} = 153.2\ (\text{KDSI})^{1.05}$$

where KDSI = thousands of delivered source instructions
and MAN-MONTHS = manpower expended to carry out the effort from the start of System Design to the end of System Test

Clearly, this algorithm provides an estimate for only three of our seven stages. The algorithm for man-month estimation is independent of the actual source language used, since naturally a higher-level language should speed up the development process. This will be reflected in the results of using the algorithm. From my experience, four additional, subjective factors must then be applied to these numbers, since the figures only represent the average project for the organization. These factors include the project's size, its complexity, the number of users, and the particular environment.

Size of project: The size is strictly based on an estimated number of lines of code and is necessarily suspect in terms of accuracy. If the estimated size of the project is the same or less than the average project in the organization described above, the estimate should not be changed.† If it is larger than

*Boehm defines an average system to be one that has no unusual aspects in its development, such as use of a completely new database or an untried set of resources (a new group of contract programmers, for example).

†My definition for an average project in an organization is phrased in terms of the project's size and complexity and is necessarily a somewhat subjective measurement. The average size is simply a numerical average of the lines of code of all of the organization's installed systems (or of similar systems from other organizations). The average complexity is a measure of the logical complexity and the number of files, databases, and so on, that the DP organization usually deals with in one system.

average, project estimates and schedules should be increased in direct proportion to the increase in size over the average. For example, if the estimated number of lines of code is fifty percent greater than average, all resource estimates and schedules should be increased by fifty percent.

Complexity of project: If the project appears to be significantly more complex in its technical requirements than the average, twenty percent should be added to all estimates and schedules. If the project is significantly less complex than average, twenty percent should be subtracted.

Number of users: If more than one user organization is involved with the new system, five percent should be added to all estimates and schedules for each additional user organization after the primary user.

Project and system environment: Three important environmental factors that affect the length of the development effort are the operating system software, the hardware, and the project staff. For *each* factor that is new or unknown, the estimates and schedules should be increased by twenty percent.

Therefore, if we apply these factors to a project that is ten percent larger than average, is significantly more complex, has three user organizations, has all new operating system software and hardware, and has completely new project staff, the original base estimates should be doubled! (In fact, the project manager might well consider dusting off his resume.)

After the project estimate has been developed, the new system's benefits are described. The benefits can be tangible or intangible. Tangible benefits are essentially those that can produce specific, identifiable cost savings. Reductions in staff and in fixed assets or increases in production with the same resources are examples of tangible benefits. Intangible benefits are those things that are difficult to quantify, especially on a monetary basis, such as improved morale and enhanced working conditions. Some intangible benefits, however, create greater income over the long term than many tangible benefits. Although the intangible benefits are always difficult if not impossible to justify, they should be described and quantified as closely as possible even if this quantification is only an educated guess.

Once all of the benefits have been quantified, a payback schedule can be generated to indicate when the organization can expect to see the new system's total development costs repaid by the benefits accruing from the system's use. Figure 6-1 illustrates a typical payback schedule. Line A on the diagram represents the accumulated running costs plus the total development costs after implementation. If we assume that the new system starts to save some money immediately, line B shows how those savings accumulate.

According to the diagram, the direct savings generated by the new system will pay for the total development costs and the accumulated running costs by about fourteen months after implementation. If the intangible savings can also be quantified as shown here, the break-even point occurs after only approximately eight months.

In addition to the total project estimates, the Feasibility Study also includes a detailed estimate of the next stage, the Requirements Definition stage. Also, the next stage's estimate can be determined by approximating the time, costs, and resources needed for each task on the Requirements Definition task list, as contained in a standard SDLC. The list includes three major groups of activities to be carried out during the Requirements Definition stage: analysis of the current system, interviews with system users and operators, and development of the requirements document. Since some of this work is carried out superficially in the Feasibility Study, estimating these activities should not be terribly difficult.

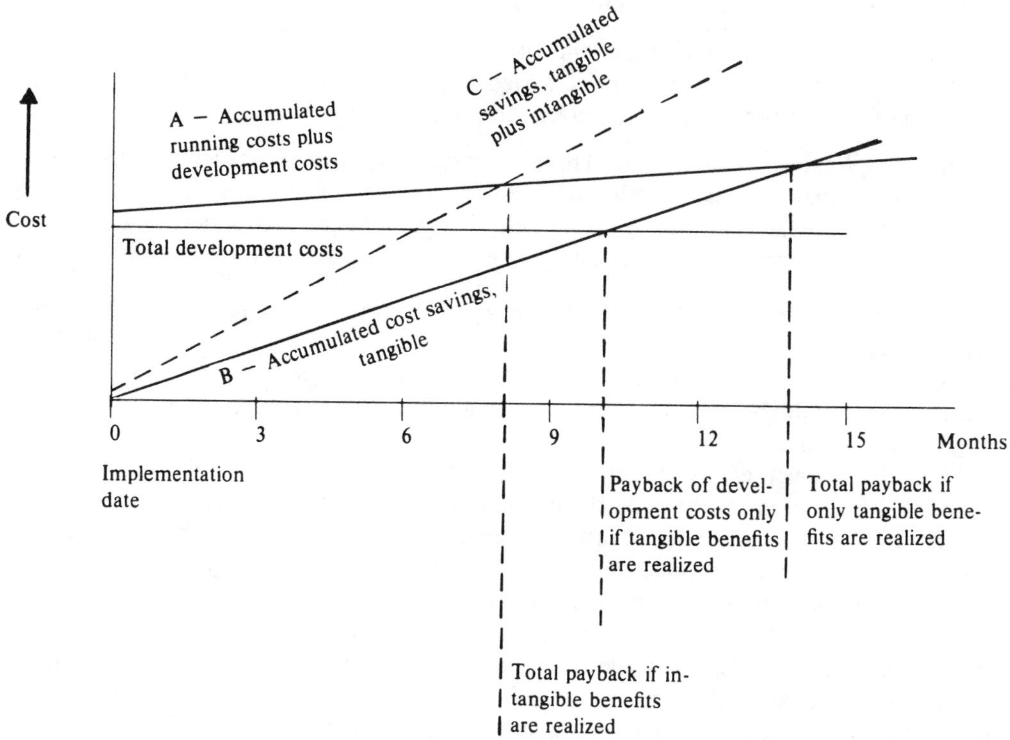

Figure 6-1. Typical payback schedule.

6.4 Documentation

The documentation produced in the Feasibility Study is largely written or narrative-style documentation. Graphs and diagrams, such as Figure 6-1 and Table 6-1, are useful to demonstrate estimates and schedules. Normally, the only formatted piece of documentation required is the original Project Request, which could take the shape of Figure 6-2.

STATEMENT OF ISSUE

____

PROJECT # ________________

DATE ________________

Name of Proposed System or Partial System __________________________

Replacement? ____ ☐ Yes ____ ☐ No ____ (Check One)

If Yes, System Being Replaced __________________________

Primary User Organization __________________________

Main Contact __________________________

Secondary User Organizations __________________________

APPROVAL FOR FEASIBILITY STUDY

	Signature	Date
Controller's Dept.	__________	_____
Primary User	__________	_____
DP Dept.	__________	_____
Project Review Board	__________	_____
	__________	_____
	__________	_____

Projected Date of Completion of Feasibility Study: ___ /___ /___

Figure 6-2. Example of a Project Request form.

6.5 End-stage activities

The final set of activities in the Feasibility Study involves presenting the results of the study to the Project Review Board. All of the documentation produced is distributed to the Board as far in advance of the actual review date as possible. Then, in the presentation itself, the Feasibility Study manager, usually the senior user representative, gives an overview of these items:

- a brief description of the proposed system
- the benefits, both tangible and intangible, of the proposed system
- the disadvantages of not developing the proposed system
- a cost-benefit analysis, including the payback schedule
- an overall cost estimate of the project and an estimate of schedules
- an estimate of the next stage
- a recommendation for the project manager

In the last item, a senior user is appointed to be responsible for the complete project from this point until implementation. Ideally, the project manager also participated in the Feasibility Study. In future stages, when the stage manager is not the project manager, this stage manager is responsible to the project manager for his assignments.

6.6 Summary

The Feasibility Study provides the starting point for the project and the documented justification for it. The Project Review Board members, who are responsible for approving the funding of the new system, make their decision based on that information. If all of the required information is well prepared and well presented, the Project Review Board's task is made that much easier. Of course, there is always a chance that the Board may not approve the next stage of the project, and in that case, the project team at least will have the satisfaction of knowing that the decision was based on good, complete data.

7

Requirements Definition Stage

If you would be pungent, be brief; for it is with words as with sunbeams — the more they are condensed the deeper they burn.

— Robert Southey

7.1 Objectives

In the Requirements Definition stage, the simple description of the required system generated during the Feasibility Study is expanded to form a detailed set of user requirements. This set covers all aspects of the system from the user's point of view, including not only functional requirements (*what* the system does) but also physical requirements (*how* the system does it) and constraints (such as timing and performance needs), in addition to external interfaces with other systems.

The major intended audience for the Requirements Definition document consists of system users, who must approve the document. Users wish to see a description of what the proposed system will do for them in clear, unambiguous, everyday language. Consequently, the document should be as free from technical jargon as possible, particularly "computerese," which DP professionals love to use. If either business or DP-related technical terms are used, they must be explained the first time they appear.

Although the Requirements Definition document is nontechnical so that users can understand it, it also must contain sufficient technical detail so that DP people can use it in the next stage to produce the new system's detailed specification. Even though the Requirements Definition needs to be fully comprehensive, the overly long, boring "Victorian novel" method of defining the system's requirements is probably as ineffective as an overly abbreviated set of system needs.

7.2 People involved

The team that develops the Requirements Definition document is critical to the project's success, and so the team members are carefully selected. Despite the common belief that the users don't know what they want, the majority of the participants in this stage are chosen from the users' ranks. The number of people required for this stage can be derived from the estimate of the resources needed, which was developed during the Feasibility Study.

Often, more than one discrete user area forms the complete set of users for the proposed system, and so the user team consists of at least one person from each of the user groups. If possible, the users involved in this stage should be those who work with the system being replaced or who have worked with similar systems. More importantly perhaps, the team also includes those users of the proposed system. Knowing that one will have to live with an implemented set of requirements is a powerful incentive to achieve accuracy and completeness in the definition of those requirements. Normally, the manager for the Requirements Definition stage is a senior user manager, who also serves as the project manager for the total project life cycle.

A great danger during this stage is that the team developing the set of requirements for the proposed system can get carried away with enthusiasm and define a system that would be totally impossible or impractical to implement. In order to prevent this kind of science fiction from being presented as a valid Requirements Definition, at least one senior DP manager or system analyst who is familiar with the type of system being defined must join the team. He not only advises on the practicality of the requirements, but also instructs the user staff about what is possible with current DP technology. In this way, DP involvement may actually expand the capabilities of the proposed system, rather than simply limit them. Another technical staff member — the data administrator, whose primary concern is the data dictionary — is involved during this stage to assist with informational needs. Not all organizations are sufficiently large to have this function.

Much interaction between the user and DP groups is necessary during this stage, as both groups gain confidence in the ability of the team to produce a valid Requirements Definition document. The composition of the team remains fluid during the early parts of this stage, as any proverbial bad apples are removed from the team as soon as they are detected. Once an effective team is developed, the user representatives in this stage should be retained for all remaining stages that require user involvement to help ensure continuity and consistency in interpreting the requirements and in translating them into specific program and module designs in the implemented system.

7.3 Activities

The major activities of the Requirements Definition stage are these:

- identify the scope of the proposed system by defining its major functions
- identify the key users of the current and new systems
- review the above information for completeness
- interview the key users (including secondary users and operations staff) to determine use of the current system and requirements of the new system
- develop the description of the current system and review it with team members
- define the functional and informational requirements of the new system and rank them by priority

- review user requirements of the new system by the project team, the interviewed users, and the Project Review Board
- develop a complete description of the benefits provided by the new system
- produce estimates of the next stage and of the rest of the project
- produce and review the end-stage document with the Project Review Board

One of the first activities is to identify the scope and boundaries of the proposed system. From the basic information developed in the Feasibility Study, the team generates a list of major functions to be performed by the system. Then, all of the individual users and the organizations that the system will serve are identified, including their relationships to the system. The key users include both primary and secondary users, as illustrated in Figure 7-1. Primary users interact directly with the system. Secondary users are those who do not provide direct inputs to the system and are not directly affected by the system outputs but who use information generated from further processing of the direct inputs and outputs.

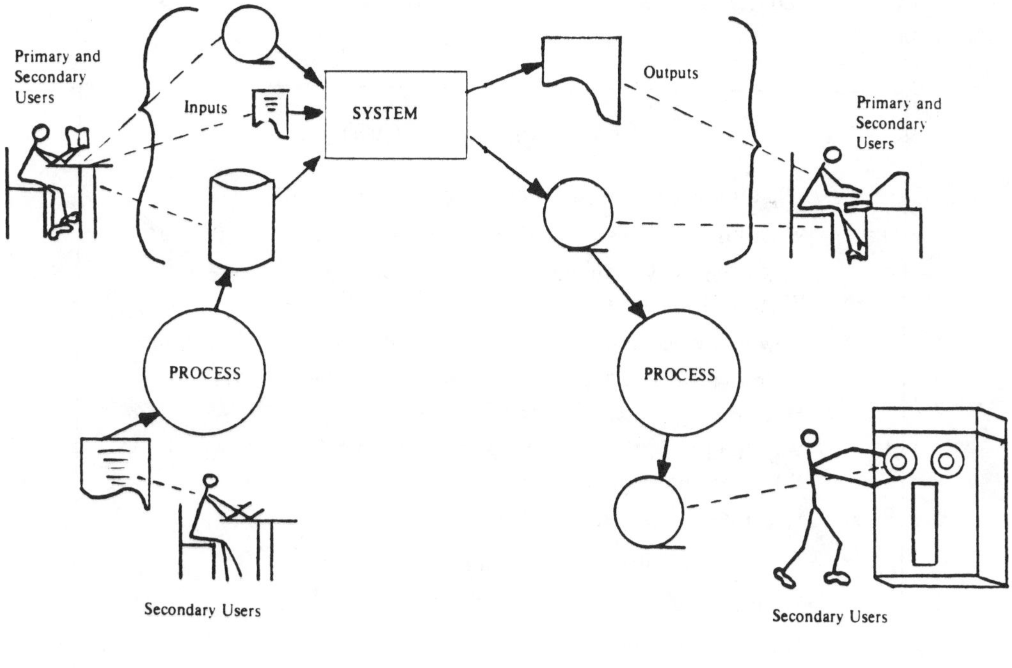

Figure 7-1. Primary and secondary system users.

Next, the rest of the activities for the Requirements Definition stage are identified, and the responsibilities for completing them assigned. As in the first stage, a standard SDLC with a complete task list for the Requirements Definition stage is extremely useful. This list should include specific activities to define security, privacy, and recovery requirements.

These three lists — of major system functions, of key users and their organizations, and of tasks and responsibilities for the rest of the Requirements Definition stage — are reviewed by the data processing and user staff team members and by other senior representatives from the key user organization and from the DP group. Once all reviewers are satisfied that this information is complete, accurate, and unambiguous, the stage activities continue. Several iterations of this process may be necessary, with information being added, deleted, or changed each time, until all users agree.

The next activities involve interviewing the key users of the proposed system in depth to discover their use of the current system and their requirements of the new system. Since changes to the system inputs and outputs will affect secondary users, they are interviewed to obtain a complete picture of the system requirements. DP operators also are interviewed at this time, since they work closely with the current system and know the problems and difficulties in running it.

Use of a standardized, detailed questionnaire for each interview assures consistency of the information obtained, and speeds up the interviewing process. The standard form includes questions that elicit information about the current system's deficiencies and problems, as well as the users' recommendations for improvements. All information gathered during these interviews is recorded on paper or whatever medium is appropriate. The information is analyzed later, during the next stage.

A purchased SDLC package often provides a standard list of questions. If not, an internally generated list can easily be created. A sample starter set of questions is shown below:

Sample Set of Interviewing Questions

- ☐ What information or data do you provide to the system?
- ☐ What information or data that you use does the system provide?
- ☐ How often do you interact with the system?
  What information or data do you use?
- ☐ How many people in your department use the system?
- ☐ What deficiencies do you believe the system has?
  How would you resolve them?
- ☐ What additional features should the system have?
  Which are most important?
- ☐ Which features of the current system are unnecessary?
- ☐ What operations could be automated?
- ☐ What is your general opinion of the system?
- ☐ How could a new system benefit your operation?

Figure 7-2. Sample list of questions for user interviews.

As the interviews progress, new questions may become necessary and can be added to the list. The previous interviews should then be reassessed to determine if these new questions are necessary in all interviews, with the goal to obtain a consistent set of information about the current and proposed systems from all users.

With the information gathered from all interviews, a complete user-oriented description of the current system — warts and all — can be developed. It is important at this stage that both the functional and physical operations of the current system are fully described. The description normally takes a narrative form, but it should include whatever diagrammatic notation the user is comfortable with. Flowcharts, data flow diagrams, structure charts, and HIPO charts are all suitable types of notation.* The content, not the format, is important. When completed, the current system description is reviewed with all of the users who were interviewed. Once again, this review is an iterative process until the current system description finally represents a completely approved users' view of the system.

Producing the complete description of the current system is immeasurably easier if its documentation has been regularly updated. Then, only those enhancements and other modifications that have been made to the system since the last update to the documentation need to be considered in addition to the information obtained from the interviews. Unfortunately, most DP system documentation is abysmal, if it exists at all. Since producing documentation is not the favorite task of many DP professionals, it is often given short shrift or sometimes completely ignored.

However the description of the current system is produced, its review by the Requirements Definition team prepares the team sufficiently to begin the next major task: to produce a comprehensive and accurate set of the user requirements of the proposed system. All of the current system requirements, along with any required changes and recommended resolutions of current deficiencies gathered during the user interviews, are now merged with the new system requirements defined in the original Project Request. A detailed review can eliminate duplications.

If there is no current equivalent system or if the current system is completely worthless, the list of the new system requirements is simply a detailed expansion of the requirements outlined in the Project Request and the Feasibility Study. The same procedure is followed in this case: by extensive interviews of key users of the proposed system, compilation of the information obtained in these interviews, and a detailed review to eliminate duplications. However, this situation is unusual, for some sort of system is almost always being used already, albeit rudimentary and perhaps totally manual, but a *system* nevertheless with some very useful parts to it.

An important category in the list of requirements is the informational needs of the new system, preferably in the form of a formatted list or a data dictionary. The definition of what information, how much information, and how often it should be accessed, changed, replaced, and so on, are determined during this stage, although the specific storage media and accessing method will be decided later. For example, in a payroll system, the Requirements Definition stage defines that the information in the system must include staff names, social security numbers, salary grades, titles, and actual salaries. At the same time, sensitive data that needs to be protected is identified, along with other security, privacy, and recovery needs, so that the system controls can be specified in the next stage.

If the organization has a data administrator who is responsible for monitoring data naming standards and for minimizing data redundancy, he should be involved now to

---

*A HIPO chart, which stands for Hierarchical and Input-Process-Output, conveys much of the same information as a structure chart, but does not indicate module interfaces or any procedural details.

assist in defining the informational requirements and to ensure use of the corporate data dictionary wherever relevant. (This function is discussed further in Chapter 8.)

Once the total list is compiled, the user requirements are ranked by priority. The reason for this activity is that if trade-offs are required — for example, if the project's budget is reduced and a scaled-down version of the system must be developed — the system developers can know which requirements take precedence and the requirements with the lowest priority could be eliminated.

The list of functional and informational requirements of the new system from the users' viewpoints is reviewed for completeness and accuracy by the project team, by all interviewed users, and by the Project Review Board. Because of the widespread interest in and importance of this particular set of information, many iterations of review and change may be necessary before the new system requirements are satisfactory to all concerned.

Once the full list of user requirements has been reviewed and approved by all of the reviewers, a detailed description of all benefits that the new system will provide is developed; this description expands on the preliminary list of tangible and intangible benefits produced during the Feasibility Study. The purpose of this activity is to provide the system users with an unambiguous statement of how they will receive and be affected by these benefits. Since more information is known at this point, this activity will probably change the cost-benefit analysis and the payback schedule developed in the Feasibility Study. If so, these changes are recorded as part of the Requirements Definition document. Again, the project team, all interviewed users, and the Project Review Board informally review the complete description of the benefits to ensure that they are valid and do not result in false or unachievable expectations. These groups also review any changes to the cost-benefit analysis and the payback schedule at this time.

Finally, a detailed estimate is made of the next stage (System Specification), when the user requirements are translated into system requirements. This translation is essentially a transformation from nontechnical language into DP language. If the project team has done a good job in the Requirements Definition stage, the next stage's estimate is easy to do because it can be based on the detailed list of requirements: The effort needed to specify each requirement can be estimated separately. If a good SDLC methodology is being used, the task list for the System Specification stage is also of great assistance in estimating that stage. The estimate of the remainder of the project is further refined at this point, because new information now is available to make it more accurate.

The last major task in this stage is to produce the Requirements Definition document and to present it to the Project Review Board for approval. But prior to this formal review, this document is informally reviewed for completeness and accuracy by all interviewed users, the project team, and representatives on the Project Review Board. The document contains all of the results of the activities carried out in the Requirements Definition stage and includes these five sections: summary of proposed system, analysis of current system, new system user requirements, estimates of next stages, and index (see Section 7.5). If all of the activities in this stage have been carried out fully, the production of the final document is largely a word-processing exercise. This is particularly true if a format for the contents of the document has been agreed to at the beginning of the stage.

Figure 7-3 shows the sequence and relationships of the various activities during the Requirements Definition stage.

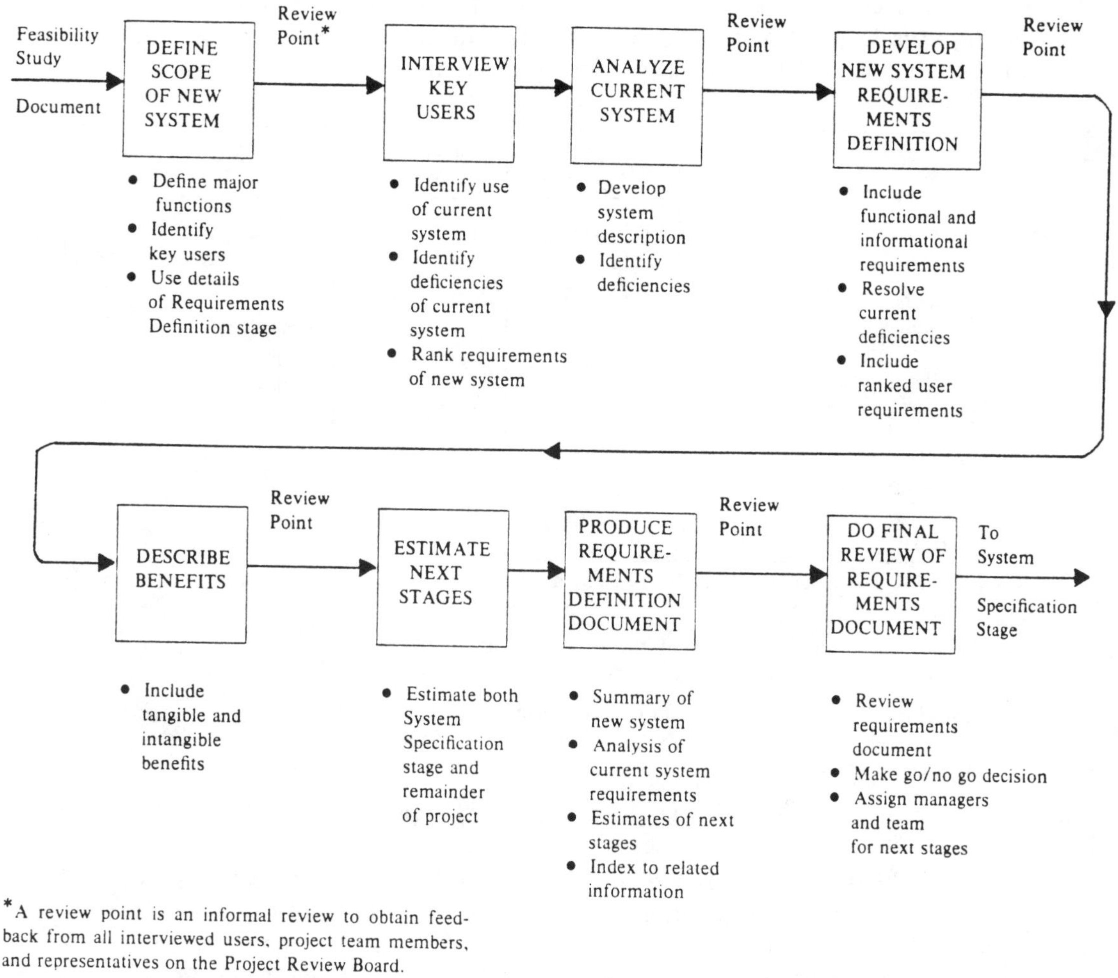

Figure 7-3. Requirements Definition stage activities.

7.4 Tools and techniques

The tools and techniques needed during the Requirements Definition stage mainly involve ranking techniques and documentation tools such as data dictionaries and charts. Since the majority of the activities involve talking to users of the current and proposed systems, interviewing techniques and interpersonal communication skills are critical during this stage. Many corporations have their own in-house training programs for teaching these skills. Also, most vendors of training courses offer video-and-workbook-based courses on these topics in addition to classroom-style seminars.

In addition, the techniques of business system analysis, such as IBM's BSP, can assist team members to identify the major functions of their organization. These techniques are aimed primarily at producing a high-level analysis of the major functions of a complete business enterprise, rather than a subset of that entity. Nevertheless, their underlying principles can be applied to analyze all of the many requested user needs of a business system in order to produce an itemized, distilled, and ranked set of requirements.*

One such simple technique is a Ranking Matrix, which can be used to order, by priority, the long list of specific and separate requirements that inevitably results from the Requirements Definition stage activities. The matrix is shown in Figure 7-4.

REQUIREMENT	USER 1		USER 2		USER 3		SCORE
	RI	WEIGHT	RI	WEIGHT	RI	WEIGHT	
1. 24-hour access to data	7	3	5	1	8	2	42
2. Ability for non-DP trained personnel to modify the system	8	3	1	1	5	2	35
3. Facility to identify out-of-line data values	6	3	8	1	7	2	40
N . . .							

LEGEND

RI = Relative importance, 1 to 10, 10 being most important.

Weight reflects the importance of the user. In this case, the range is 1 to 3, 3 being the most important.

Score for each requirement = Sum of (RI × Weight) for each user. Then, the requirements must be ranked in order of the scores.

Figure 7-4. Ranking Matrix.

If there is only one user of the system, ranking is usually relatively simple; but sometimes, even in this situation, the user will insist that all of the requirements are equally important. This is of course unrealistic, because there must be some requirements that are more important than others. After the ranking is agreed upon, and as the development of the new system progresses, business needs will change, budgets will be altered, priorities themselves will change, and market-driven needs unknown at the start of the project will impose themselves onto the new system. Many DP managers will insist, "We have to freeze the requirements at the end of the Requirements Definition stage." My only response is, "Try it!" Since the Ranking Matrix is so simple and easy to use, the requirements' priority can be checked and rechecked throughout the development effort as circumstances change.

Team members also need to be familiar with certain documentation tools. For example, in order to describe the logical and physical flow of both the current and the proposed systems, data flow diagrams could be used if the users understand them. Or, rudimentary structure charts, HIPO charts, and sometimes traditional flowcharts can be

*I know of no specific texts on business system analysis to recommend, but IBM does offer a comprehensive set of materials that provides rules and techniques for developing ranking methods, work flow diagrams, control paths, and so on, from a list of detailed user requirements.

employed, again, if they are acceptable to the users. In practice, whatever notations that the users are most comfortable with are used to describe the system at this stage.*

A high-level, user-friendly data dictionary is extremely effective in recording all of the informational requirements at this stage. A data dictionary is simply a repository of data about data, "meta-data," as it is sometimes called. In order to be useful at this point in the SDLC, the data dictionary must be able to deal with high-level overviews of the system, and it must be automated and accessible on-line to both technical as well as non-DP personnel. There are many data dictionaries on the market that meet these requirements and many more that do not. Probably each different environment would require a different type of data dictionary, but two that seem to be gaining wide acceptance are the University of Michigan's PSL/PSA [51] and MSP, Inc.'s, Data Manager [45].

7.5 Documentation

The Requirements Definition document is composed of these five sections.

- *Summary of the proposed system:* a brief explanation of the reasons for requiring a new system, a nontechnical narrative overview of this system, and a summary of the tangible and intangible benefits of the proposed system.
- *Analysis of the current system:* a detailed narrative and graphic description of the current system that is being replaced or enhanced by the proposed system; this section includes flowcharts, DFDs, structure charts, or similar representations, which depict the functional operation and the physical operation; a list of all affected users and business functions with all relationships to the current system identified; and a list of the deficiencies of the current system and the required changes and additions. (If no current system exists, this section of the Requirements Definition document is clearly unnecessary.)
- *New system user requirements:* a complete and accurate users' view of the proposed new system, including overall objectives of the new system and a list of its major functions. Every major function is decomposed into its individual requirements, which are ranked by priority. All operational and environmental requirements and constraints are itemized, including all performance constraints, physical limitations, and timing considerations. Timing factors include system operational timings, in addition to the required implementation timetable.

---

*Many texts and methodologies recommend the use of structured analysis and particularly data flow diagrams during the Requirements Definition stage. Although I believe the technique to be valid, I also believe that structured analysis is more of a design technique. If DFDs can be used so effectively at this stage, then much of the Requirements Definition, System Specification, and System Design stages will have effectively been combined and many design questions will have already been answered. If, on the other hand, what is meant by structured analysis is using DFDs simply to organize the requirements of the system into an accurate, functional DFD, then this is what I have already described as being part of the Requirements Definition stage activities.

One or more of the major functions of the new system inevitably involves manipulating data or information. The informational requirements are fully described in this section in the form of a data dictionary, specifically in terms of what the user expects to provide as input and what he expects to receive as output. At this stage, this list of informational requirements does not pre-empt any system design decisions about logical or physical data configurations, types of storage media, or use of files or databases. What *is* included are the user requirements in terms of frequency of data access, required response times to information requests, general recovery requirements such as how much old information to retain, and allowable tolerances in the accuracy of the information generated by the system. Finally, the new system's tangible and intangible benefits are explained in detail.

- *Estimates of the next stages:* the detailed estimate of the System Specification stage and a revised estimate of the remaining stages of the SDLC.
- *Index to related material:* an index to all information produced during this stage, residing on paper in filing cabinets, on disk files (floppy and rigid), and on various other recording media. The index also includes references to all related manual and automated systems that the proposed system will interface with, both directly and indirectly. (Naturally, all this information need not be included in the Requirements Definition document; otherwise, the much-maligned Victorian novel specification would have to take second place to the Requirements Definition document in terms of voluminousness, repetitiousness, redundancy, and sheer boredom.)

  This index is necessary so that statements in the Requirements Definition document can be justified by references to accessible supporting documentation. In addition, since much of the information collected and generated in this stage, as in all stages, may be used in subsequent stages, a good index to this information saves time later.

Because the Requirements Definition document is so critical to the development of the new system, a summary of the contents list is shown in Figure 7-5.

7.6 End-stage activities

The end of the Requirements Definition stage is marked by the formal review and approval of the Requirements Definition document. If all of the activities and informal reviews detailed earlier have been carried out correctly, this final review by the Project Review Board should be a formality. Nevertheless, the document should be distributed to the Project Review Board members and to all involved management prior to the scheduled review. The formal review should take place one week or more before the scheduled end of the stage to allow time for any changes, corrections, or improvements to the document.

Contents List

1. Summary of the proposed system
   - □ Reasons for new system
   - □ Description of new system
   - □ Benefits of new system

2. Analysis of the current system
   - □ Current system description
     - Narrative
     - System functional flow diagram(s)
     - Operational description and flow diagram(s)
   - □ User areas and functions
   - □ Current system deficiencies
   - □ Required changes and additions to current system

3. New system user requirements
   - □ Objectives of new system
   - □ Major functions (in order of priority)
     - Detailed requirements for each function (in order of priority)
   - □ Operational constraints
     - Performance
     - Timing
     - Physical
   - □ Informational requirements
   - □ Benefits of new system
     - Tangible benefits
     - Intangible benefits

4. Estimates of the next stages
   - □ Detailed estimate of System Specification stage
   - □ Revised estimate of remainder of project

5. Index to all related material
   - □ Working papers
   - □ Relationships to other systems

Figure 7-5. Requirements Definition document contents list.

At the review, the users, DP organization, and the controllers must be satisfied that all user requirements are described adequately, that the system is technically feasible, and that the financial parameters are accurate and make economic sense. Specifically, the Project Review Board must be satisfied with the answers to at least the following questions:

- Is the description of the current system accurate and acceptable to all users?

- Are all of the functions and requirements of the proposed system adequately described?
- Are the priorities that have been established for the proposed system's functions and requirements agreeable to all users? (This question may prove to be more difficult to resolve than all the others combined.)
- Are DP operations staff and users of the proposed system satisfied with environmental, physical, and operational constraints of the proposed system as described?
- Are the users satisfied that the informational requirements as specified are complete?
- Do the benefits described agree with the cost-benefit analysis outlined in the Feasibility Study? If not, have the cost-benefit analysis and the payback schedule been altered to reflect them?
- Is the estimate, including schedules, of the System Specification stage acceptable to all reviewers?
- Are the DP development manager and the user manager for the next stage assigned? Do they both accept the Requirements Definition document and the estimate of the System Specification stage?
- Is the estimate of the remainder of the project acceptable to all reviewers?
- Is sufficient staff (in terms of number and levels of experience) available for the System Specification stage?

As can be seen from the above questions, one of the final acts of the Requirements Definition stage is to assign the manager from the user organization for the next stage and the DP development manager for the project.

The Requirements Definition document is a key document in the life of the proposed system. Therefore, several subsequent reviews of the document may need to be scheduled before all parties are fully satisfied with it. If the document is not accepted even after several reviews, the project will either be canceled or postponed, or the Requirements Definition stage extended to allow for the requirements to be further defined to the satisfaction of the Project Review Board. When the document is accepted, the Project Review Board issues a letter of approval, which is signed by the following persons: every member of the Project Review Board, the stage manager of the Requirements Definition stage, the stage manager of the System Specification stage, the project manager, the DP development manager, and the DP operations manager. Following the acceptance of the requirements document, the project team is ready to move on to the System Specification stage.

8

System Specification Stage

We must not hope to be mowers,
And to gather the ripe gold ears,
Unless we have first been sowers
And watered the furrows with tears.
— Johann Wolfgang von Goethe

8.1 Objectives

The Requirements Definition document contains a set of user requirements and constraints. The team's primary objective in the System Specification stage is to specify the data processing system to meet those detailed user requirements. The System Specification stage, then, embodies an important shift in emphasis in the SDLC. Up to this point, the activities have been heavily user-oriented, with assistance from the DP development staff required only during the Requirements Definition stage to ensure that a realistic and achievable set of requirements was defined. Now, those requirements must be translated into terms that accurately reflect the user requirements, but that are expressed in terms the system designers, coders, and testers can understand. They must be translated into discrete system specifications such as performance criteria, operational parameters, security and privacy needs, geographical dispersions, and many other physical requirements. From these criteria, networking, telecommunications, and distributed processing requirements can be generated to form part of the detailed System Specification. In addition, the data requirements now are specified from the informational requirements in the previous stage. Therefore, this stage is regarded as a technical stage, although it is managed by the user organization to ensure that the users' needs continue to be fully met in the translation. The greater than one-to-one ratio of user staff to DP staff in the Requirements Definition stage now is reversed, as explained in Section 8.2.

If the Requirements Definition stage has been carried out in detail and if its end-stage document is accurate and comprehensive, the task of translating those requirements into specific system needs is relatively straightforward and simple. If, even better, the system users are comfortable with DP terminology and fully conversant with

DP system capabilities, the system specification becomes a one-for-one translation of the detailed user requirements. Unfortunately, most of the time neither of the above is true. As a result, the production of the system specification is typically a significant effort, constituting a substantial segment of the SDLC and absorbing fifteen percent of the total time and resources, as suggested in Chapter 6.

Although the system specification should not define *how* the system will work, it must define *what* the system will do to meet the user requirements. In Chapter 5, I used the analogy of a potential automobile purchaser's definition of his requirements and the car manufacturer's translation of them into automobile specifications. In DP terms, Table 8-1 provides some examples of translations from user requirements to system specifications. Although the examples are much simplified, they illustrate the differences between requirements and specifications.

Table 8-1
Examples of Translation from Requirements to Specifications

USER REQUIREMENTS	SYSTEM SPECIFICATIONS
• 24-hour access to data	• On-line database environment
• Users must have immediate access to data and remote response time less than five seconds	• On-line network of user terminals with internal mainframe response time of less than two seconds, network delay of less than three seconds
• User-oriented, dynamic reshaping of files, reports, displays, etc.	• Relational or inverted-list database system
• Ability for non-DP trained users to modify the system	• Interface with a nonprocedural language, such as MARK IV or INQUIRE
• Facility to identify out-of-line data values	• Editing of input data against a table of valid ranges to produce a listing of out-of-range fields and a file of records containing those fields

The final documentation produced during this stage is such that the system in subsequent stages can be designed to its most detailed level. By the end of this stage as part of the System Specification document itself, a high-level design chart or picture of the proposed system is produced. This overview design will be expanded to form the complete system design during the next stage.

8.2 People involved

As a final activity of the preceding stage, two managers, one each from the DP and user organizations, were selected for this stage. The overall manager of the stage and the ultimate authority is a senior manager from the user organization. With the assignment of the DP development manager, the stage is set for a dual act between the user and DP organizations. A DP professional himself, the DP development manager is usually the manager of the technical members of the project team. Often the DP team leader or his manager assumes this role. Both of these managers are responsible to ensure that this act is one of cooperation and not one of conflict. Too often, the relationship between the users and the DP professionals is an adversarial one, and clearly such a relationship is destructive to the perceived professionalism and integrity of both groups and can prevent an effective system from being developed.

In addition to the two principal managers, someone must actually do the work. The estimate produced at the end of the Requirements Definition stage identifies the number of people required to carry out the System Specification tasks. As in the previous stage, a mixture of user staff and DP development staff is required. In this case, however, since the System Specification document to be produced is largely a technical document, the majority, or approximately seventy-five percent, of the total staff are DP members and the remaining twenty-five percent are users. Explanation and interpretation of the user requirements are provided by the users for the DP professionals who, in turn, translate those requirements into technical system specifications. Consequently, the DP skills required are mainly those of DP system analysis and design. To assist in specifying the system's controls in detail, the corporation's DP auditing function, if one exists, becomes involved in this stage.

Because the users' physical and operational system constraints are being translated into actual system characteristics in this stage, some involvement from the DP operations staff is also necessary, though not on a full-time basis. At key points within the stage and at the end-stage review of the System Specification document itself, the DP operations representative reviews the operational and control characteristics of the specified system to ensure conformity with required operational standards and to ensure the practicality of those specifications.

A major role to be filled during this stage is that of the data administrator. Since much of the information being handled is key to the business operations of the modern enterprise, some function must act as custodian of the information. Increasingly, that responsibility is given to the DP organization. DP cannot and should not be made solely responsible for this business information. The data administrator is therefore intended to fill this role of information custodian for the corporation as a whole. This function differs from that of the database administrator, whose responsibility is limited to one particular system and its database. The data administrator's responsibilities are to enforce corporate data naming standards and procedures, to minimize corporate-wide data redundancy, and to maintain the general integrity and security of the business data. As mentioned in Chapter 7, the data administrator may have already become involved in this information handling role. During the System Specification stage, this role is expanded and becomes more specific as the data defined becomes more specific. The major tool of the data administrator is the data dictionary, as explained in Section 8.3.

In those organizations with a successful corporate-wide data administrator, data administration is regarded as a major business function, such as financial or marketing, and is independent of the data processing function. The advantages of such an approach are that it provides a control point in terms of enforcing standards and controlling access to business information, and it also offers a means for designers to determine the existence of available, relevant data for new business systems. As a result, duplication of critical business data in the corporate data dictionary is minimized and security of the data is maximized. Moreover, use of high-level, nonprocedural decision support system languages enables authorized personnel to access the data dictionary and thereby gain accurate corporate information quickly and easily to assist them in executive decision making. Without this central, independent data administration function, however, the long-held dream of an accurate, easily accessible, secure, and up-to-date corporate information database probably never can be realized.

The skills required for a data administrator are mostly those associated with business system analysis, although familiarity with the general concepts of database management systems and database structures is a definite asset. Additionally, the data administrator or his staff needs to be very familiar with the specific data dictionary and database management system that the enterprise is using. Furthermore, an in-depth knowledge of the business operations of the enterprise and an ability to interact positively with all levels of management are essential characteristics of the successful data administrator — he is clearly an unusual individual! (The person to fulfill the role of data administrator probably wears a red cape and performs quick changes in telephone booths. Mild-mannered cub programmers will almost certainly not succeed at data administration and need not apply.)

The database administrator does not need to be completely involved until the System Design stage, but he works alongside the data administrator in this stage, ensuring that the system database specification is defined to be compatible with the corporate data dictionary. He also ensures that the system data dictionary is compatible with the corporate data dictionary. In addition to possessing system analysis and design skills, the database administrator is an expert on the physical and logical characteristics of database management systems and advises on the need for and the use of a DBMS within the organization.

8.3 Activities

The first activity during the System Specification stage is the analysis of the users' physical, environmental, and operational requirements and their translation into the specification of the new system. This translation gradually helps to clarify the view of the system until the actual system type required (batch, on-line, file- or database-oriented, centralized, distributed, and so on) becomes clear by the end of this stage. The preliminary definition of possible system types performed in the Feasibility Study serves as a basis for this activity.

When all of the requirements have been translated like the examples in Table 8-1 and the type of system defined, this information is reviewed informally by the project team and by the Project Review Board. Any disagreements as to the type of system proposed are resolved at this time.

Next, a high-level diagram of the proposed system is produced. Several types of diagrams are suitable for this purpose, but it is best to use a notation that is compatible with or even the same as the notation used for the high-level design of the system in the next stage. The most popular and user-friendly of the currently available techniques is that of data flow diagrams, but more information regarding timing and sequencing, if available, can be included on a hierarchical structure chart, HIPO chart, or flowchart.

Whatever technique is used, more detailed analysis of user requirements identified in the previous stage is carried out. For example, the user requirements are grouped so as to logically represent major system functions, which correspond to form major "boxes" or "bubbles" in the system diagram. Figure 8-1 is a simple example of the first version of such a high-level schematic of a system. Each bubble in the diagram could represent one or more discrete user requirements translated into discrete system functions. Several iterations of this diagram are usually necessary before project team members are satisfied that it represents the system they want to build.

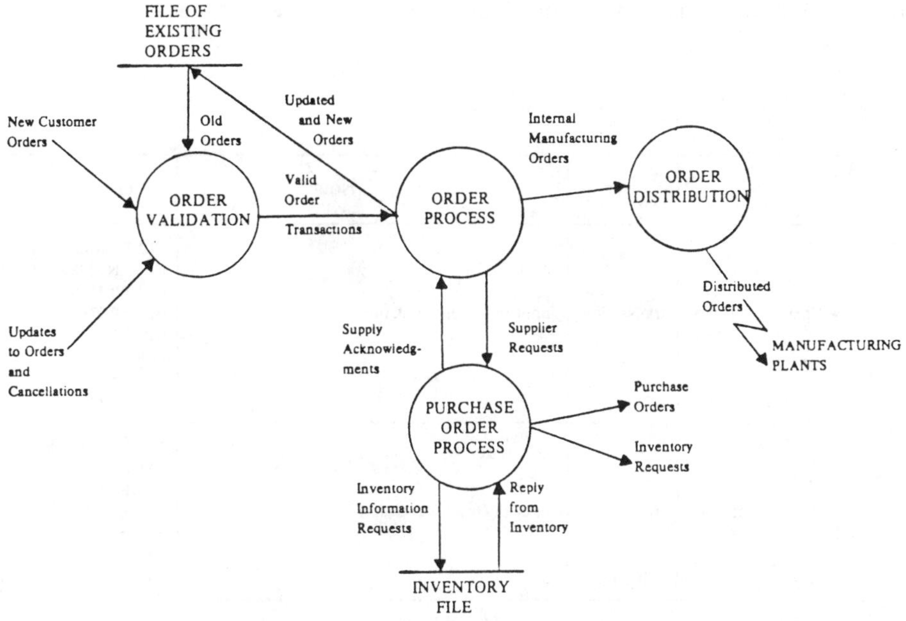

Figure 8-1. Example of a high-level data flow diagram of a system.

From the definition of the information requirements in the previous stage, the data requirements now are defined with the aid of the database administrator and the data administrator. One issue to be resolved, for example, is whether a database and a database management system are required. If a database is needed, what type should be chosen — hierarchical, network, or relational? Although some preliminary thought may be given to the choice of a database management system, the database designer doesn't recommend a specific DBMS to implement his design until the next stage. The database-related tasks in this stage are to enforce the use of data naming standards and procedures and to describe the data requirements specified in the corporate data dictionary.

A natural consequence of developing a high-level schematic view of the system is that the data requirements start to be automatically specified; that is, the data inputs and outputs of the system, as opposed to the intermediate data requirements, are clearly identified on the diagram. For instance, in Figure 8-1, the inputs to the system are New Customer Orders, Old Orders, and Updates to Orders and Cancellations. Outputs from the system are Distributed Orders, Purchase Orders, and Inventory Requests. It is also clear from the diagram that File of Existing Orders is updated and that Inventory File is accessed. From this modest start, the system's complete data requirements can be developed. These requirements are expressed in physical terms as files, forms, reports, transactions, screens, displays, and so forth, both in the system data dictionary, which was begun in the previous stage, and on the DFD.

Each of the data requirements on the DFD must then be decomposed into separate data items: What data items exist in each transaction? Which specific pieces of data are required in each report? and so on. All this information is recorded in the data dictionary to expand the previous entries. The data dictionary must contain an entry to define each bubble and arrow in the high-level data flow diagram and its relationship to other entries in the dictionary. Data dictionary entries for part of the system illustrated in Figure 8-1 are shown in Figure 8-2.

ENTITY	TYPE	RELATIONSHIP	CONTAINS
New Customer Orders	transaction	input to Order Validation	CUST.NAME CUST.NUMBER ORDER.NUMBER ORDER.ITEM ORDER.QTY PRICE ORDER.DATE DELIV.DATE
Updates to Orders and Cancellations	transaction	input to Order Validation	ORDER.NUMBER UPDATE.CODE ORDER.ITEM ORDER.QTY PRICE UPDATE.DATE DELIV.DATE
Old Orders	record	input to Order Validation	
Updated and New Orders	record	output from Order Process	see New Customer Orders
Valid Order Transactions	transaction	output from Order Validation	
Order Validation	process	inputs: New Customer Orders, Updates to Orders and Cancellations, Old Orders outputs: Valid Order Transactions	
Order Process	process	inputs: Valid Order Transactions, Supply Acknowledgments outputs: Updated and New Orders, Internal Manufacturing Orders, Supplier Requests	

Figure 8-2. Partial system data dictionary.

As you can see, the data dictionary contains descriptive information about the processes in the system in addition to the system's data. The CONTAINS part of the process descriptions will eventually list the subprocesses, which may not be fully defined until the System Design or the Program Design and Development stages. As the system-level data dictionary is developed, the data administrator ensures that any entries corresponding to information in the corporate data dictionary conform to the corporate data naming standards, and that the corporate data dictionary is updated to include new entries and related references. The ultimate objective of the corporate data dictionary must be that it can refer to any piece of business data, either directly or through a cross-reference to a particular system data dictionary.

The first version of the system data dictionary is completed when all of the data elements in the high-level system diagram are described as fully as possible. Then, the project team reviews the diagram and the system data dictionary for accuracy and completeness. Several iterations of this review may be necessary before the project team is fully satisfied. Next, representatives from the Project Review Board review these documents before work continues.

Now that all the data requirements are known, a related activity involves controlling access to that data. Much of the data being processed in modern systems is sensitive, such as personal, financial, marketing, and business planning data to which access needs to be controlled. All such data types are identified in this stage and the allowable forms of access defined by the users on the team. Protection of data in a teleprocessing network environment is particularly critical, as unauthorized access to data is easier in this situation. Data encryption is a technique often used in this environment.

Another type of control that is specified now is audit trails. Generally, any system consists of a series of actions performed upon data to transform it from input data to output data. For technical and legal reasons, a separate record of these actions must be kept. In the case of a system crash, for instance, the audit trail allows a retracing of steps to the point at which processing can safely restart. From a legal point of view, the user often needs to demonstrate precisely what happens to a piece of information as it passes through the various transformations in the system to verify the validity of the system's processes.

Finally, required levels, or "generations," of files and databases are specified. For instance, if a system is to perform a daily file update, the specification may be that three generations of all files be available at all times. Therefore, if today is Wednesday, then Monday's, Tuesday's, and Wednesday's versions of all files must be available. This provides a certain level of recoverability in the case of a system breakdown, a natural disaster, or a straightforward creation of bad data. In planning for a natural disaster, a copy of the most current generation of the data should be forwarded regularly to a remote location.

As mentioned in Chapter 7, the task list for the Requirements Definition stage provided by the SDLC methodology should have included specific activities to define security, privacy, and recovery requirements. If so, the system controls are simply an elaboration of these previously defined requirements. If these requirements have not yet been defined, the specification of system controls can absorb a significant portion of the resources allocated to the System Specification stage.

The next major activity in the System Specification stage is to revise the cost-benefit analysis and payback schedule, which were developed in the Feasibility Study and possibly modified in the Requirements Definition stage. Since much more detailed information about the new system is now available, the estimates of costs and benefits can be redeveloped with much more accuracy. If the new estimates vary significantly from the original figures, they are assessed by the Project Review Board, particularly if the changes would lengthen the payback schedule. A project that appeared at the start to be attractive financially may now look marginal, and agreement to continue with the project may depend upon criteria that are nonfinancial in nature, such as regulatory demands or market-driven reasons. Or, perhaps what originally seemed to be an attractive product for sale in the market has since been produced by a competitor in the interim and has turned out to be a disaster, because of various unforeseen political happenings, for example. Consequently, the market for this product now has shrunk dramatically. The board must assess all such considerations to confirm the continued viability of the project.

As before, an estimate of the next stage is developed. It can be based on the high-level diagram of the system. Each entity in this diagram needs to be designed in detail, and the DP professionals on the project team can assist in estimating the amount of effort required in each case. Remember that in the System Design stage, several design alternatives may emerge that will affect the estimates; for example, they will vary in terms of whether to use in-house versus subcontract design and development work, whether to buy off-the-shelf packages, and whether to install versions of the system first. The alternatives will have a multiplying effect on the schedules of the System Design stage, but it would be a mistake to develop the estimate by multiplying the number of people required simply to accommodate several different alternatives. Since the project team at this stage does not know what the design alternatives are, or how many there are likely to be, the estimate should indicate that only one alternative is being assumed and that if more emerge, the actual effort and resources expended during System Design will be increased accordingly.

When the estimate of the System Design stage is complete, a revised estimate of the remainder of the life cycle stages also needs to be made based on the Requirements Definition document. By now, with real experience, a good project team should have detected any tendency to over- or underestimate, and it can make corrections to help counter this tendency in subsequent estimates.

The next activity generates the end product of all of the previous activities: the System Specification document. All of the documentation produced so far in this stage is consolidated into the following seven sections: system description, data requirements, network and telecommunications requirements, system controls, revised cost-benefit analysis and payback schedule, estimates of next stages, and index to related material (see Section 8.5).

In parallel with the other activities of the System Specification stage, the users on the project team *start* to develop the detailed system test plan to fully test the system against its complete set of approved user requirements. The critical parts of a test plan identify the following information: test input data, expected test output, list of test criteria with cross-references to corresponding input and output data, levels of acceptance or nonacceptance for each of the test criteria and for the complete test, schedule for starting and completing the test, and resources required to carry out the system test. The system test plan is not a *required* deliverable until the end of the System Design stage.

Finally, during this stage, the System Specification document is reviewed and approved by the Project Review Board, and the manager for the next stage is recommended and assigned. (These end-stage activities are described in detail in Section 8.6.) Figure 8-3 summarizes the main activities required in the System Specification stage.

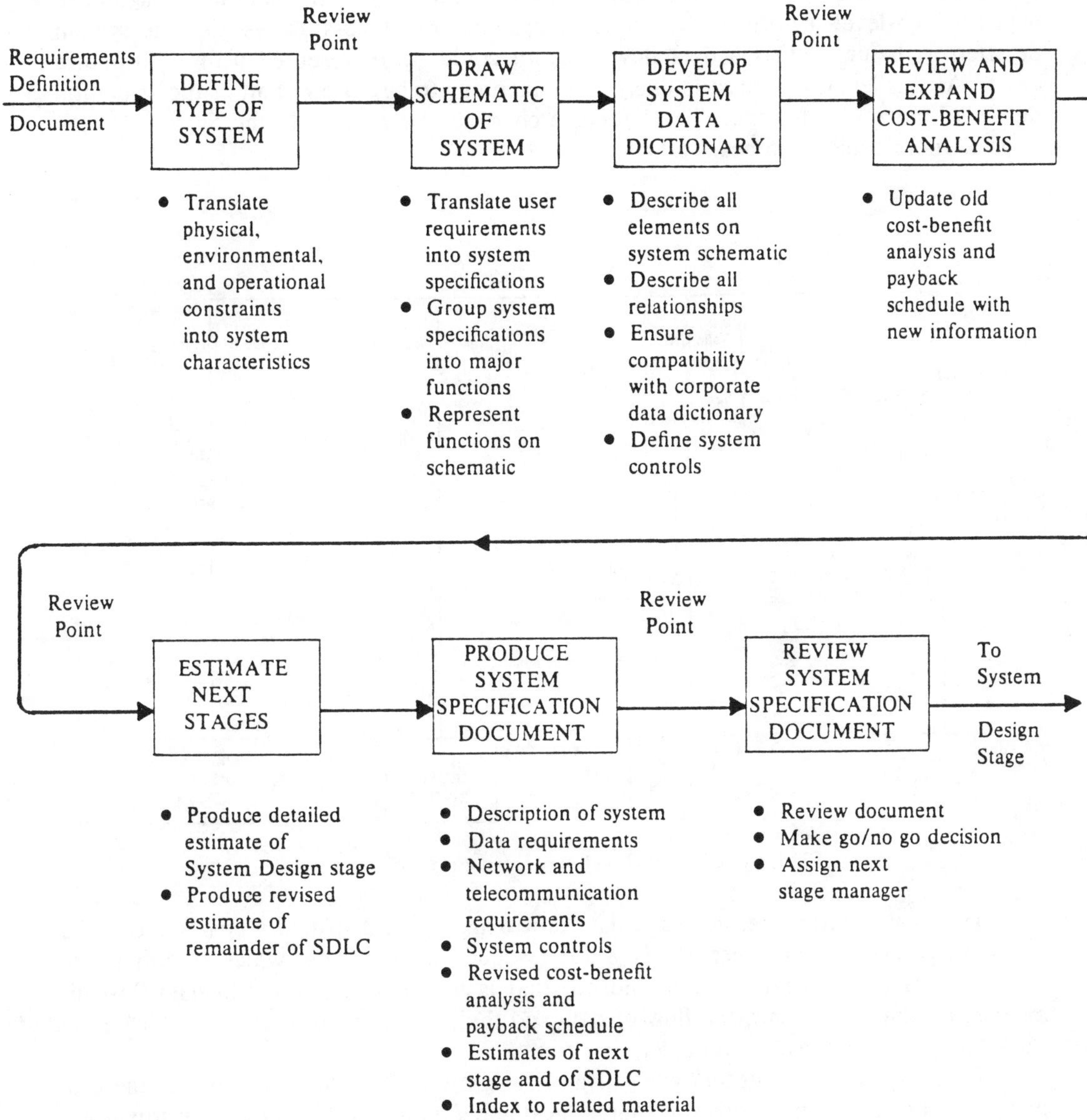

Figure 8-3. Summary of the System Specification stage activities.

8.4 Tools and techniques

While business system analysis is a useful skill during the Requirements Definition stage, in this stage the emphasis moves toward DP system analysis skills and techniques. Specifically, team members must be able to analyze stated user needs and to specify an actual DP system that, when implemented, will fulfill those needs. The staff also needs to be familiar with certain documentation tools and techniques. As already mentioned, the high-level system diagram can take the form of a data flow diagram. Alternative diagrammatic techniques are those of structure charts and HIPOs.

The structure chart can be used in essentially the same way as the data flow diagram to depict a high-level picture of the proposed system. Figure 8-4 shows how the system depicted in Figure 8-1 as a data flow diagram could be represented using a structure chart. At this level, the chart is likely to be incomplete because not all of the structural detail is known at this time. The structure chart can be revised in the System Design stage as more detail becomes available.

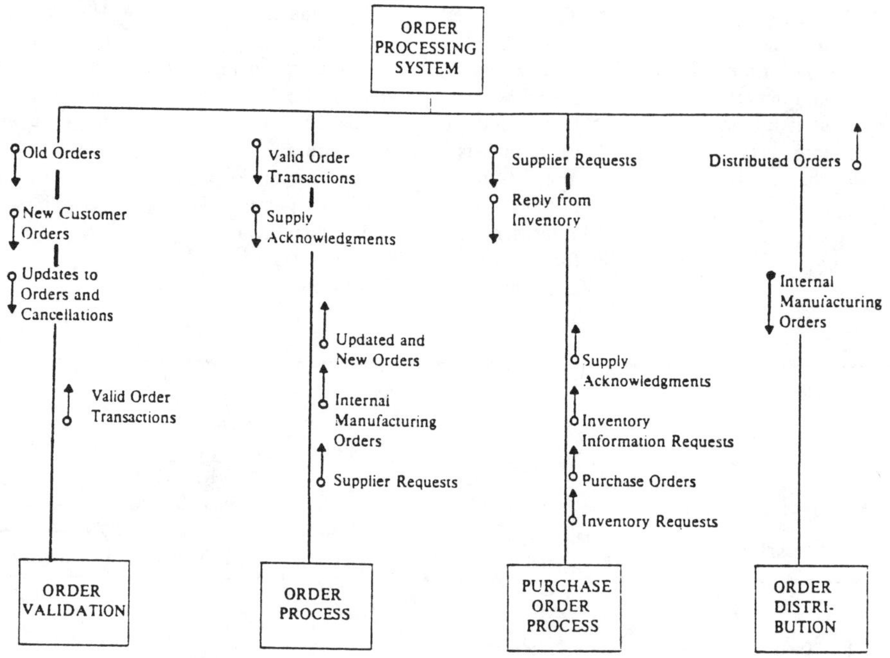

Figure 8-4. High-level structure chart of a system.

Two major differences between data flow diagrams and structure charts should be apparent: Structure charts can imply a strict sequence of events, which is difficult to denote in data flow diagrams and, indeed, that is not their purpose. In data flow diagrams, on the other hand, the flow of data and the positioning of files and databases in the system are much easier to depict.

The HIPO chart is another analysis and design tool, introduced by IBM in the early 1970s. The acronym stands for *H*ierarchical and *I*nput-*P*rocess-*O*utput. In this notational scheme, a simple hierarchical diagram of our order processing system is shown in Figure 8-5.

Figure 8-5 represents the "H" of HIPO, which shows how each function is decomposed into subfunctions. Then, for each box or component (function or subfunction) in the diagram, an IPO diagram is drawn, such as those in Figure 8-6 for the sample system. The HIPO notation cannot really claim to be a design method because it only depicts what the designer already knows before he starts to design. However, it can be an effective design documentation tool and is readily understood by nontechnical users.

Any one of these three notational tools can be used in this stage to serve as a high-level diagram of the system. Whichever one is used, the structured techniques used in later stages are compatible with them all. Therefore, the choice of data flow diagrams, structure charts, or HIPO charts can be made on the basis of which documentation makes the readers of the System Specification document most comfortable. Increasingly, data flow diagrams are being chosen at this stage because they are not cluttered by procedural details and are therefore more readily understandable.

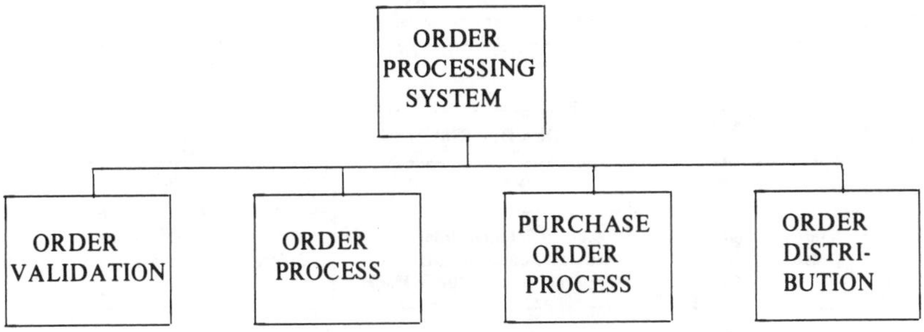

Figure 8-5. A simple hierarchical diagram of a system.

(a)

ORDER PROCESSING SYSTEM		
INPUTS	PROCESS	OUTPUTS
New Customer Orders Old Orders Updates to Orders and Cancellations	Order Validation Order Process Purchase Order Process Order Distribution	Distributed Orders Purchase Orders Inventory Requests

(b)

ORDER VALIDATION		
INPUTS	PROCESS	OUTPUTS
New Customer Orders Old Orders Updates to Orders and Cancellations	validates customer information; updates eligibility and some data ranges	Valid Order Transactions

(c)

ORDER PROCESS		
INPUTS	PROCESS	OUTPUTS
Valid Order Transactions Supply Acknowledgments	updates File of Existing Orders and sends Internal Manufacturing Orders to Distribution; sends out Supplier Requests and receives Supply Acknowledgments	Updated and New Orders Internal Manufacturing Orders Supplier Requests

Figure 8-6. I-P-O diagrams (a) through (c) of the system.

(d)

PURCHASE ORDER PROCESS		
INPUTS	PROCESS	OUTPUTS
Supplier Requests Reply from Inventory	processes requests for parts and components that will be supplied by vendors; checks Inventory File to find out if items are available and and either produces Purchase Orders or Inventory Information Requests, depending upon inventory status	Inventory Information Requests Supply Acknowledgments Purchase Orders Inventory Requests

(e)

ORDER DISTRIBUTION		
INPUTS	PROCESS	OUTPUTS
Internal Manufacturing Orders	splits up Internal Orders and distributes them to relevant Manufacturing Plants	Distributed Manufacturing Orders

Figure 8-6 (continued). I-P-O diagrams (d) and (e) of the system.

Other notational techniques can be used in this stage, such as Warnier-Orr diagrams [29] and Nassi-Shneiderman charts [28].* But the three techniques described earlier are the diagrammatic methods currently most in favor. Of course, simple narrative, without diagramming techniques, is often used to specify a system, but this lacks the power of pictures. A picture is indeed worth a thousand words in this case. In addition to the diagrammatic tools that can be usefully employed during the System Specification stage, the data dictionary, as described earlier, is an essential mechanism for recording system entities and their definitions and characteristics.

8.5 Documentation

The major documentation is the System Specification document, which consists of seven sections:

- *System description:* This section contains a clear, nontechnical narrative description of the new system such that user management can understand what the system will do without having to read any other documentation. This narrative description is very similar to that produced in the previous stage. The high-level system diagram is included with a brief explanation of the notation used, and each of the system functions is described in terms of the user requirements being met by the function.

  Any user requirements that are not being met and any plans to meet them in later versions of the system are also explained here. If different versions of the system are to be implemented at different

*Warnier-Orr diagrams are described in Chapter 3. Nassi-Shneiderman diagrams, or Chapin charts, are used to describe the detailed procedural logic within a module; they are similar to conventional flowcharts but force the designer to use the three basic constructs of structured programming. They are described in Chapter 10.

times, each version is described in terms of its functions, the specific user requirements being met, and their approximate implementation dates.

- *Data requirements:* All data requirements of the system identified so far — all files, databases, transactions, reports, screens, displays, and other similar data-oriented system entities — are described here. The system data dictionary also is included, the specific relationships between it and the corporate data dictionary are identified, and any system data elements that are also entries in the corporate data dictionary are listed.
- *Network and telecommunication requirements:* The environmental and operational constraints of the system impose performance and geographical requirements, which, in turn, demand certain networking and telecommunication characteristics. These characteristics are expressed in terms of where and when access to the system is needed, how it is needed, and what performance is required, including response times, transaction processing rates, and similar system attributes.
- *System controls:* This section describes three types of controls: sensitive data and processes to be made secure; audit trail requirements; and levels of security, including the generations of backup needed and recovery specifications.
- *Revised cost-benefit analysis and payback schedule:* An updated version of the cost-benefit analysis from the Feasibility Study is included with more details of the financial benefits accruing from the new system and of the costs to implement and operate this system. All changes to the payback schedule are described here and the revised payback schedule presented. Any changes from the original cost-benefit analysis and payback schedule should be highlighted.
- *Estimates of next stages:* The detailed estimated costs and schedules for the System Design stage are included here as well as in the updated cost-benefit analysis and payback schedule section. Additionally, the revised estimate for the remainder of the project is contained in this section with the planned implementation schedule for the system. Again, this estimate and schedule must correlate with information in the revised cost-benefit analysis and payback schedule.
- *Index to related material:* As in all stages, much material and documentation that is generated during the stage is not included in the finally approved end-stage document, but it all must be accessible for reference and for use by subsequent life cycle stage participants. Therefore, an index to the working papers of the stage is included.

8.6 End-stage activities

Prior to the formal review by the Project Review Board, the System Specification document is reviewed by all members of the project team for completeness and accuracy. Finally, the System Specification document is reviewed and approved by the Board before the project team can move onto the next stage. Again, if all of the necessary activities have been carried out successfully, the review is simply a formality. The formal review is scheduled to occur long enough before the planned end of the stage to allow significant changes to be made to the document, if necessary, without the need to change the end-stage date. This period of time can range from a few days to several weeks depending on the size and importance of the project.

At the formal review, the users, controllers, DP organization, DP operations staff, and DP auditors must be satisfied that the following are true:

- The specified system meets the user requirements stated in the Requirements Definition document. If requirements are missing, they are documented and the schedule for their ultimate implementation is acceptable. All of the informational requirements are represented in the list of data requirements. The network and performance characteristics as specified are practical and achievable, and they meet the users' needs.
- The installed system will be compatible with and supportable by the planned hardware and software environment.
- System controls, in terms of data security, data auditability, and data recovery, are adequate as specified.
- Financial information contained in the estimates and the cost-benefit analysis is acceptable, as are the estimates themselves of the System Design stage and subsequent stages. The cost-benefit analysis and the payback schedule are also acceptable.
- The narrative description of the proposed system is understandable and acceptable.
- A senior DP development manager is assigned as the next stage manager, and he specifically accepts the System Specification document and the estimate for the System Design stage.
- Sufficient staff in terms of number and level of experience are available for the System Design stage. (The users on the project team are expected to stay with the project for reasons of continuity and liaison.)
- Preliminary work on the system test plan by the users on the team is acceptable.

The review of the System Specification document may need to be repeated several times before a complete consensus is reached. Cancellation of the project because of nonapproval at this point in the SDLC is unusual, but it can happen. More likely, however, are a commitment for further work on the System Specification and a rescheduled review of the corresponding documentation.

When all reviewers are satisfied with the document, the Project Review Board issues the usual approval letter. The letter contains a description of any concessions that the Project Review Board has approved and of any System Specification omissions that are expected to be corrected in subsequent stages. Signatories of the System Specification approval letter include every member of the Project Review Board, the stage manager of the System Specification stage, the stage manager of the System Design stage, the project manager, the DP development manager, the DP operations manager, and the DP audit manager.

If the System Specification is approved, three of the seven SDLC stages are accomplished. The project manager can feel more confident of success as he hands over the next major activity, developing the system design, to the DP professionals.

9

System Design Stage

"The time has come," the Walrus said,
"to talk of many things:
of shoes and ships and sealing wax,
of cabbages and kings.
And why the sea is boiling hot,
And whether pigs have wings."
— Lewis Carroll

When the System Design stage is reached, the time has indeed come to talk of many things. Often during this stage, more talking is done than anything else. Adding to the conversational level, the data processing organization becomes heavily involved during this stage and, in fact, many DP professionals feel that System Design is when the life cycle really starts. This is of course not true, for system developers must have a very good idea of the problem before they start to design a solution. Typically, as illustrated in Chapter 6, 27 percent of the resources and 40 percent of the time allocated to the complete project have already been expended by the time the System Design stage is started.

Much public discussion has been devoted to what techniques should or should not be used in the System Design stage, and many developers advocate a good system design methodology as sufficient to provide techniques for all life cycle stages. This is not true! No matter how good the methods used in the System Design stage, their results are useful only when they are combined effectively with the results from all other life cycle tasks.

9.1 Objectives

This stage's primary objective is to develop a comprehensive technical description of the proposed system. That is, the System Specification from the previous stage defines *what* the system will do; the objective of this stage is to define *how* the system will do it. The technical description must be sufficiently detailed so that in the next stage, all of the programs can be completely designed and coded from their technical specifications, contained in this overall system description.

All programs and modules in the system are defined in terms of their inputs, outputs, and required internal functions and processes. All relationships between each of the system's programs and modules are defined explicitly, and all timing and performance requirements are extrapolated down to the program level in terms of the individual program's performance needs.

With the definition of the data requirements and the specification of the system's database from the previous stage, the goal now is to design both the logical and physical structures of the data. This task belongs to the database designer, who takes the complete set of data entities specified in the System Specification stage and develops a detailed integrated logical view of all of the data to be processed by the system. This provides a clear picture or description of all the system's data and the interrelationships.

In parallel with the logical view of the system's data being developed, both the system and the corporate data dictionaries are updated: All new processes, procedures, programs, and modules identified during the design process are included in the system data dictionary so that by the end of the stage, it represents a complete and accurate picture of the system's data. Also all cross-references to and new required entries in the corporate data dictionary are entered.

When a technical picture of the system is available in some form, boundaries can be drawn around the parts of the system that can be implemented using commercially available software packages. In some cases, the complete system can be implemented with a package. For example, packages for payroll systems, accounts payable systems, and manufacturing control systems are among those readily available. The project team identifies several alternative packages with different boundaries, involving varying amounts of detailed design and development effort by the DP organization. The team evaluates these alternatives and recommends the best one, using a procedural decision making technique, such as the Kepner-Tregoe technique [22] (see Section 9.4.2). Another aspect of the decision regarding packages is whether to develop the programs internally or externally.

The detailed system test plan, begun in the System Specification stage, is a deliverable of the System Design stage. Its purpose is to direct the system test activity in assuring that the original objectives of the system are met.

Too many technical descriptions of systems produced in this stage resemble complex engineering or mathematical treatises with an abundance of impressive formulae and equations. Often, the system designers omit important practical details in the rush to impress the world with their esoteric technical abilities. Unfortunately, the design is likely to be picked up in the next stage by a group of absolutely normal programmers who would not recognize a differential equation or a Fourier polynomial if they tripped over one — nor should they. The System Design document is intended to be a technical document, but with a purpose: to provide an unambiguous and complete road map for the coders and implementers of the system to follow.

With this in mind, one more essential objective of the System Design stage is to produce a complete system flow diagram. Not to be confused with a data flow diagram, the system flow diagram is a flowchart depicting processes and physical entities included in the system, such as printers, tapes, and disks. It demonstrates the operational and physical flow of processes and data in the system. All timing constraints and processing sequences are shown on the diagram, and the man-machine boundaries and interfaces also are clearly delineated. All of the physical requirements (such as amounts and types of storage media required, access equipment, and core needs) are described or at least estimated. This set of requirements, of course, can be shown separately from the diagram as supplemental narrative information. Figure 9-1 is a system flow diagram of the order processing system of Chapter 8.

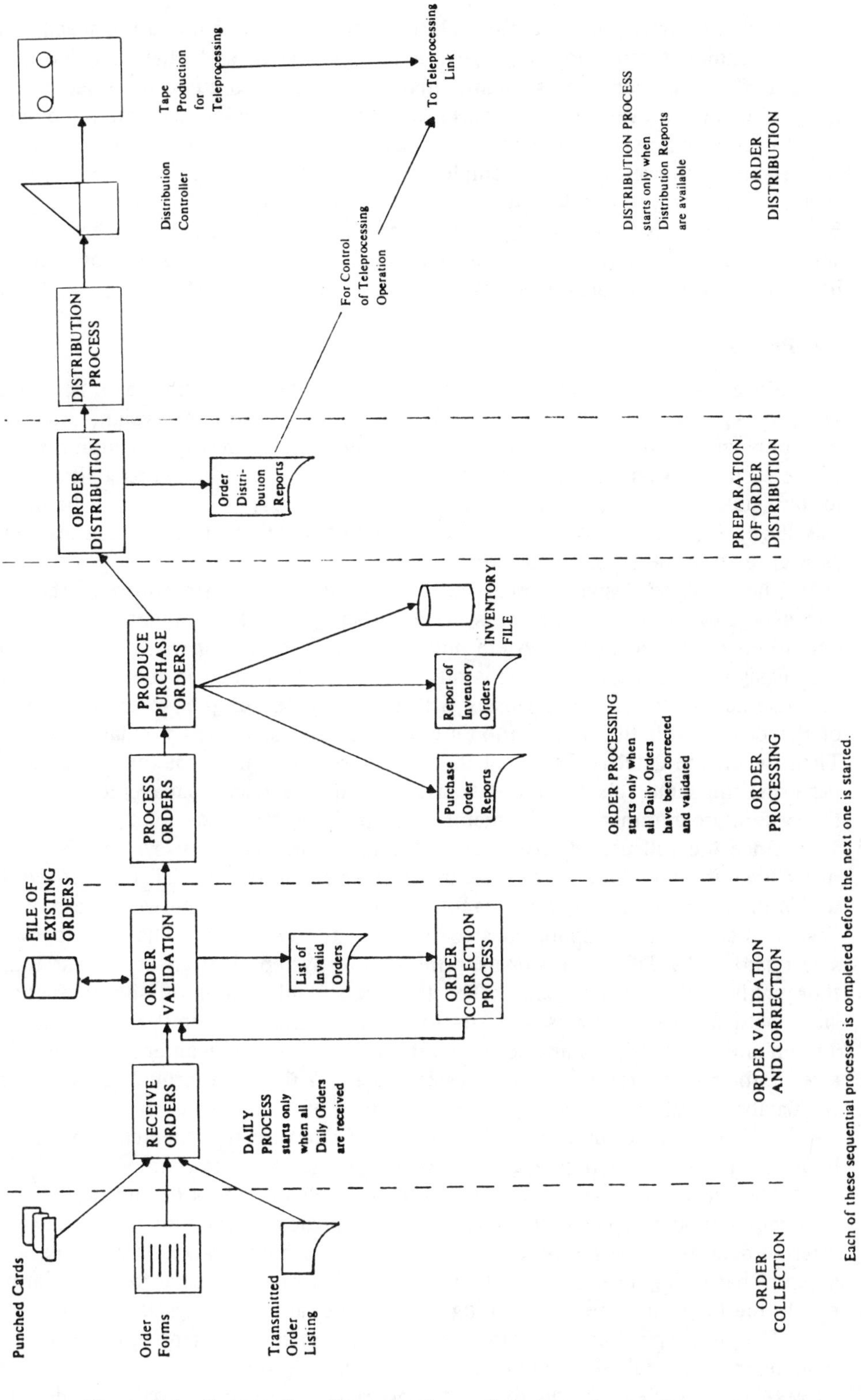

Figure 9-1. System flow diagram of an order processing system.

A final objective of the System Design stage is to recommend the specific program design techniques, program languages, coding standards, and other detailed guidelines to be used. Some company standards may already exist to guide the selection of these things; but in the ever-changing world of application development methodologies, it is wise to re-examine such standards with each new system. Some newly developed application generator package, for example, may render those old structured programming standards not only obsolete but completely unnecessary. ("Oh sacrilege!" do I hear Edsger Dijkstra say?) No coding is necessary in the System Design stage, although in some modern environments with user-friendly, high-level languages, some coding may be carried out to form prototypes of the system (see Chapter 16).

9.2 People involved

Since this stage is a technical one, most of the system design team is composed of DP professionals, trained and experienced in business system design, system design methodologies, system documentation, and system test planning. In addition, members of the system design team require some prior experience in developing similar systems, ideally, successfully implemented ones. A nucleus of users continues to be involved in this stage, and their responsibilities include the completion of the system test plan, with assistance from the system designers.

The database designer details all logical and physical structures of the data files and databases to be used by the system. Also, the data administrator completes the definitions contained in the system and corporate data dictionaries. The roles of database designer and database administrator are often embodied in the same person. The database administrator works closely with the database designer to ensure compatibility of the design with the organization's guidelines and standards for data and databases. Then, when the database is installed, the database administrator must maintain it. He performs the same role for the databases and the database management system as do the system programmers for the mainframe operating systems.

Since the full use of databases and database management systems is still new to many organizations, here is some guidance in selecting the specialized staff required. If this is the corporation's first courageous step into the forbidding wilderness of database design, there are three approaches to assigning the two roles. The first approach is to select two lucky DP professionals prior to the System Design stage and train them thoroughly in the required skills. The training should include off-site instructional sessions with hands-on exercises, visits to organizations with similar data requirements, and on-site investigations and tests of various database management systems using subsets of their organization's actual system data. With this thorough database training, the database staff should be capable of designing and supporting the required databases and of effectively deciding between competing database management systems. A few hours spent watching video tapes does *not* constitute adequate training.

The second approach to acquire database professionals is to hire them. The same skill requirements apply to these potential candidates as they do to the newly trained internal database experts. Since these skills do not come inexpensively, please do not assume that hiring an experienced database professional will save the corporation money. In the long run, effective training of personnel almost always saves money.

The third approach is to hire a suitably qualified consultant to carry out the database design. A database administrator, in this case, still is required once the database is successfully installed. Many excellent and reliable consulting database designers are available; the good ones are very expensive and, of course, only a temporary resource.

Even though the major deliverables from the System Design stage are considered to be technical, some repetitive, clerical tasks (such as editing and typing documentation and recording the completion of specific tasks) need to be carried out. Since these activities will increase greatly in the next stages, initial assignments of people to perform them, such as technical clerks and program librarians, are especially important now.

Managing the System Design stage activities falls to the lot of the senior DP development manager, who has already been working with the users during the Requirements Definition and System Specification stages. This manager is also responsible for taking the project through the next stage (Program Design and Development). In addition to being knowledgeable and experienced in all of the technical demands of System Design, this DP professional needs to be an accomplished administrator and people manager. The choice of this manager is not one that can be made lightly. The personalities involved in the System Design stage normally constitute an unstable, even explosive, mixture, which is rendered even less stable by the pressures of deadlines and changing specifications often experienced in this stage. The stage manager needs to anticipate problems, whether technical or people-oriented, and prevent them before they develop or at least be able to defuse problems before they reach a critical point.

The DP team began to be formed during the System Specification stage, and all of the DP professionals assigned to the project by the end of the System Design stage tend to stay with the project until after implementation. As the skills required in the System Design stage are varied but the life of the project is finite, formal matrix management of the entire project team may be necessary. This type of management structure is desirable when certain skills are needed only temporarily on a project; personnel are assigned on an as-needed basis and are supervised by a technical manager, rather than the particular project manager. In fact, for many projects, a matrix management structure may be desirable across the complete system development life cycle. Chapter 13 provides a more complete discussion of various management structures.

9.3 Activities

The first activity in the System Design stage is to generate an overall system diagram, based on the high-level system schematic produced during the System Specification stage. If the structured techniques are being used, this is when a hierarchical structure chart is now developed to show the main subcomponents of the components in the high-level system schematic.

An important part of this initial design activity is to determine suitable software packages that can be used to implement the system either wholly or partially, although this activity could be carried out during the System Specification stage. Following this search, the designers determine the impact of the software package or packages on the boundaries of the other parts of the system. The purchase of packages need not have any major effect on the overall design of the system, but physical and logical interfaces between packages and other parts of the system may need to be designed and implemented. Figure 9-2 shows how the choice of various software packages shown on a structure chart would affect design decisions.

The technical differences between each packaged alternative are described in detail so that the project team and the Project Review Board can choose intelligently between them, as described later in this section. An effective way to make an objective appraisal is to describe a general system design and then compare each alternative to this general design.

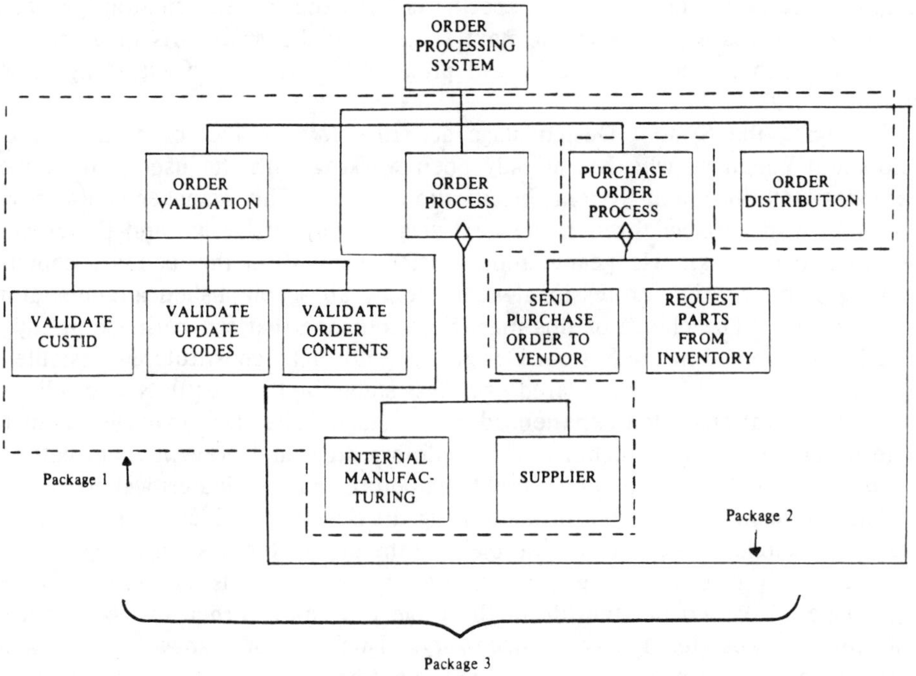

PACKAGE	SYSTEM FUNCTIONS IMPLEMENTED BY PACKAGE	SYSTEM FUNCTIONS TO BE DEVELOPED
1	Order Validation Order Process Order Distribution	Purchase Order Process
2	Order Process Purchase Order Process Order Distribution	Order Validation
3	All	None

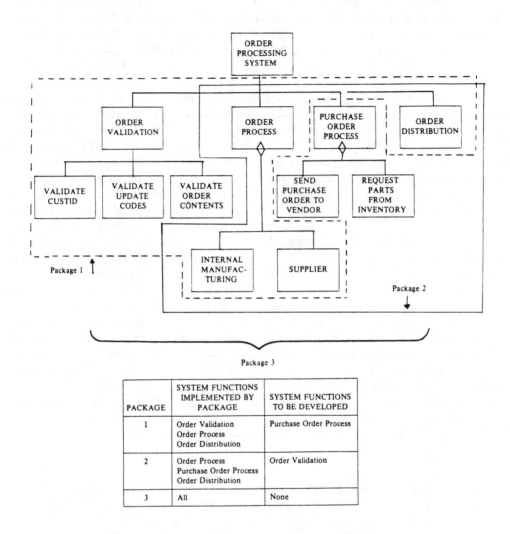

Figure 9-2. Effects of software package decisions on a system design.

Simultaneously with developing the overall system diagram, the designers now detail the type of hardware and software environment based on work done in previous stages. Details of that environment must be clearly defined in terms of what levels of the specific operating systems are required, and in terms of the specific mainframe, type of mini- or microcomputers, primary and secondary storage, and all other related requirements. (An initial determination of this environment was begun as early as the Feasibility Study.) In addition to the specific needs of the system, two other major factors influence this determination: First, there may already be a well-established hardware and software environment into which the new system must fit snugly and smoothly. For example, there may be no choice on the operating system to be used since the existing software environment will support the proposed system and most other systems in the organization. Second, some of the software packages being considered may demand specific hardware or software. Therefore, if alternative software package solutions are being considered, several alternative hardware and software environments may also need to be defined in detail.

The overall system diagram, with its identification of package boundaries and hardware and software environments and technical descriptions of each package, is now reviewed and approved by the complete project team before the stage activities are continued.

The next major activity in the System Design stage is to produce the complete set of detailed system design diagrams. This involves decomposing every component of the high-level system diagram produced in the previous stage into subcomponents and each subcomponent into sub-subcomponents, and so on, until the lowest-level components can be regarded as elementary components, or those that need not be decomposed any further. Sometimes, these elementary components are called "system primitives." An elementary component can be directly developed into program code by the development team in the next stage. In those parts of the system for which a package is being recommended, the package itself could be regarded as an elementary component. Depending upon the specific programming techniques being used in the next stage, the elementary components may need to be very simple or could be quite complex. For instance, if the Jackson or Warnier-Orr methodologies are used in the Program Design and Development stage, the elementary components produced in the System Design stage can remain quite complex, each representing several hundred lines of COBOL, PL/I, or FORTRAN code. On the other hand, if no effective program design techniques are being used in the next stage, the elementary components produced at the lowest levels of the system design diagram must be quite simple, each representing perhaps only 25 to 100 lines of code, or even fewer. In the latter situation, the dividing line between system design and program design becomes somewhat fuzzy.

The guidelines of structured design should be used in this decomposition process. Experience has proved over the last few decades that this top-down approach is more reliable than other approaches in producing an accurate and detailed picture of a system. This activity produces a set of structure charts.

In order to facilitate the translation from the system design to code, each component, from top to bottom of the system flow diagram, is accompanied by a narrative description of that component. These narratives are variously referred to as pseudocode, structured English, or minispecifications (minispecs), among others. So the set of charts plus the minispecs describe the complete system design.

Another major activity, as noted earlier, is developing the detailed integrated logical view of the data to be processed by the system. This provides a clear picture or description of all the system's data and the interrelationships. In modern parlance, the totally integrated logical view of the system's data is known as the schema, or conceptual schema. The individual, program-oriented logical views are known as subschemas. A clear description of the differences between conceptual schemas and subschemas can be found in James Martin's excellent book *Computer Database Organization* [25]. This logical view can be implemented by a database management system that not only effectively and efficiently stores all of the system's data, but also provides the means to extract the individual logical views of the data required by the individual programs.

As stated earlier in this chapter, as each component of the system flow diagram is developed, all new identified entities, processes, and data items are incorporated into the system data dictionary. The corporate data dictionary is updated when it is affected by the new elements. The data administrator ensures that the data naming and data definition standards are being met, and the database designer combines the data subschemas into a system conceptual schema. At the end of this activity, the database designer recommends to the project team the specific database management system to be used to implement this schema most effectively.

All of the communication and network requirements generally specified in the System Specification stage for performance and geographical considerations now are defined in detail. All communication lines and their transmission capabilities, modems, terminal controllers, satellite and microwave links, and all other teleprocessing equipment are specified and possibly ordered, because of the long delivery times associated with some of this equipment. In some cases, it may be necessary to order a general set of items at an earlier date and refine the order during the System Design stage when the details become clearer.

After the communication requirements have been detailed, the man-machine boundaries of the system are identified along with any affected manual procedures, either new or existing. All interfaces with other manual or automated systems also are defined in detail, as well as all data entry and data correction procedures.

The users on the project team compare the set of detailed System Design diagrams and narrative information with the System Specification document to ensure that all of the specified needs of the system are being met in the design. With all of the technical details completed, the detailed design for each design alternative is now reviewed by the project team for accuracy, completeness, and appropriateness. There should be no intent to eliminate or choose a specific design alternative at this review, because financial, timing, and resource characteristics for each alternative must first be determined. Increasingly, financial considerations are at last playing an important part in the decision to implement DP systems. In particular, a cost-benefit analysis, payback schedule, estimate of the next stage (Program Design and Development), and estimate of the remainder of the project must be developed for each alternative, since the various packages selected vary not only in how much of the proposed system requirements they each meet but also in their costs. In general, the more sophisticated and comprehensive the package, the more expensive it is and the fewer internal programming resources are required to develop the remaining parts of the system.

The benefits defined for each alternative should not vary significantly. If significant variances are found, then even at this early stage of the development process, some of the alternatives can no longer be considered viable. Overall costs do not normally vary a great deal, as higher internal resource expenditures usually compensate for the lower costs of simpler packages and vice versa. One significant variation to be expected is in the cost estimates for the next stage for each alternative. Clearly, if an off-the-shelf software package meets all of the proposed system requirements, the Program Design and Development costs will be minimized, but the purchase and maintenance costs of the package itself could be considerable.

An additional factor to be considered is whether the programs are developed internally or externally. Body shops that employ multitudes of programmers can provide staff to produce the required code from the program specifications. Depending upon available programming resources and company policy, some or all of the detailed program design, coding, and testing may also be carried out by these outside workers.*

---

*An increasing and encouraging trend is to provide users with user-friendly programming tools such as report writers and application generators so that they can develop the systems themselves. Many programmers find this trend alarming; I believe that it is healthy and inevitable. After all, where would the automobile industry be today if only experienced engineers could drive cars?

If, as is usual, some program design and development will be carried out in-house, the detailed system design diagrams can be used as a basis for the estimate of the next stage. If structured design techniques are being used, each module defined in the structure chart can be fairly accurately estimated in terms of the effort needed to produce program code and full documentation for each module. Additionally, the estimate must include costs and delivery schedules for any special equipment, such as telecommunications hardware, required to implement the system.

Since the required amount of in-house development affects the length of the next stage, it also correspondingly affects the schedules of subsequent stages, especially the implementation dates. Obviously, these effects must be considered in the estimate of the rest of the project for each of the alternative designs.

Now that every design alternative is complete in terms of technical and financial details, each design is evaluated by considering the following three major factors: first, the proportion of user requirements being met and their relative importance; second, the costs, benefits, and payback schedule; and third, the probable user acceptance level of the new system. The first two factors have already been defined in detail. The third factor, user acceptance, is subjectively measured and the users on the project team must make the assessment.

Except for this last factor, the alternatives should be evaluated as objectively as possible by the project team. Unfortunately, DP professionals are not known for their dispassionate objectivity; for instance, the fact that the president of a particular software house regularly plays golf with the DP director is not a good reason for choosing a particular software package. However, decisions often are made on such a basis. To prevent such an event, the team needs a procedure that minimizes all subjectivity in making its evaluation. The Kepner-Tregoe Decision Analysis Matrix, described in the next section, is a good example of an objective evaluation methodology.

Whatever the methodology used, it must provide a clear ranking of the design alternatives and a clear explanation of how this ranking was derived. If the highest ranking alternative seems to have only one thing going for it — the golfing ability of its vendor's president, for instance — the ranking process should be questioned.

Once the various design alternatives have been evaluated and ranked, the complete project team recommends the best one. In practice, the best two or three are usually recommended, with the final decision being left to the unanimous approval of the Project Review Board, the System Design stage manager, the Program Design and Development stage manager, the project manager, the DP development manager, the DP operations manager, the DP audit manager, and the DP standards manager at the end of the System Design stage.

Next, the system test plan for each recommended alternative is completed in detail. As described earlier, the main objective of the System Test stage is to ensure that the new system meets its objectives, namely, the system requirements contained in the Requirements Definition document. When there are several design alternatives, there are at least two parts of the system test plan: Part 1 is a plan to test the general parts of the system that are common to every recommended design alternative; and Part 2 is a plan to test, for each recommended alternative, those parts of that alternative design that are different from the common system.

For each recommended design alternative, the system test plan contains at least the following:

- *Test input data:* Sufficient data is included to ensure that every specific function and characteristic as defined in the Requirements Definition document is tested.
- *Expected test output:* For every specific function and characteristic that is tested, there is a specific result that is proof of the correct operation of that function or characteristic.
- *List of test criteria:* A list is prepared of those specific, detailed user requirements that the user wishes to see demonstrated in the final test of the system. The list is cross-referenced to the individual corresponding items of test input data and expected test output data. It is provided by the user organization and is based directly on the Requirements Definition and System Specification documents. Several items of input and output data, when considered together, may constitute one test criterion. For example, the inputs of hours worked, pay rate, regular work week, and overtime rate should generate one weekly pay amount within a certain range of accuracy. (See Chapter 11 for a discussion of test data generators and related tools.)
- *Levels of acceptance:* The values of the test input data can be precise, but the required test output values may often vary over a range of tolerances. The allowable range of these tolerances, for each "piece" of expected test output, must be stated. For one defined test criterion, for instance, there may be several discrete outputs, each with different allowable tolerances. These must be defined either separately or as an integral part of that test criterion.
- *Test schedule:* A detailed schedule is given for the start and finish of the system test, including the time needed for testing individual functions and the people, hardware, and software resources needed to carry out the system test within the prescribed schedule.

A valuable set of guidelines and criteria for performing system testing is found in Myers' *The Art of Software Testing* [27]. After the system test plan is completed, it is reviewed in detail by the complete project team.

Inevitably, a new system requires new methods of operation and use, and so the user representatives on the project team should now identify the training they need so as to use the new system when it is installed. An essential part of this training is having clear documentation of the system, documentation that not only describes the system in user terms, but also provides detailed, nontechnical instructions on how to actually use the system. Since operators are also users of the system, their training needs must be identified, along with the requirement for operator manuals. The user training and documentation requirements need not be fully developed during the System Design stage, because the detailed content depends largely on the design alternative chosen. However, the schedules and extent of user training can be outlined, and the general content of the documentation decided upon. Details of the recommended System Design documentation are provided in Section 9.5. Figure 9-3 summarizes the main activities to be carried out in this stage.

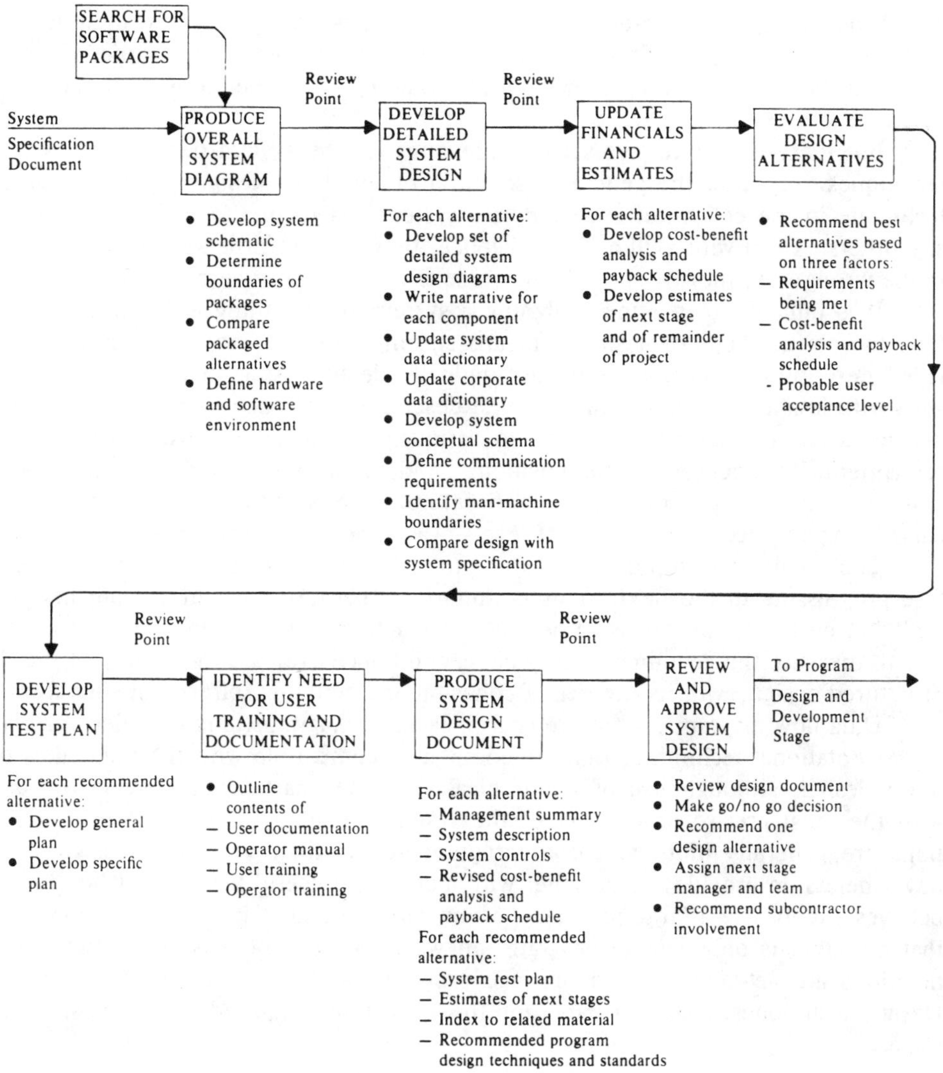

Figure 9-3. System Design stage activities.

9.4 Tools and techniques

In this section, I discuss two categories of techniques that can be applied in the System Design stage: a set of top-down design techniques and tools, and an evaluation technique developed by Kepner and Tregoe [22].

9.4.1 Design techniques

If the late 1960s and early 1970s was the era of new *program* design techniques, then the late 1970s and early 1980s seems to be the period when multitudes of *system* design techniques emerged. To the casual observer, many of these techniques seem to be much like many of the earlier program design techniques. In fact, even to the non-casual, deeply involved observer, many of these new "panaceas" for all system design problems are exactly like some program design techniques of the earlier period; only the word "program" has been changed to "system" to further confuse the already confused DP professional.

But there is an effective set of techniques for the system designer to use. These techniques fall under the general description of top-down design, even though no one technique in the collection is a complete system design method. These tools are like any others: Used with skill and intelligence, they can perform well; used foolishly and in the wrong way, they often perform worse than if no tools were used at all.

It is difficult to imagine designing a system (or anything else) in any other way than top-down. Top-down simply means starting with the most abstract and least detailed description of the system and gradually decomposing that description, step by step, into less abstract and more detailed descriptions of each part of the system. This general technique has been referred to variously as "levels of abstraction," "stepwise refinement," "functional decomposition," and many other terms, all meaning essentially the same thing. Top-down design naturally lends itself to hierarchies, a structure chart being an effective depiction of levels of abstraction, as shown in Figure 9-4.

The intention of top-down design is to enable the designer to verify each level before progressing to the next. This is important, because what may seem like a trivial omission on level 1 may cause a design catastrophe at level 7. So, the designer needs a way to measure the decomposition process and hence evaluate the quality of the design. Structured design, with its metrics of cohesion and coupling, offers just such a way.

Data flow diagrams, structure charts, Jackson diagrams, and Warnier-Orr diagrams all are notational techniques that are completely compatible with the guidelines of top-down design, although use of hierarchical structure charts does provide the designer with the most precise description of the system. The Jackson and Warnier-Orr notations are generally more suited to program design than to system design, but they nevertheless do provide the designer with a clear and useful technique when the system behaves simply like a large program. Many Jackson and Warnier-Orr proponents insist that a system is only a large program, anyway. (Details of how these techniques and notations are actually used to produce programs and systems appear in Chapter 3.) Design techniques, however, are not the only tools required in the System Design stage.

9.4.2 Kepner-Tregoe Decision Analysis Matrix

The evaluation technique devised by Kepner and Tregoe [22] is useful when a choice must be made between a number of alternatives and when it is important to minimize the subjective influences in the evaluation process. The key to this technique is defining a complete list of each alternative's required characteristics. This list is separated into two parts: a *must* part consisting of those requirements that must be met in each alternative; and a *want* part, consisting of the remainder ranked in order of importance. Any alternative that does not meet every one of the must characteristics is eliminated from the reckoning. Each of the want characteristics is then given a weight, usually an integer from one to ten, with ten denoting the highest priority characteristics, and one the lowest. The evaluators analyze each alternative and score to what extent each of the want requirements is met by each alternative. (Scores are also from one to ten, ten being best.) Then, for each alternative, the products of weight times score for all want characteristics are summed to obtain a performance total. Theoretically, the alternative with the highest performance total is the recommended alternative. Figure 9-5 shows how the technique could work for a simple system with three alternative designs.

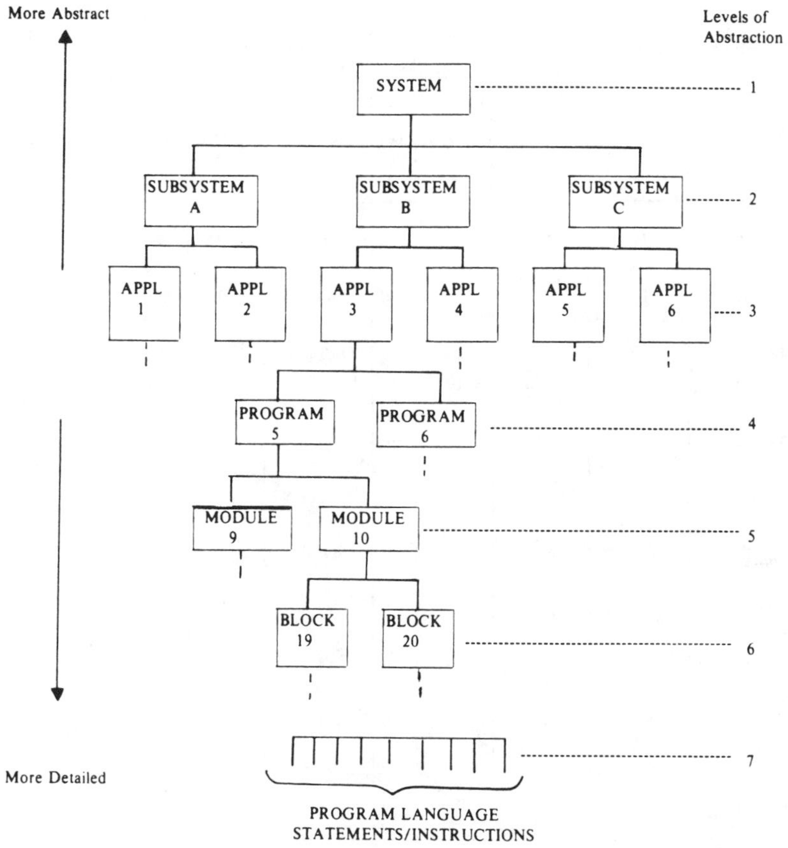

Figure 9-4. A top-down, hierarchical structure.

From the performance totals calculated for alternatives A, B, and C, B appears to be the winner. C was eliminated before the weighting and scoring exercise, because it did not meet all of the must requirements. DEC hardware, in this case, was incompatible with IBM hardware. Clearly, some subjective judgment must be involved in providing weights and scores for each characteristic of each alternative. In a real situation, the system would have many more required characteristics than in our example, and the users on the project team would be heavily involved in the weighting and scoring process.

MUSTS	ALTERNATIVE A		ALTERNATIVE B		ALTERNATIVE C	
• On-line access to live data	YES	√	YES	√	YES	√
• Compatible with IBM hardware	YES	√	YES	√	NO	×
	(IBM)	√	(AMDAHL)	√	(DEC)	
• Total estimated cost less than $200,000	$180,000	√	$160,000	√		
• Process greater than 25,000 transactions per hour	35,000	√	40,000	√		NO GO

WANTS	WEIGHT	DETAILS	SCORE	WT x SC	DETAIL	SCORE	WT x SC	DETAIL	SCORE	WT x SC
• Requires less than 5Mbytes core	10	4.8	7	70	4.0	10	100			
• Maximum transaction processing rate	10	35K	8	80	40K	10	100			
• Written in COBOL	9	COBOL	10	90	FORTRAN	0	0			
• Documented to QA standards	8	YES	10	80	PARTLY	6	48			
• Uses Jackson design method	8	NO	0	0	YES	10	80			
• Meets all security requirements	7	PARTLY	5	35	PARTLY	7	49			
• Uses latest DBMS technology	7	NO	0	0	SOME	6	42			
• Is designed for expandability	7	YES	10	70	YES	10	70			
• Package needs no modifications	5	NO	0	0	YES	10	50			
• Package meets all editing requirements	1	NO	0	0	YES	10	10			
PERFORMANCE TOTAL				425			549			

Figure 9-5. Example of the Kepner-Tregoe evaluation technique.

Once the alternatives have been scored in this way, the team should analyze them further, using a similar worksheet for potential problems. For instance, in the example above, the winning alternative B is written in FORTRAN and requires AMDAHL hardware in its original form. If modifications must be made to alternative B to make it actually run on the in-house IBM equipment, then perhaps the choice between using COBOL and FORTRAN is more serious than it first appeared. The want requirement of using COBOL should be reevaluated – perhaps it really is a must.

Figure 9-6 demonstrates these concerns. In this figure, although alternative B is the better technical choice, it has a high probability of implementation and support problems as compared with alternative A (195 against 25). As anyone familiar with

Murphy's Law knows, a potential problem has a very good chance of becoming a real one at the most inopportune moment. So, as a result of potential problem analysis, what clearly appears to be a favorite *technical* alternative may be usurped in favor of an apparently political choice. This illustrates that perhaps some of the so-called political decisions are in fact technical decisions based on more extensive technical analysis.

	ALTERNATIVE A			ALTERNATIVE B		
POTENTIAL PROBLEMS	PROBABILITY P	SERIOUSNESS S	P × S	PROBABILITY P	SERIOUSNESS S	P × S
Will require programming work to implement on IBM	2	5	10	9	5	45
Will require additional training for software support staff	3	5	15	10	5	50
Will require hiring of FORTRAN (or any non-COBOL language specialist)	0	10	0	10	10	100
PPA SCORE (P x S TOTAL)			25			195

NOTE: Probability and seriousness are both scored from 1 to 10, with 10 being the highest probability and the most serious.

Figure 9-6. Potential problem analysis worksheet.

9.5 Documentation

All of the technical activities in this stage produce various pieces of documentation, which are collected and organized into the System Design document. It contains at least the following nine sections:

- *Management summary:* a general technical description of the system with its objectives and how these objectives will be met. The differences between the various design alternatives are highlighted, especially those differences important to management — namely, differences in terms of costs, benefits, and schedules.
- *System description:* a detailed technical description of the system for each design alternative, including a narrative description of the system along with the detailed set of system design diagrams and a complete list of all system inputs and outputs. The system data dictionary should be included here, if used, as should any database design description and database management details. All technical descriptions of the telecommunication aspects of the system are included, along with details of the required hardware and software environments. All manual procedures and interfaces with other systems must be documented.
- *System controls:* a description of how each of the proposed alternative designs will meet all data security, privacy, and recoverability requirements, specified in the previous stage.

- *Revised cost-benefit analysis and payback schedule:* a description of any changes, good or bad, to the cost-benefit analysis caused by each design alternative; this description serves as critical input for evaluating the design alternatives. An important part of the cost-benefit analysis is the payback schedule; it varies as a function of the implementation timetable for each alternative.
- *Recommended design alternatives:* a summary of the evaluation process used to arrive at the ranking of the design alternatives. If a proprietary or previously published methodology is used, a reference to its use with the results is sufficient. The top two or three recommended designs are briefly described with an equally brief comparative analysis of their characteristics.
- *System test plan:* the plan for testing and scheduling each of the top two or three recommended alternatives.
- *Estimates of the next stages:* For each recommended alternative design, an estimate of the next stage includes the usual resource expenditure estimates and schedules, as well as a recommendation of the parts of the required Program Design and Development activities that could be carried out by subcontract programmers. Also included in this section is an estimate of the remainder of the project for each design alternative, including the implementation schedules, with implementation and conversion plans for the new system. A detailed, step-by-step plan for the implementation activities plus a schedule and plan for all of the required file, data, and procedural conversion tasks is included here as a basis for the estimate. These plans will be revised as necessary in subsequent stages.
- *Index to related material:* This section contains the usual references to all of the working papers produced during the System Design stage. In addition, the documentation for all of the recommended packages is reproduced, or at least referenced here. If any information about potential programming subcontractors is available, this information, too, is referenced to assist in later decisions about which subcontractors to use in the Program Design and Development stage.
- *Recommended program design techniques and programming standards:* If program design standards and a standard programming language for the development organization exist, they are stated here. If, however, no standards exist as is so often the case, the design team recommends them. These recommendations may vary slightly with each design alternative but the overall objectives are to reduce development time; improve program quality and documentation; and produce programs that are easily tested, maintained, and modified. To fulfill these exacting requirements, the program design and development techniques should include a nonprocedural, user-friendly, interactive, high-level, self-documenting application generator that produces structured, modular programs and that uses the corporate data dictionary to control data definition and naming standards. Simultaneously, this tool generates the system data dictionary. (Clearly, this application generator is not Assembler language, COBOL, or even ADA.)

Typically, the recommended standards for the Program Design and Development stage include the following: programming language or languages with a list of proscribed commands, statements, or operations; recommended methods of implementing standard program structures; maximum and minimum sizes of programs; preferred linkage mechanisms between programs and operating systems; and data naming standards.

After the System Design document has been completed, the Project Review Board must review and approve it. This and other end-stage activities are described below. Prior to this formal review, however, project team members themselves review the document to ensure that no surprises, to them at least, occur during the final review.

9.6 End-stage activities

After the project team completes the System Design document and informally reviews it, the document is subjected to a formal review and approval by the Project Review Board. Because many of the details contained in the document will probably be challenged at the final review, the review must be scheduled well before the end of the stage to allow for rebuttals or resolutions of these challenges. For a system development life cycle of greater than six months elapsed time, the final review should be scheduled several weeks before the planned end of the stage.

The task for the reviewers is to choose which of the recommended alternative designs best meets all of the detailed requirements defined in the System Specification document and recommend that alternative to be implemented. They also must decide whether program development will be done in-house or subcontract; and if subcontract is chosen, which subcontractor will be used. Each part of the System Design document must then be minutely reviewed and changed if necessary.

Once the System Design is approved and a specific design alternative is agreed upon, the manager for the next stage is selected and the Program Design and Development team assigned. If he has survived the design activities, the System Design stage manager usually becomes the Program Design and Development stage manager. This person is usually a senior manager from the DP development organization. He must be in total agreement with the estimate of the next stage and the recommended program design techniques and standards. The user members of the reviewing group must be fully satisfied that the system test plan will in fact test all of the user requirements for the system.

When all reviewers are satisfied with the System Design document, probably after several iterations of the review process, a letter is issued by the Project Review Board. This letter, which grants approval to proceed to the next stage, is signed by at least the following individuals: all members of the Project Review Board, the stage manager of the System Design stage, the stage manager of the Program Design and Development stage, the project manager, the DP development manager, the DP operations manager, the DP audit manager, and the DP standards manager (quality assurance).

9.7 Summary

The System Design stage is a critical point in the system development life cycle because it is the final stage before the implementation of the new system. All of the thinking is done and now the doing begins. The Program Design and Development stage is when, in most people's perceptions, all of the real programming is done. As mentioned before, if all of the specifications and design work have been carried out correctly, the programming stage should be easy. But, as I am sure Murphy once said, "If everything is going well according to plan, you must have forgotten something."

10

Program Design and Development Stage

The man who makes no mistakes does not usually make anything.
— Edward John Phelps

10.1 Objectives

In this stage, the primary objective is to produce and test the programs that make up the system. Since so much confusion and mystique surround the terms *program* and *programming,* let's begin with a definition:

> **program,** *n.* a logically related order of actions to be performed by a computer either to solve a problem or to process data; the instructions and data, reduced to computer code, for such a series of actions.

The "computer code" in the definition is, of course, the programming language or languages that the programs are written in. Clearly, the programs that are the final products of the Program Design and Development stage must meet this definition; together, they constitute a fully coded system in the target language or languages, as specified in the System Design document. However, that is only part of the story.

The activities performed in this stage are those most often referred to as "programming." What does that term mean? The popular images of a programmer include the technician, in communion with the computer, keypunching furiously until the wee hours of the morning; and the computing superstar, creating weird and wonderful products that seem closer to art than engineering in terms of structure and usefulness. Both of these images are correct to a degree, but successful programming today means not only coding, but also designing, testing, and documenting. Coding is probably the least important of those skills. All of the programs must be designed, coded, tested, and documented; and all of the programmers must be skilled in each and every one of those functions.

To achieve the objectives in this stage, project members use structured programming. This much vaunted, oversold technique is really in practice only a disciplined coding technique and it cannot be usefully employed as a design or a testing methodology. Unfortunately, in the early days of the structured revolution, structured programming was offered as a total panacea for all of DP's problems. When it did not work out that way, structured programming gained a bad, undeserved reputation, a reputation that its proponents are still trying to overcome. Nevertheless, when used for coding and for program documentation, structured programming is extremely effective in improving the quality and readability of programs.

The purpose of the documentation at this level is to explain, in nontechnical language, the processing logic of the program in enough detail to allow a future maintenance programmer to make changes easily, to fix errors, to add enhancements, and so forth. Despite many claims to the contrary, there is no popular programming language that can be seriously regarded as self-documenting. In general, the higher level the language is, the less detailed explanatory documentation is required. Program documentation is discussed in Section 10.5.

In the traditional system development life cycle, the Program Design and Development stage normally consumes the most time and resources. In Chapter 6, I estimated that 25 percent of the total project's resources and 30 percent of the time available will be spent in Program Design and Development. With the advent of software packages, this stage can become progressively shorter. Additionally, with the use of languages that are more user-friendly than today's commonly used languages, and with the use of application generators, this stage could disappear altogether sometime soon (see Chapters 16 and 17).

10.2 People involved

In the Program Design and Development stage, the project team is likely to be at its largest, with the majority of the members being programmers. Because of the team's size, various organizational structures to manage the team are likely to be used.* The users still are involved in this stage but obviously not in creating the programs; their role is as advisors, reviewers, and interpreters of user requirements when needed. The manager for this stage is the senior DP development manager, the same as for the last stage, since this is a technical stage as well.

Since the programmer is the most important worker in this stage, we must consider carefully, what is a programmer? A debate that has raged for decades is over the issue of whether programming is a science or an art. Many programmers like to consider themselves artists, as they feel that artists are more creative and less well organized than engineers or scientists. One only has to review the history of scientific invention to realize the fallacy of that argument. Leonardo da Vinci, for one, certainly did not restrict his immense creativity to his paintings, sketches, and sculptures; he presented many beautifully inventive solutions to technical problems of the day. Yet, within all da Vinci's creativity, he was well organized and his creations themselves possessed a high degree of order. Many other highly creative people are also extremely well organized — something the self-styled programmer-artist would do well to remember.

Because of the extremely rapid growth of the DP industry and because of the lack of good, formal DP education, the ranks of programmers are filled with people from many different original professions. They may have been accountants, economists,

*Possible structures are matrix management, egoless teams, and chief programmer teams, as described in Chapter 13.

teachers, mathematicians, engineers, commercial artists, truck drivers, or almost anything else. Of course, some have been trained from the start in computer science and have continued in the field. The net result of this mixture of origins is that imposing a disciplined, consistent style of working on such a variety of individuals is difficult. Additionally, there is the well-known phenomenon that the most productive programmer can be ten or more times more productive than the programmer with the lowest rate of output. This productivity difference seems to be connected to the individual programmer's particular mindset, which itself is often related to his previous experience and training. Conversely, simply because programmers originate from such a mixture of disciplines, a well-enforced set of standard programming procedures is all the more necessary.

But, back to the original question of what a programmer is; the answer, as I said earlier, is that he is a designer, coder, tester, and documenter. The program designer is the most important member of today's program development team; ideally, he is knowledgeable in program design methodologies, such as the structured design techniques discussed in Chapter 3, and is experienced in successfully building programs.

Coders are of course required in this stage, as the final product always is code. They are familiar with all of the programming languages being specified for the proposed system. These languages typically include a main language such as COBOL, FORTRAN, PL/I, or even BAL, and may include subsidiary languages for specific purposes for some input-output routines or teleprocessing protocol handling. Finally, there is always the ubiquitous system control language, usually IBM's JCL or a derivative of it. Increasingly, user-friendly, high-level languages are being used for specific types of applications; these include financial application languages, manufacturing control languages, and many, many others. To be a successful program coder today, therefore, requires a knowledge of many different languages and an ability to use more than just a few of them. Because of this rapid expansion of needed skills, the job of program coder is being merged with that of the program designer and, in some cases, with that of the *system* designer.

A large amount of testing is carried out in this stage, both by individual programmers and by a group separate from the programmers. This group could be a team of programmers whose individual programming assignments are completed, a team from another project, or a team of specifically assigned testers. Whoever these testers are, they must have a good understanding of the total system's objective in order to ensure that the system is being built correctly. For this reason, it is often advantageous to recruit members for the test group from the system design team assembled during the previous stage.

Sometimes in very large projects, separate assignments are made to "documenters" to explain the programs as they are written. This is not a recommended way of creating documentation, as something is inevitably lost in the translation between the programmer and the documenter. The best method is to have the programmers themselves document their own work.

Since a large amount of detailed documentation is produced in this stage, increasingly specialized staff members are being hired to keep the documentation accessible, consistent, and up-to-date in a manual or automated library. These persons are usually referred to as program librarians or project librarians. They often share with the project leader the control of access to the source code of programs that are in the integration testing process.

In every DP system, there are many levels of software and corresponding levels of responsibility (see Table 10-1). Many DP organizations were set up with a distinct separation between analysts and programmers: Analysts carried out the design work, and programmers did the grunt work of coding and implementation. Because the increased use of higher-level languages and increased automation of coding-related activities today has gradually started to eliminate much of the need for significant coding efforts, the tasks of analysts, designers, and programmers have become increasingly inseparable. Although this trend is healthy and inevitable, some negative reaction in the programmers' ranks has resulted. Every week some new method of programming seems to be marketed. Not only is the programmer's job changing rapidly and at a greater rate, but with the introduction of high-level languages, application generators, re-usable program libraries, and other productivity enhancers, the programmer's control over his own career path seems to be more and more tenuous.

Table 10-1
Levels of Software Responsibility

<table>
<tr><th>LEVELS OF SOFTWARE/OPERATIONS</th><th>RESPONSIBILITY</th></tr>
<tr><td>Nontechnical instructions</td><td>Operators, users</td></tr>
<tr><td>System control languages (JCL)</td><td>System analysts</td></tr>
<tr><td>High-level languages (PL/I, COBOL)</td><td>Users, system analysts</td></tr>
<tr><td>Assembly-level languages (BAL)</td><td>Programmers</td></tr>
<tr><td>Machine languages</td><td rowspan="2">System engineers</td></tr>
<tr><td>Logic boards, circuits</td></tr>
</table>

A typical situation for an Edgar Allan Poe hero or heroine is to be trapped in a room in which the walls, ceiling, and floor are all inexorably closing in; desperate measures are called for! The programmer often feels this way, with his responsibilities being squeezed out of existence by application generators and user-friendly languages at one end and customized firmware at the other end. The desperate measures he resorts to fit into two categories: first, making the job appear more difficult than it really is, and second, acquiring training in other related disciplines.

The first is only a short-term solution but one that the programmer can implement alone quite easily. A cryptic comment here, no comments elsewhere, and an unnecessarily complex use of a little-known program instruction can make an otherwise simple routine appear to be an esoteric, state-of-the-art use of a software engineering technique. Of course, some programmers have been doing this for years in order to make their craft appear much more difficult than it really is.

Or, secondly, the programmer can get additional training — a considerably more long-term and effective solution but one that cannot be implemented by the programmer alone. DP management must decide to provide training and education in system analysis, system design, business fundamentals, management principles, and other subjects for the programmers. In this way, the concept of DP professionalism can take on a new meaning in terms of the formal training acquired, in addition to the current, somewhat subjective qualifications based on educational degrees and experience.

10.3 Activities

In terms of activities, the Program Design and Development stage is almost certainly the busiest, since more detailed work is carried out here than in the other stages. This is probably why most programmers feel that this stage is when all of the real work is done. Because of the increased amount of activity, the first task is to produce a work plan based on the detailed set of system design diagrams (usually the structure charts) and the estimate of the Program Design and Development stage produced in the previous stage. This work plan must include assignments of personnel to design, code, document, unit test, and integration test every entity identified in the set of system design diagrams. If either the Jackson or Warnier-Orr program design methodology is used, an individual work plan can be developed for each program because of the extreme procedurality of these techniques.

There are many ways to represent this work plan, including precedence diagrams that show dependency relationships between tasks, balloon charts, and critical path charts.* One of the simplest and best methods is the Gantt or bar chart. Figure 10-1 demonstrates how this type of chart provides a clear overview of a sample work plan, because both planned and actual schedules are shown, along with special events such as team reviews and members' vacations. Most programmers, even with interactive development facilities, work on more than one program at time; this, too, can be shown on the bar chart. Any task dependencies can be highlighted by special notes, as in Figure 10-1.

In addition to the work plan, a method is needed for recording resource expenditure and the project's progress on at least a weekly basis. Expenditures and progress can be tracked by setting up a system that requires project team members to record their time spent on specific tasks on standardized forms or on time cards so that the hours or days worked can be accurately charged against the project budget. In this way, actual progress can be compared with planned progress at least every week. Such a detailed recording mechanism may have been used in previous stages, but it certainly is needed in the Program Design and Development stage because the volume of activities is so much greater and because the cost of these is normally charged to the users' organization. All three of these entities — the work plan and the time recording and the status reporting procedures — should be automated with on-line data entry facilities to ensure that the required information is obtained as painlessly as possible from all project team members. If reporting progress is difficult and time-consuming, team members probably will not record the needed information.

In some organizations, the System Design stage produces documentation that defines the programs in the system but does not provide the detailed logic and operational descriptions of each program. When examined closely, some of the so-called logic descriptions are not detailed enough to provide an unambiguous guide for the coders, and so the incomplete programs must be subjected to further design. The next task, then, is to ensure that every program identified in the detailed set of system design diagrams is designed down to the pseudocode, structured English, or schematic logic level.

---

*Because of their potential for complexity, all of these charts have a nasty habit of doubling as wall-coverings and sometimes as desk and floor coverings, too!

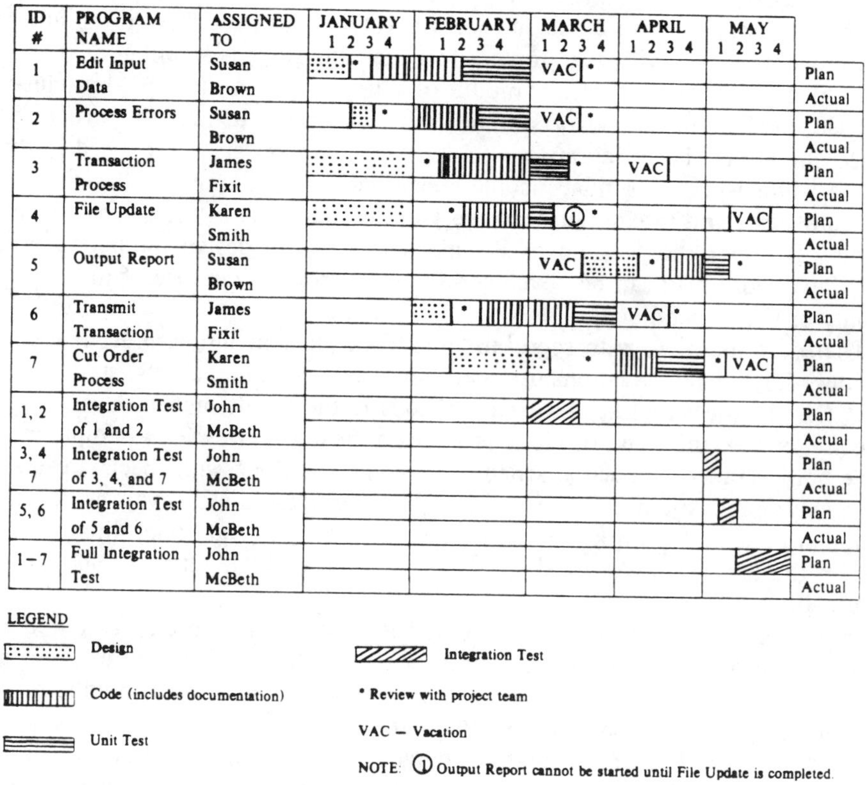
ID #
PROGRAM NAME
ASSIGNED TO
JANUARY 1 2 3 4
FEBRUARY 1 2 3 4
MARCH 1 2 3 4
APRIL 1 2 3 4
MAY 1 2 3 4
1 Edit Input Data Susan Brown
2 Process Errors Susan Brown
3 Transaction Process James Fixit
4 File Update Karen Smith
5 Output Report Susan Brown
6 Transmit Transaction James Fixit
7 Cut Order Process Karen Smith
1, 2 Integration Test of 1 and 2 John McBeth
3, 4, 7 Integration Test of 3, 4, and 7 John McBeth
5, 6 Integration Test of 5 and 6 John McBeth
1–7 Full Integration Test John McBeth
VAC
Plan
Actual
LEGEND
Design
Code (includes documentation)
Unit Test
Integration Test
• Review with project team
VAC – Vacation
NOTE: ① Output Report cannot be started until File Update is completed.

Figure 10-1. Sample program development schedule in the form of a Gantt chart.

At this point, each program is reviewed by the project team for accuracy, correctness, and adherence to programming standards. The recommended technique for program reviews is the walkthrough (see Chapter 14). This review process occurs throughout the stage because development activities for each program start at different times (see Figure 10-1).

Once each program's design has been reviewed and approved by the project team, it is coded. At this point, the infamous structured programming techniques can be applied, depending upon the practices followed within the organization or those followed by the individual programmer. At its best, structured programming is a set of rules to ensure standardization, efficiency, and clarity of the coding. Certain program design methodologies, such as Jackson and Warnier-Orr, almost force structured programming rules upon the coding process. What is needed, however, is a set of rules for consistently translating the basic structured programming constructs into the "local" language. This set of rules should follow naturally from the particular program design methodology being used.

Producing good, accurate program documentation should be considered a parallel task with coding, and the coding itself should include any JCL or similar control statements required to make the program run in the system environment. The next activity involves program testing, which includes two types of testing: *Unit testing* tests each program to ensure that it meets its own individual specification as represented by the diagrams and minispecs in the System Design document; and, second, *integration testing* is carried out to ensure that the system (all of the programs together) also behaves impeccably, according to its specification in the System Design document. After all this testing, the user should be able to have the fully coded system installed in a system test environment and run through the system test schedule with absolutely no problems.

When the coding for any one program is complete, or at least complete enough to represent an initial version of the program, the programmer begins the unit testing process. Unit testing simply pits the program against its own specifications to ensure completeness and accuracy. Inevitably, unit testing is iterative, as errors and omissions are found in the original code and the code is corrected and tested again. At the successful conclusion of unit testing, the complete program, with its design documents, source code, program documentation, and unit test results are reviewed for completeness and accuracy by the project team. Next, the program is entered into a library, preferably an automated one, whose access is controlled by the project librarian and by the project leader, as stated earlier. The programs in the library are used to build the simulated system during integration testing.

The integration testing of the emerging system is usually carried out by a separate test group of programmers, who test and build the system, piece by piece, as each program is successfully unit tested. The system's structure has a great deal of influence upon the sequence of integration testing and on the timing of individual program development activities. If the top-down development approach is being used, the objective is to gradually build the complete system from top to bottom, testing each level as represented in the hierarchical structure chart produced in the last stage.

Consider the simple hierarchical system structure shown in Figure 10-2. Assume that as each program represented by a box in the diagram is coded and unit tested, this system is integration tested in a top-down manner. In the strictest sense, this means that modules A through M are developed, unit tested, and entered into the growing system structure in that strict alphabetical order. But, typically, one "leg" of the structure needs to be developed first, because the user needs it to form a first version to be demonstrated to the user organization.

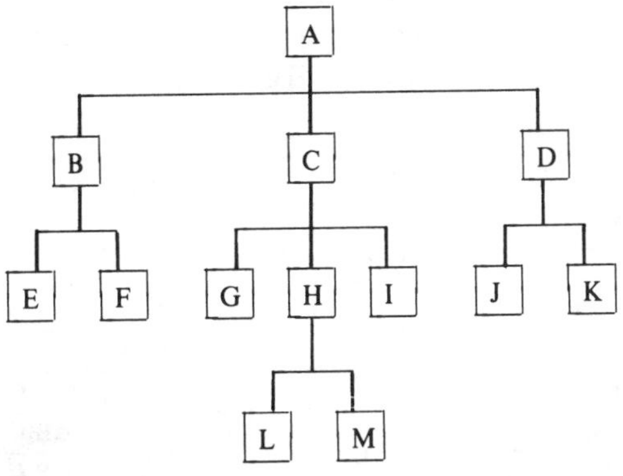

Figure 10-2. System structure example.

In this case, let's say that leg A-D-J-K must be coded and tested first. The sequence of development and test activities shown in Table 10-2 depicts the probable resulting schedule of events. Modules A, B, C, and D are developed and tested first, in that order. As soon as two modules have been successfully unit tested, integration testing can start (modules A and B, in this case). As the development builds up, the amount of integration test activity increases rapidly so that at any one time, there are a number of different activities occurring.

Table 10-2
Top-Down Development Sequence

DEVELOPMENT SEQUENCE NUMBER	PROGRAMS DEVELOPED	TEST SEQUENCE NUMBER	PROGRAMS UNIT TESTED	PROGRAMS INTEGRATION TESTED
1	A	–	–	–
2	B	1	A	–
3	C	2	B	–
4	D	3	C	A,B
5	J	4	D	A,B,C
6	K	5	J	A,B,C,D
7	E	6	K	A,B,C,D,J
8	F	7	E	A,B,C,D,J,K
9	G	8	F	A,B,C,D,J,K,E
10	H	9	G	A,B,C,D,J,K,E,F
11	I	10	H	A,B,C,D,J,K,E,F,G
12	L	11	I	A,B,C,D,J,K,E,F,G,H
13	M	12	L	A,B,C,D,J,K,E,F,G,H,I
–	–	13	M	A,B,C,D,J,K,E,F,G,H,I,L
–	–	14	–	A,B,C,D,J,K,E,F,G,H,I,L,M (full integration test)

In practice, these activities occur in parallel rather than in sequence, because the available resources allow several programmers and testers to work simultaneously. The development sequence could then be optimized, as shown in Table 10-3.

Table 10-3
Optimized Top-Down Development Sequence

DEVELOPMENT SEQUENCE NUMBER	PROGRAMS DEVELOPED	TEST SEQUENCE NUMBER	PROGRAMS UNIT TESTED	PROGRAMS INTEGRATION TESTED
1	A,B,C,D	–	–	–
2	J,K	1	A,B,C,D	–
3	E,F	2	J,K	A,B,C,D
4	G,H,I	3	E,F	A,B,C,D,J,K
5	L,M	4	G,H,I	A,B,C,D,J,K,E,F
–	–	5	L,M	A,B,C,D,J,K,E,F,G,H,I
–	–	6	–	A,B,C,D,J,K,E,F,G,H,I,L,M

The above description implies that the system structure being used to "drive" the integration testing activities includes the complete system: programs, system control statements (JCL), operating instructions, manual procedures, and every entity required to run the new system in full. Therefore, the test that occurs at the end of the integration test sequence is actually a test of what is the closest thing to the real system as possible, with users and operators given the opportunity to play their roles in this final integration test of the system.

Any required program changes identified during integration testing as a result of approved changes to the original system's requirements are fed back to the original programmer, or whoever is responsible for the program, with a complete copy of all relevant documentation. The programmer makes the necessary changes, carries out the unit testing for the program, and when the tests are completed satisfactorily, returns the updated program plus updated documentation to the librarian, who reenters it into the library for the next pass of the integration test. Of course, this library could be none other than an extended version of our old friend, the system data dictionary, expanded to include not only the names and descriptions of the components of the system, but the components themselves.

When the integration testing is completed and all involved are satisfied with the results, the tests are fully documented to describe the test results. The objective of this test documentation is to demonstrate that the system does meet its specifications. These test results are then reviewed for completeness by the project team, particularly the user members of the team.

In parallel with the testing, the project librarian updates the system and corporate data dictionaries with any new identified data and process entities that are introduced as a result of the testing activities. This is to ensure that all parts of the library are recorded in the system data dictionary and can be referenced from the corporate data dictionary.

While the development and testing activities are being performed, the project team develops a first draft of the training manuals and the guides for the users and for the system's operators. If the top-down techniques are being used, the user guides can be tested for accuracy by actually being used to run the system during some of the later, more comprehensive integration tests.

Since the users will be heavily involved in the remaining development activities, they develop a detailed estimate of the next stage, System Test, based on the system test plan. They should also refine the estimate for the remainder of the project, including the implementation schedule and conversion plan, in particular. The implementation schedule contains a list of specific activities for successfully installing the new system, including dates and responsibilities for each activity and the approved fallback procedure in case the new system fails for whatever reason. The conversion plan contains similar information for all of the data conversion activities, which ensure that all production input and reference data are compatible with the new system. (The implementation and conversion activities are described in Chapter 12.)

Finally, the various pieces of the documentation are finalized and assembled to be reviewed and approved by the project team. The last activity in the stage is the end-stage review, described in Section 10.6. Figure 10-3 summarizes all of the required tasks for this stage.

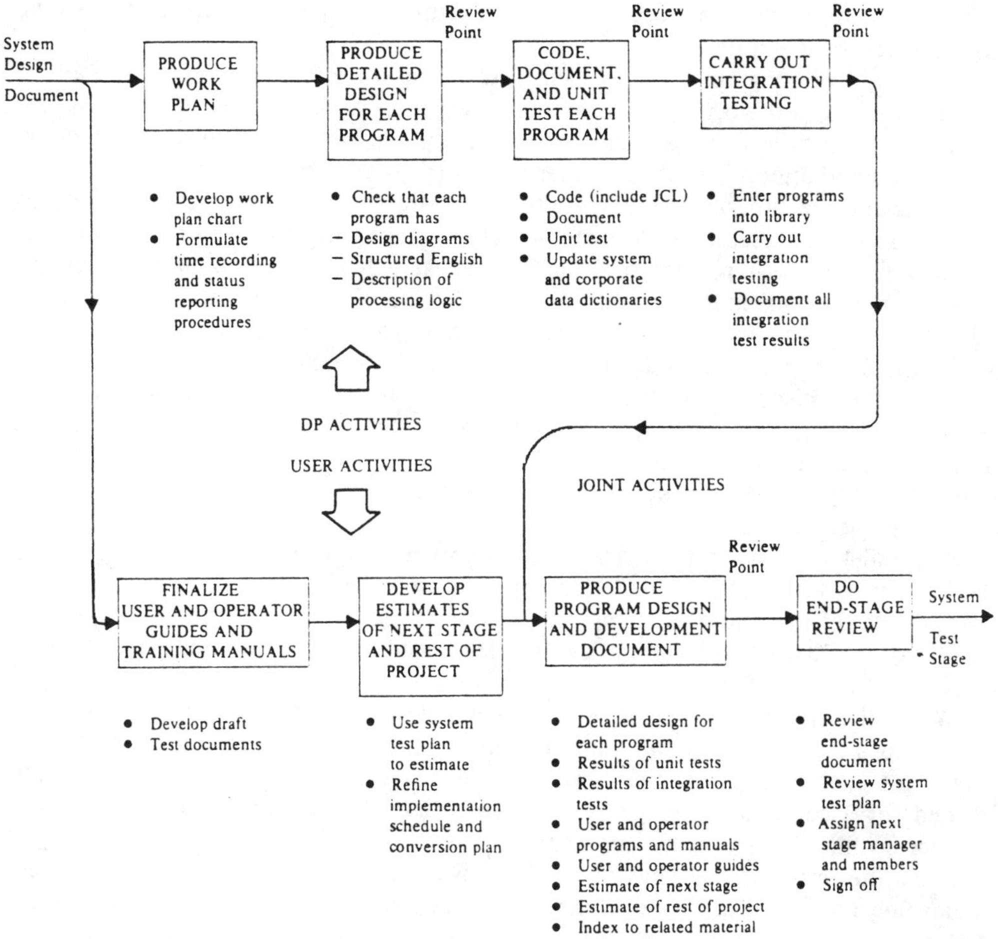

Figure 10-3. Program Design and Development stage activities.

10.4 Tools and techniques

Most of the techniques and methodologies used in this stage are discussed in detail in Chapters 3 and 4. Nevertheless, good things bear repeating, so a summary of the various aids for programmers is provided here. But rather than simply repeating them, I have also provided my humble opinions of the methods and my assessment of their advantages and disadvantages.

Since *top-down development* has been described fairly extensively earlier in this chapter, I need only say that it is a generic development procedure by which a complex problem is broken into its major functions, each of which is decomposed into simpler, solvable problems. Any or all of the specific design and programming techniques fit quite comfortably within it. With minimal modifications, I believe the top-down development philosophy can be used in all system development situations with very effective results. It is difficult to find a disadvantage of a technique so universal as top-down development other than its informality, but one specific disadvantage is that if an error is made in the top-level structure, that error stands a good chance of being propagated down through all the lower levels of the system structure.

Functional decomposition is the most generally accepted design technique because, as a form of top-down development, it offers guidelines for correct decomposition of systems not offered by the general top-down method. It uses structure charts and program narratives, often in the form of structured English. A major advantage of functional decomposition is that it reflects the "natural" way that designers view systems — as a series or group of functions. There are many textbooks that describe this technique, but I believe that the best one now is *Structured Systems Analysis: Tools & Techniques,* by Gane and Sarson [17]. Unfortunately, this methodology is more suited to system analysis and system design than to program design, and I feel that at the program level it leaves much to the individual programmer's intuition. The technique has also been used extensively for requirements definition and system analysis; DeMarco's *Structured Analysis and System Specification* [11] is an excellent description of this use of functional decomposition.

One of the good things from Great Britain, the *Jackson design methodology,* often referred to as JDM or SSP, is extremely effective at the program design level. Many large organizations in Europe have adopted it as a program design standard, but it has not yet attained an equal level of popularity in the United States, probably due to a mixture of chauvinism by American DP professionals and a lack of marketing push from Jackson's organization. A major advantage of JDM is its procedurality; the programmer must follow five steps every time a program is designed. This procedurality generates consistent program structures and tends to eliminate logic errors at an early stage of development. In a perverse way, this very procedurality is also one of JDM's disadvantages. As mentioned before, programmers tend to be a mixed bunch and they often react unfavorably to the imposition of procedures and disciplines, even if these things will assist them to perform more productively. Therefore, a methodology such as JDM needs strong and continuous management commitment, a constant training program, and an automated documentation update and retrieval facility in order to succeed. This last documentation-related success factor is required because JDM, like many other effective structured methodologies, does produce a significant amount of documentation. The Jackson methodology is one of the most effective program design methods available today and it deserves at least a trial in most large DP organizations.

The *Warnier-Orr design methodology* is based upon the same premise as JDM: The program structure can be derived directly from the structure of the data that the program will process. Warnier-Orr has a similar set of procedural steps as in JDM, but the diagrammatic notation is different. Whereas JDM uses hierarchical structure diagrams to represent data and programs, Warnier-Orr uses bracket diagrams (see Figure 3-16). Warnier-Orr is less procedural and less rigorous than JDM, but its bracket notation, which is less intimidating than the Jackson notation, is sometimes more acceptable to the user community; this type of notation is also easier to update.

Many of the same arguments that support the use of JDM also support the use of Warnier-Orr. A decision between the two is often based on personal preference and availability of support and training facilities. Both Warnier-Orr and JDM proponents claim that systems, in addition to programs, can be designed using these techniques.

This has not been proved yet, although Orr himself has written a book on system design using the Warnier-Orr technique entitled *Structured Systems Development* [29]. Jackson's new book *Systems Development* [20] expands the basic JDM to include the development of system specifications. It seems that if the data requirements of the system at least on the output side are well known, both the JDM and the Warnier-Orr techniques can be used to design the total system, including the individual programs (see Chapter 3).

Nassi-Shneiderman diagrams are not a design method, but they are an improvement over the traditional flowchart [28]. The Nassi-Shneiderman diagram is often referred to as a "structured flowchart" because it allows only the three structured constructs – sequence, selection, and iteration. There is no method to represent a GOTO in this diagram. (Of course, none of the other structured techniques has a satisfactory way of representing GOTOs, either.) Figure 10-4 shows how a Nassi-Shneiderman diagram represents a simple program.

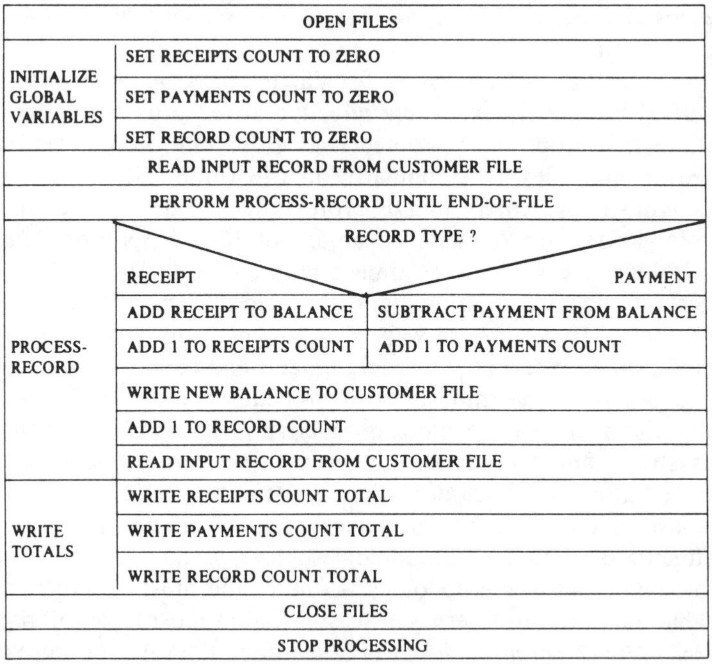
OPEN FILES
INITIALIZE GLOBAL VARIABLES
SET RECEIPTS COUNT TO ZERO
SET PAYMENTS COUNT TO ZERO
SET RECORD COUNT TO ZERO
READ INPUT RECORD FROM CUSTOMER FILE
PERFORM PROCESS-RECORD UNTIL END-OF-FILE
PROCESS-RECORD
RECORD TYPE ?
RECEIPT
PAYMENT
ADD RECEIPT TO BALANCE
SUBTRACT PAYMENT FROM BALANCE
ADD 1 TO RECEIPTS COUNT
ADD 1 TO PAYMENTS COUNT
WRITE NEW BALANCE TO CUSTOMER FILE
ADD 1 TO RECORD COUNT
READ INPUT RECORD FROM CUSTOMER FILE
WRITE TOTALS
WRITE RECEIPTS COUNT TOTAL
WRITE PAYMENTS COUNT TOTAL
WRITE RECORD COUNT TOTAL
CLOSE FILES
STOP PROCESSING

Figure 10-4. A Nassi-Shneiderman diagram.

In the diagram, blocks of processing are represented by rectangles. A vertical rectangle on the left side of the diagram denotes a logically grouped set of processing actions. Often, this part of the diagram represents logic that is iterative, as in Figure 10-4 with PROCESS-RECORD. Here, all of PROCESS-RECORD is iterated until the END-OF-FILE condition is reached, as denoted by the rectangle directly above PROCESS-RECORD which says PERFORM PROCESS-RECORD UNTIL END-OF-FILE. Conditional statements are represented by inverted triangles, as in the RECORD TYPE? selection. The alternate processing paths are separated by vertical lines.

Nassi-Shneiderman diagrams are a useful notational technique, especially in depicting the detailed logic of a program. As such, they are an alternative to detailed Warnier-Orr or Jackson diagrams at that level. Like Warnier-Orr diagrams, they are relatively easy to modify.

When many DP professionals refer to structured programming, *structured coding* is often what is really meant. It is simply a discipline of using a restricted set of statements of a particular programming language. Only the three basic structured constructs are generally allowed, and GOTOs are severely restricted. Each functional block of code must have only one entry point and, if possible, one exit. All coding must be explained by embedded comments, and there are usually some local rules about formatting the code in a consistent manner for each program.

Although it is not a design technique, I definitely recommend use of structured coding as it makes programs much easier to understand and consequently much easier to maintain and update. (Structured coding is explained in more detail in Chapter 4.)

The intent of *program documentation* is, of course, to render the program more easily understood, updated, changed, and maintained — a laudable intent indeed. Some program design techniques ask the programmer to produce pseudocode or structured English versions of the program prior to coding. A useful procedure is to enter a copy of this pseudocode as a sort of super-comment at the beginning of the source library listing of the program.

Even though many user-friendly and high-level programming languages are now available, most big DP systems installed in the United States were written in COBOL and many new systems continue to be written in COBOL. Despite its original claim of being self-documenting, COBOL needs a great deal of explaining to be understood by nontechnical people, and some additional clarification even to those trained in the language. Therefore, some program documentation in the form of comments embedded in the code is required. With a language such as COBOL, it is superfluous to write one comment for each line of code, but a paragraph of explanatory comments for each ten- to fifteen-line block of code is in order. A complete set should be maintained as program documentation.

Software in the form of *test pathing packages* is available to monitor the operation of a program and to produce a report with information on which logic paths in the program have been exercised and which have not. These packages are very useful in determining if the test data is adequate and if there are any unnecessary or nonworking patches of code in the program.

A good *data comparison program* or facility is almost a must when changes to a program or system are being made, because it produces a listing of the data before and after the change and identifies all differences. Using such a program enormously reduces the amount of manual data checking required and helps to ensure the completeness of the testing of changes.

With the realization that a great deal of programming can be proceduralized, entrepreneurs have developed software systems or *application generators* that automate the application programming process. The most effective systems provide an interactive screen-based menu selection type of facility for building application code. I believe that along with pre-packaged software, application generators are the wave of the future. (This subject is discussed in Chapters 16 and 17.) Suffice it to say at this point that I definitely recommend an investigation into application generators as a means to increase programmer productivity.

Similar to application generators, *report writers* can be effectively utilized to improve productivity, but they are usually less sophisticated and limited to producing highly formatted reports from information in an existing database. Almost every database management system has an associated report writer package with its own user-friendly language.

There are many other tools and techniques available to programmers. I assume the common availability of interactive, video-terminal-based program editing and operating facilities as a must. The preceding list of tools and techniques is not comprehensive, but is intended to give the DP professional an idea of what is available to enable him to be more productive.

10.5 Documentation

If one of the recommended design techniques described above is used, a significant amount of design documentation is produced. A finalized set of this design documentation should be maintained in addition to the program documentation.

As the iterative process of unit, integration, and system testing begins in this stage, the programs need to be changed to fix errors, make enhancements, resolve ambiguities, and so forth. These changes to the programs subsequently require changes to the set of design diagrams and to the program documentation. In the good old days when there was no documentation and no design diagrams (except disposable flowcharts), there was nothing to change. Now, with these modern, newfangled methodologies, there is much to update in addition to the code. Four possible ways to handle the problem of maintaining documentation are these:

- Insist that the documentation be done as part of the program updating procedure. This is unpopular if many updates become necessary; also it requires very strong and competent project management.
- Leave the documentation as it is and allow it to become out of date and irrelevant until the next major release of the system. This is often the course taken and it works only if most of the enhancements and changes are synchronized with the major system releases.
- Throw out the methodology because the programmers complain about the need to keep the documentation up-to-date. (Of course, no rational organization would take this step.)
- Automate the documentation process using word processing and graphics systems integrated with on-line, interactive program development facilities. This is clearly the optimum solution.

Although these suggestions apply mostly to the program documentation produced during the Program Design and Development stage, the principles apply equally to all system documentation. Most of the documentation contents have been discussed earlier and Figure 10-5 summarizes these pieces of documentation.

The only piece of documentation that has not been discussed earlier is the index to related material, which contains references to any proprietary and internally developed design methodologies and techniques used during this stage. The working papers section includes the usual index to all of the documentary information produced during this stage but not included in the end-stage document.

Contents List

- □ Detailed design
  - design diagrams
  - logic descriptions or explanations
  - program documentation — narrative
  - input-output data descriptions
  - program source listings, including embedded comments
  - JCL listings
  - operator guide
  - user guide
  - results of unit tests
- □ Results of integration tests
- □ User training program and manuals
- □ Operator training program and manuals
- □ System user guide (for complete system)
- □ System operator guide (for complete system)
- □ Estimates of next stage and of remainder of project, including the implementation and conversion plans
- □ Index to related material
  - references to techniques, tools, and methodologies used
  - working papers

Figure 10-5. Program Design and Development document — contents list.

10.6 End-stage activities

The major purpose of the final activities in the Program Design and Development stage is to ensure that the system is complete and ready for system testing and to reassure the users of that fact. Therefore, as the final task, the system is proved to be fully written and documented to the end users' complete satisfaction. Additionally, that special user, DP operations, must be equally satisfied that the system is viable and operable from its point of view.

The Program Design and Development document is reviewed by the Project Review Board for completeness. However, the users represented on the Project Review Board and on the project team are specifically interested in the integration test results to ensure that, as far as possible at this point, the system meets all of its design specifications and it will perform as specified (within user-defined allowable tolerances). All questions directed at the developers during this review are based on a comparison with the System Specification and System Design documents.

The training manuals and the operating guides for users and system operators are reviewed in detail by both groups to ensure that they believe not only that the system works, but also that they will be able to use and operate it successfully.

The system test plan, having been developed and refined by the system users during the last two or three life cycle stages, should consequently be completely acceptable to them. Nevertheless, the plan is reviewed in detail once more at this point, since it will be implemented in the next stage. In addition, the detailed system description from the System Design document is reviewed once more to ensure that no final changes need to be made to it.

Special attention is paid to the estimate of the System Test stage to ensure its complete conformity with the system test plan. Also, the estimate of the remainder of the project is examined in detail, and the users must be in total agreement with the implementation and conversion plans.

During the review, the manager for the System Test stage is assigned. Normally, this manager is a senior user, since the final sign-off at the end of the next stage is effectively an acceptance of the complete system by the user. The team members for the System Test stage also are assigned. Usually, an equal number of DP development and user staff members are involved in the System Test stage activities with the users actually controlling the system test. DP development personnel are available for technical assistance in making changes and correcting errors. As many DP operators participate as are expected to be involved when the system is in production.

This particular end-stage review is often a harrowing experience for both users and technical members. The DP organization wants the users to be convinced that they are indeed getting a good system. Because of this, the review often consumes a considerable amount of time and proceeds through a number of iterations. Therefore, as usual, the review should be scheduled in plenty of time before the planned end of the stage — at least two weeks in advance of that date.

When the review is completed and all parties are satisfied with the system so far, the usual approval letter is issued by the Project Review Board and contains the signatures of at least the following as an indication of their approval: each member of the Project Review Board, the stage manager of Program Design and Development, the stage manager of System Design (if different from above), the stage manager of System Test, the project manager, the DP development manager, the DP operations manager, and the DP standards manager (quality assurance).

10.7 Summary

Completion of this stage is always a great relief to the DP development organization. However erroneous the feeling, the major effort on the system development required from DP is over for all intents and purposes. *If* all of the previous stages have been carried out to perfection and *if* all requirements of the system have been fully met, there will be little work left for DP — at least until well after implementation, when the first of the users' requests for enhancements start rolling in.

However, perfection is not often attained, certainly not in the system users' eyes and, after all, they *are* the judges. Therefore, relieved or not, the DP organization must prepare for yet more battles to win and fires to extinguish during the System Test stage.

11

System Test Stage

A great part of courage is the courage of having done the thing before.

— Ralph Waldo Emerson

The System Test stage is a transitional one in that it represents the time when the newly developed system passes from the control of the DP organization to that of the end users. As such, it is an extremely critical stage, because it is the last chance for the users to check the system before they start to live with it.

If all of the tasks in the previous stages have been carried out successfully and to the satisfaction of all concerned, the system will already have been tested thoroughly. In addition, the system test plan will have been desk-checked several times by users and DP staff. Therefore, the users should be confident that the system is perfectly acceptable. As the above quotation from Emerson suggests, the level of their courage during this stage will indeed be augmented by virtually "having done the thing before."

11.1 Objectives

The major objective of the System Test stage is to prove the system meets every user specification. All of the original system requirements, as contained in the Requirements Definition document, are tested and proved to the users' satisfaction to have been achieved, and by the end of the stage, the users must be perfectly confident that the system will operate satisfactorily in production. In this context, the system consists of the following:

- programs (source and load modules)
- program documentation (source comments and narrative)
- control code (JCL)
- system documentation (diagrams plus narrative)

- manual procedures
- user guide } including troubleshooting procedures
- operator guide } including troubleshooting procedures
- operator training manual
- user training manual

The full system test is not simply a repetition of the final integration test. Specifically, this test fulfills five needs:

- *Testing the system's objectives and requirements:* As approved in the last stage, the system test plan ensures the obvious purpose of system testing: to test all of the system's requirements, including specifically the usability of the system (see documentation testing below); security and audit requirements; performance requirements; reliability, which can be measured by the mean time between failures (MTBF), although this test may only be practical as part of volume testing; error recovery requirements; and manual procedures.
- *Volume testing:* The system is designed to handle certain maximum volumes of data in terms of file size, number of transactions, and so forth. Included in the system test is a series of tests that provides greater (by 10 to 20 percent) than the absolute maximum volumes of data that the system must handle in real life. The system, of course, must be able to process satisfactorily these over-maximum volumes. The volume test inevitably lasts a considerable amount of time, and, for this reason, it can also be used sometimes to measure the MTBF of the system. If one or more system failures occurs during the test, the data can be used to estimate the likely MTBF when the system is in production. This measurement can then be compared with the allowable MTBF specified earlier.
- *Stress testing:* Stress testing has objectives similar to those of volume testing. During stress testing, the system is forced to operate at its absolute maximum processing rate. If the system in production must process at a maximum rate of 25,000 on-line transactions per hour, for example, a suitable stress test is to test the system at a rate of 35,000 transactions per hour or typically forty to fifty percent above maximum. If the system operates at greater than 25,000 transactions per hour, the stress test is a success. This type of testing is particularly important for on-line, real-time, transaction-driven systems.

  To illustrate the difference between a volume test and a stress test, let's look at an analogy: A volume test of an automobile would be to drive it, fully loaded with passengers and luggage, at a steady speed of 55 mph for 8 hours each day for 2 weeks. A stress test of the same automobile would be to drive it for one hour at 100 mph over a rough, dirt road. With automobiles as with DP systems, it is unreasonable to expect the user (purchaser) to be the first to find out that the product does not meet the specified requirements.

- *Configuration testing:* In developing systems to be installed in today's distributed processing environments, the designer often must design the system so that it can operate in several, or even many, different hardware and software situations. And so, the system's behavior is tested by running it in simulations or facsimiles of each environment. Setting up these simulations or facsimiles can range from simply utilizing a vendor's simulation software package to laboriously building a carbon copy of the production environment.
- *Documentation testing:* The user guide and operator guide are both used at the same time to "run" the system test to ensure not only that the tests are carried out in a controlled manner, but also that by the end of the system testing, the guides themselves have been tested for completeness and accuracy.

These five needs are expressed in terms of specific goals to be achieved in the system test plan.

11.2 People involved

Since full responsibility for system testing belongs to the users of the system, a team of users is appointed to carry out the system test plan, using the plan itself as a schedule of events and the draft user guide as a procedures manual. A team of operators from the DP operations staff, who are directed by the user team, use the draft operator guide as a procedures manual.

The users and the DP development staff work closely together in this stage. Specifically, those DP professionals involved with the integration testing of the system are available, as are the DP members from the System Design and Program Design and Development teams, to assist in the testing, to interpret test results, and to answer questions.

The manager of this stage is normally a user, but the DP development manager also participates, regarding the system test as a personal responsibility. After all, if the test is a failure, guess who gets the system to fix it? Obviously, the DP department must bear the brunt of the responsibility.

11.3 Activities

The System Test activities consist of three major phases: The first phase consists of a full system test carried out by the development team. The same test is repeated twice by the users, who control the test, and by the DP operators, who run the system. So, in the second phase, the users carry out an acceptance test, still in a test environment; in the third phase, they perform an installation test to ensure the viability of the system in the production environment.

Many new systems require the installation of new or additional hardware and software. Even if new mainframes are not required and the system can reside comfortably within the available processing and storage capacity, new terminals and telecommunications equipment may be required so that users can communicate with the system. Installation of the new hardware and software could be carried out during this stage. In fact, if the hardware and software are significantly different from that in the existing environment, they should be installed before the system test begins so that it is carried out in a realistic environment.

Normally, the major hardware vendors are responsible for installing their own hardware and associated software, *if* that software is also produced by the manufacturer. Software vendors also install their own software unless the purchased software needs no special technique or skill to install (currently an uncommon situation but one that is likely to change in the future). The trusty DP professionals on the project team are intimately concerned with the hardware and software installation. To completely understand the new environment, they work with the manufacturer's installers and watch the installation procedures. At this time, the DP personnel also implement the system generations and the production JCL for the new system.

As specified in the system test plan, the actual test output data are compared closely with the expected system test output. Any variations are closely investigated by the system test team and, if necessary, changes are made to the system and the relative part or parts of the system are tested again. This process is repeated until there are no discrepancies between the actual system test output and the expected output, *or* any remaining discrepancies are understood and approved by the users and by all others involved in the system test activities. All test results, including all iterations and the reasons for them, are fully documented.

Following this first system test by the DP staff, the users take control and run the same test with DP operators assuming their eventual roles. This second acceptance test is normally performed in a test environment. Finally, for the third test, a subset of the acceptance test is performed in the production environment.

The drafts of the user guide and the operator guide are used to actually run the system test. Any resulting changes required to these guides are documented, the changes made, and the relevant part or parts of the system test are repeated to ensure that the documentation changes are effective.

The drafts of the training manuals for both the users and the operators are checked out during the system testing at the same time as the user and operator guides. Again, all changes are fully documented. While the training manuals are being tested, both users and operators should be trained before system installation so that they can operate the system fully and continuously from day one of its production.

At the end of the system test, all of the documented testing results are reviewed in detail by the System Test team and approved as being complete and accurate. Then, the implementation schedule developed in the previous stage is reviewed and approved by the users and DP operations management responsible for the system. As part of this review, the users define the fallback procedure if the system should fail after implementation. That generally involves saving the latest possible version of the old system, with all of its data and documentation, so that processing can be restarted if a failure occurs during the early days of the new system's life. Figure 11-1 summarizes the major activities of the System Test stage.

Normally, a DP system operates in a repetitive, cyclical manner. If an early failure occurs, however, too few complete cycles may have been processed to produce enough back-up data to effectively back out the system and to restart it from a known safe point in the processing sequence. Also, the system's recovery procedures may be regarded with some skepticism by the users. From their point of view, *any* part of a system that has just failed is not to be trusted. Therefore, it is advisable, if not essential, to develop an initial fallback procedure that does not rely on the new system if it fails. This procedure usually depends upon some form of parallel running of the old and new systems for a predefined period of time. Then, if the new system fails, all of those involved — DP development staff, users, and DP operators — can revert to the old system until the new system is fixed. If parallel running cannot be implemented, the fallback procedures must include a regular reconversion of the system's inputs and outputs to the old format so that an old safe point can be reverted to if necessary. The period of time for these fallback procedures to be in operation is determined by the users, DP operators, and the Project Review Board at the end-stage review in the previous stage.

In environments where the system test is carried out on an *exact* duplicate of the production environment, a test of the fallback procedures is included in the test. Fallback procedures are like insurance: One hopes that they will never be used, but if the need arises, all concerned will be highly pleased that the procedures exist.

Also at this point, the project team ensures that the maintenance and release procedures for the new system are developed so that implementing enhancements, corrections, and new versions of the system in the production environment can be done efficiently and safely (such procedures are discussed more fully in Chapter 12). The project library concept, as discussed in Chapter 15, is an invaluable aid in developing these procedures.

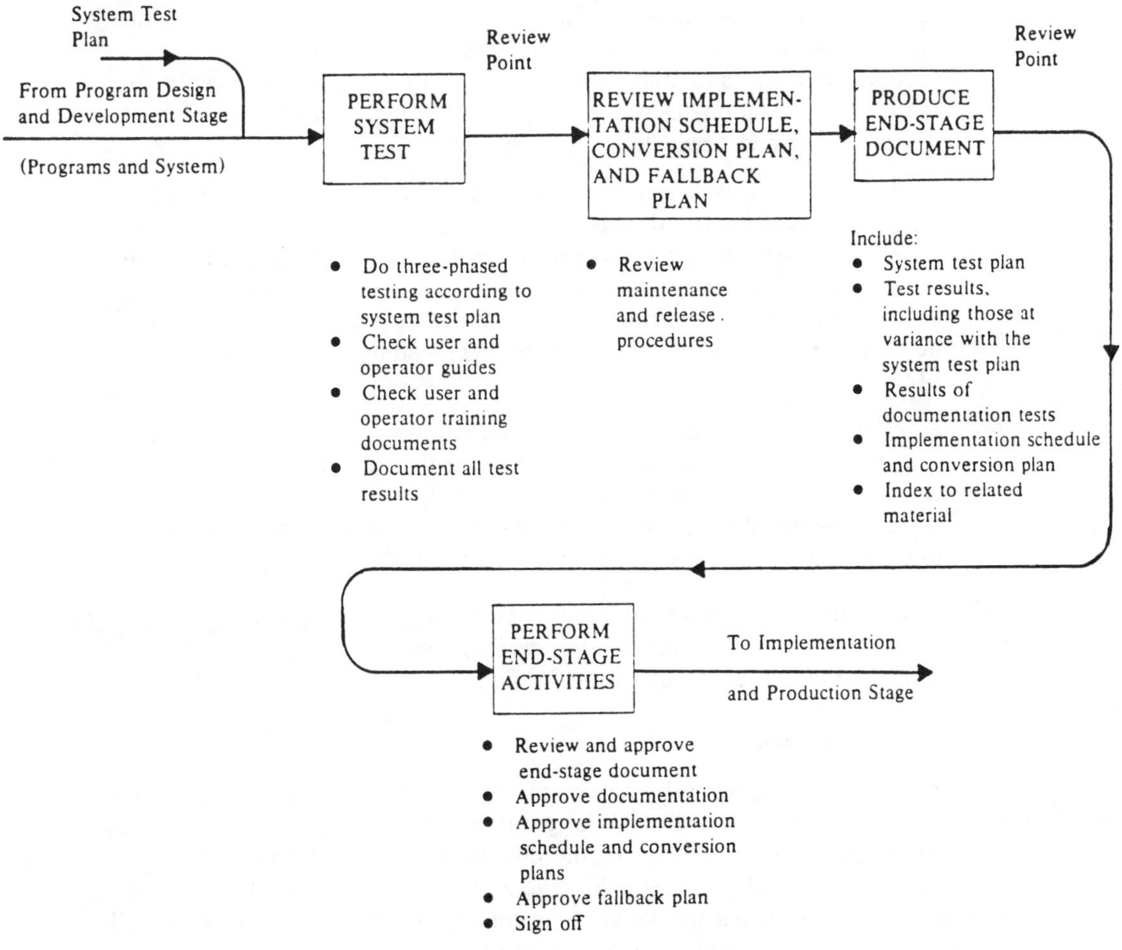

Figure 11-1. System Test stage activities.

11.4 Documentation

The System Test document contains enough information to convince the Project Review Board that the system has been fully tested and is ready to go into full production. The document consists of the following six sections:

- *System test plan:* The plan, which is developed during the System Design stage, is included here.
- *Test results:* The complete, documented, and verified system test results are listed, along with a full description of any changes made to the system as a result of the System Test activities.
- *Results at variance with the system test plan:* Some items in the system test plan may remain untested or may produce test results that vary from the originally expected results. If the user accepts these variances from the system test plan, a full explanation of the reasons for this acceptance and for the variances themselves are included here.
- *Results of documentation tests:* The documentation to be tested in simulated production mode includes the user guide, operator guide, user training manual, and operator training manual. The full results of these documentation tests, with any changes made as a result of testing, are contained here.
- *Implementation schedule and conversion plan:* The implementation schedule lists dates for the specific activities needed to install the new system successfully; the conversion plan includes any data conversion tasks that are necessary, usually the conversion of any existing files or databases to the new format and the conversion of input data to the new input requirements. The fallback procedure also is spelled out here.
- *Index to related material:* Such documentation produced in the System Test stage as status reports and time recording documents are not included in the end-stage document. An index to all these documents must be included here, as well as a list of references to all techniques, tools, and software packages used during the system test.

When the System Test document is completed with all of the above sections, it is reviewed for accuracy and completeness and approved by the project team. A final detailed review of the system test results is performed at the end of this stage.

11.5 Tools and techniques

At this time, there appear to be no automated test case generators that can receive as input a system specification in human language and that can produce as output a set of data designed specifically to test all of the details of the specification. If such a tool existed, its marketers would have made several fortunes and the development and operation of system test plans would be considerably more simple than it actually is. But although this marvelous tool does not yet exist, some test *data* generators are available. When supplied with the detailed program-level logical design of a system, these tools can generate the minimum set of test data that, when applied as input to the system, will ensure that every discrete logical path and condition is tested. Use of this type of tool will *not* ensure, of course, that all required specifications and requirements are tested. Also, these generators cannot be usefully employed until the programs have all been designed in detail. This is often late in the life cycle to start generating test data.

One of the more promising techniques being developed is that of cause-effect graphing. This sophisticated and precise technique effectively transforms an English language set of system requirements into a set of Boolean algebraic equations, which can be expressed as logic diagrams using simple AND, OR, and NOT logic operators. From these diagrams, an extremely specific, yet fully comprehensive set of test cases and subsequent test data can be derived. Cause-effect graphing has great potential for being automated. When it is, a significant manual effort will be eliminated. (This technique and many others related to testing are described fully in Myers' excellent book *The Art of Software Testing* [27].)

In Chapter 10, I mentioned test pathing packages and data comparison packages as being useful in program design and development. These software tools are also extremely useful, of course, during the System Test stage.

11.6 End-stage activities

The end-stage activities in the System Test stage have one major purpose: to ensure to the users' complete satisfaction that the system has been so thoroughly checked that absolutely nothing will go wrong when the system is installed in the actual production environment. To this end, the users as well as everyone else associated with or affected by the new system carefully review the end-stage document. The reviewers include the Project Review Board, the project team, the DP development organization, DP audit, DP operations, and DP standards (quality assurance). In particular, they compare the test results with the original Requirements Definition and System Specification documents. All variations and discrepancies are fully explained and each explanation accepted by representatives of the affected users. The users and the DP operators must be fully satisfied with their respective guides and training documents and be sure that these documents have received a thorough testing.

The implementation schedule and conversion plan are approved in detail by the relevant members of the user organization, and the fallback plan made satisfactory to them, to DP operations, and to DP audit.

As this stage is so critical, the end-stage review almost certainly requires a number of iterations before all those involved are satisfied that the system is ready for actual operation. More than the usual caution in scheduling the review is taken to ensure that an extension of the review does not cause a delay past the planned end of the System Test stage, for a delay would result in an unexpected slipped implementation schedule, a politically disastrous result.

As in all stages, if the review is not successful, some or all of the stage activities are repeated to produce a product that meets the approval of the reviewers. Then, the end-stage review needs to be rescheduled and, inevitably, the implementation of the new system will be delayed. This delayed installation, however politically unpopular, is always preferable to the forced installation of an unsatisfactory product.

If all of the above are fully satisfactory and the final implementation date is agreed upon, this stage can be completed by the usual letter of approval from the Project Review Board. As in previous stages, this letter has multiple signatories, including at least the following: each member of the Project Review Board, the stage manager of the Program Design and Development stage, the stage manager of the System Test stage, the stage manager of the Implementation and Production stage (if different from above), the project manager, the DP development manager, the DP operations manager, the DP audit manager, and the DP standards manager (quality assurance).

The next stage manager is usually the same as that of the System Test stage, a senior user manager. The DP operations organization also will be heavily involved in the implementation of the system into the production environment. Following a successful review of the System Test, the new system is ready for implementation and the next stage of the life cycle, the Implementation and Production stage, can be entered.

12

Implementation and Production Stage

Nothing ever becomes real until it is experienced — even a proverb is no proverb to you till your life has illustrated it.

— John Keats

The reader might be forgiven for thinking that when the Implementation and Production stage finally rolls around, there is almost nothing left to do but switch the system on. As I shall describe later, even just switching it on is a far from simple matter. Thoughtless and ill-prepared installations are probably responsible for more rejected and discarded but perfectly adequate systems than almost any other cause. If the software, hardware, and human environments all have not been adequately prepared for the new system, the implementation period may be longer and more costly than all of the previous life cycle stages put together. That is clearly unacceptable. The project manager cannot afford to just plug it in and switch it on, because much too large an investment has been committed to the system by this point in the life cycle to risk its being simply thrown away.

The Implementation and Production stage does require a considerable amount of effort and planning even if all of the previous stages have been one hundred percent successful and complete. Only by planning this stage and then adhering to the plan can the implementation team members be sure that they have in fact implemented the new system successfully.

It should be clear to all those who have been involved with developing a DP system that installing it is not simply a matter of plugging it in. One day, but not anytime soon, DP system requirements may be so standardized that ready-made application systems can be purchased and installed just like calculators, typewriters, and telephones. Until that day comes, however, the software, hardware, and human environments for the new system all must be made hospitable and compatible with its new procedures. Typically, there will be other separate systems, manual or automated, that will need to be connected with the new system and that will probably need modifying. Also, some existing procedures usually must be converted to be compatible with the new system.

To learn these new systems and procedures, all operators and users of the system must be trained, and many will need to be convinced that the new system is acceptable;

some who are already convinced will be eagerly waiting to use the new system. If users and operators are involved in the system testing activities as recommended, they will have advance notice of the usefulness and of the idiosyncracies of the system. If their opinion after system testing is that the system is not only acceptable but preferable to their current mode of operation, they will form a powerful lobby in favor of the new system. (It never hurts to have friends in high places.)

Fortunately, if all of the activities in all of the previous life cycle stages have been carried out as recommended in Chapters 6 through 11, much of the planning and preparation for the Implementation and Production stage will have been completed by the end of the System Test stage. The detailed implementation and conversion plans were completed in the Program Design and Development stage and reviewed in the System Test stage. The user and operator guides were tested, and the user and operator training manuals were readied for use. In fact, even among those implementation activities that have not been mentioned yet, some can be carried out in parallel with activities in other stages.

After implementation, what is next for the system and the project team? Is there life after implementation? Of course, this is the time when the system truly comes alive. If all goes according to plan, the new system after implementation will be in its longest and most productive phase. This is only to be expected; if not, why have the users and developers spent all this time and money? Soon after implementation, a production review is carried out to ensure that the system has been installed correctly and successfully and that it has performed to its users' expectations.

During the production life of the system, changes will be required, new versions installed, and, heaven forbid, errors will be found and fixed. Each activity needs to be formalized, and the written procedures made available when the system goes into production for the first time. A fallback plan has also been developed in anticipation of a disastrous system failure.

12.1 Objectives

The major objective of the Implementation and Production stage is to install the system smoothly, on schedule, without any significant problems, and to the complete satisfaction of the users and the operators of the system. With the successful completion of the System Test stage, the users are fully convinced that the system meets all of its requirements, and both users and operators are satisfied with how the system is used and operated.

After a successful implementation, the users' goal is to keep the system in an operational state for 100 percent of its scheduled up time. If the system is a 24-hour, real-time, on-line system, this objective is particularly challenging. Clearly, the users require the services of the DP organization in order to meet this objective.

Even when the system is deemed to be perfect when installed, changes will inevitably be required. For whatever reasons the changes are requested, they are implemented in a timely, orderly, controlled, and correctly prioritized fashion. Throughout the production life of the system, even with all of the changes being introduced, the original requirements and objectives of the system have to be maintained. Therefore, changes and enhancements to the system are installed only after they have undergone the same level of rigorous testing that the system itself was subjected to. Completely new releases or versions of the system are subjected to a mini-life cycle to ensure their conformance with the original System Specification document and with any new requirements that have been specified since the original installation. Of course, these new requirements, when approved by the user, are added to the Requirements Definition and System Specification documents to ensure that these documents reflect the modifications to the system.

12.2 People involved

The implementation team consists of a mixture of users, DP development staff, and DP operators, who ideally have had previous direct experience in implementing a similar system. The users take control of the system at the start of the System Test stage, and this control continues into this stage. Similarly, the operators continue their activities from the previous stage and complete their operation of the system to the point at which it becomes a natural and normal part of their professional activities. The DP development staff's involvement, by contrast, changes from a largely passive role in the System Test stage to a much more active one during implementation, because many tasks in this stage require the direct involvement of the DP professionals. Since system implementation should be a one-time event, the users and DP operators do not need to be trained in the nuances of the system generations, translation of test JCL to production procedures, and other such implementation-specific activities that are best carried out by the DP development staff.

By the end of the Implementation and Production stage, when the production review is carried out, the users and operators of the new system should be assured that the new system is an improvement over the old system in terms of its results and their own activities. Any dissent from this opinion must be mitigated as far as possible by further training, by changing the system and its procedures, or, in extreme cases, by assigning the dissenters to another function. There are always some individuals who, because of their background, beliefs, personal insecurity, or just plain irascibility, refuse to accept anything new or different. Not much can be done to change the opinions of such malcontents. As much distance as possible should be placed between them and the object of their disruptive attentions — not a simple task to be sure.

12.3 Activities

As mentioned before, many of the planning and preparation activities for the Implementation and Production stage are completed prior to the formal start of the stage. Several of these activities are described in previous chapters as being part of other stages. For instance, the conversion plan and implementation schedule are completed during the System Design and System Test stages. Nevertheless, still other activities are carried out actually at or close to the specific installation date.

Although the data conversion programs and procedures have been already implemented and fully tested as part of the system test, they must be implemented again immediately before system installation in order for the new system to start operating with fully current data in all of the required new formats and structures. Therefore, the data conversion of the production-level inputs to the system is the first activity to be carried out during this stage. Sometimes, this activity is actually an integral process of the new system itself and, in that case, it need not be carried out separately from the installation of the system. The scheduling details concerning these conversion activities are contained in the conversion plan. The implementation schedule simply consists of a list of specific activities that need to be carried out by specific dates in order to successfully install the new system. Responsibilities for each activity are also identified, as are the steps of the approved fallback procedure.

As distasteful as the possibility may be, it must be accepted that some new systems are developed, fully tested, successfully installed, and then, because of some overlooked, often apparently trivial factor, collapse disastrously with no hope of immediate recovery. Data processing systems are highly complex mechanisms whose potential internal interactions are often far too numerous to test completely. Therefore, a distinct, if unlikely, possibility is for the system to be installed with a fatal flaw. Consequently, a fallback plan to utilize the old system is formulated and reviewed in the System Test stage to anticipate this potentially disastrous crash of the system, however improbable.

Disaster recovery procedures are built in to the system as part of the control mechanisms specified in the Requirements Definition and the System Specification stages, but a complete failure of the system within a few hours or days of the installation is a unique situation, both from a practical and a psychological point of view.

The user and operator training manuals are completed prior to system testing and are tested during that stage. Simultaneously, sufficient staff is trained before system installation in order for the new system to be operated fully and continuously from the first day of its production life. Additional training of new users and operators will need to be scheduled as required. Also, as mentioned in Chapter 11, since the DP professionals work alongside the vendors when any new hardware and software is installed, they are completely conversant with the new system environment.

As mentioned many times before, very few systems go through life without being modified, fixed, or enhanced in one way or another, and, in fact, most mature DP organizations spend a majority of their resources on maintaining existing systems. Much as the tedious administration of the far-flung outposts of the British Empire was referred to as the "White Man's burden," today the DP manager's burden is the maintenance of old, outmoded, heavily patched, creaking DP systems under his care. Although the final responsibility for such systems is, of course, with the users of that system, the DP maintenance programmers must actually make the required coding changes, feverishly scanning the unintelligible listings, while frustrated operators pace about them and impatient users make telephone calls to DP management, complaining about "unresponsive programmers."

Much of the frustration and chaos so often associated with program and system maintenance results because this important activity is not planned, and because no procedures exist for the maintenance programmer to follow. Therefore, prior to the installation of the system, maintenance and release procedures must be developed. This is another activity that can be carried out effectively prior to the Implementation and Production stage; at least some of the maintenance procedures can be completed during integration testing in the Program Design and Development stage. At this time, a recommendation is that any changes made to individual programs be isolated from the system that is gradually being integrated (see Section 10.3). Only when each program is tested satisfactorily and fully documented is it integrated into the full system structure. The integration test is then carried out to ensure that the local changes are compatible with the global system environment, and the system documentation is updated to reflect the changes.

The same general procedure is adopted in production except that the full integration test of each fix and enhancement is carried out on a copy of the production system as if it were in system testing mode. This effectively isolates the fixing and testing activities from the production environment and maintains the integrity of the production system. A library of the system levels is implemented and a set of procedures developed to ensure that this testing philosophy is adhered to. As discussed in Chapter 15, several levels of the library may be required to maintain complete integrity and isolation between the testing system and the production system. The production system is the ultimate and most protected level of this library. The users and owners of the system approve each change to the system after it has been system tested and before it is finally implemented.

Changes to the system are grouped in batches, rather than small changes and updates being made continuously one at a time. Batches of updates can then be regularly scheduled as new "releases" or versions of the system, and each new release subjected to an abbreviated system development life cycle, as any small system would be. If so many changes are required to the system and resources are limited such that the changes must be ranked to provide an order of implementation, the Ranking Matrix described in Chapter 7 should be used before they are grouped in batches. The batches themselves can then be ranked into a desired chronological order of implementation.

Of course, some changes to the system must be made in an emergency fashion. In this case, much of the testing and documentation activities associated with the full maintenance procedures then must be carried out retroactively. Under no circumstances must any change be made to the system without being fully documented and tested, retroactively or otherwise.

The design and documentation methods used in the System Design and in the Program Design and Development stages have a profound effect on the maintenance activities. For example, if the structured design methods and the associated documentation techniques have been used, less error-fixing of the system probably is necessary, because the system design was so good to begin with that any changes required are considerably easier to implement than if the traditional nonmethods had been used. Many researchers, including myself, claim that in practice the use of structured design techniques has reduced maintenance activity by up to fifty percent and more from that experienced with nonstructured systems. One of the most effective tools in support of this claim is the project library. During maintenance, the library can be used effectively to control the testing and implementation of enhancements, fixes, and releases to the production system by forcing these changes to be tested in a nonproduction mode before being installed into the production environment.

After all this preparation, the system can be installed. There are at least three major approaches to system installation: parallel running, immediate cut-over, and phased installation. In *parallel running,* as discussed before, the new system is installed and the old system continues to run in parallel with it. In this way, the performance and output of the two systems can be continuously compared until the time the old system is switched off. This technique has particular advantages if the new system fails during the parallel running period. However, parallel running is only really suited to large, batch-oriented systems. On-line, real-time systems by their very nature are almost impossible to be run in parallel with each other. In addition, parallel running presupposes an existing old system of at least semiautomatic form.

If parallel running is chosen as the installation technique, the users, DP operators, and the Project Review Board decide the period of time to allow for enough parallel running and determine the criteria to judge whether the new system is performing satisfactorily. At the end of that period, the old system can be switched off. (The wise user will insist on preserving a complete copy of the latest version of the old system, if not for posterity, at least for a while.)

Immediate cut-over is the opposite approach to parallel running. When a parallel operation is impossible, then the system must be installed in one exciting, trauma-filled activity. Usually, a period of time when no significant production activity occurs is chosen. Weekends, holidays, third shifts are all possible periods when new systems can be installed, even if parallel running is to be the installation approach. The immediate cut-over approach generally requires much more detailed planning and preparation than does parallel running.

Whichever approach is chosen, the users have a set of benchmark criteria to be continuously applied to the new system during its early days to ensure that it continues to perform to all of its requirements. This set includes performance levels for the highest priority system requirements plus some time-related criteria, such as mean time between failures (MTBFs), and average transaction processing rates expected.

The *phased approach* to installation assumes that the system users agree to accept only part of the system at first and additional parts according to a schedule of phased partial installations until the complete new system is implemented. For each phase, either the parallel running or the immediate cut-over installation approach could be adopted, the choice depending upon the desires of the user and the characteristics of the specific part or parts of the system being installed in that phase.

After the successful installation of the system and any parallel running period, the production review is scheduled. The timing of this review varies from system to system, but it does not occur until the users and DP operators determine that the system is stable.

Because the production review is the final review and represents approval of the first release of the new system, the Project Review Board and *all* stage managers associated with the system life cycle attend. Specific items to be reviewed and approved by all those present include at least the following:

- performance of the new system
- acceptability of the user and operator guides
- quality of the user and operator training manuals and training programs
- data conversion problems
- installation problems
- total cost of the project
- schedule adherence

If all of these items are reviewed and the system is deemed satisfactory, the Implementation and Production stage is considered to be complete. The end-stage documentation consists of a complete report of the production review and a letter approving the system itself, signed by every member of the Project Review Board. Figure 12-1 summarizes the major activities of the Implementation and Production stage.

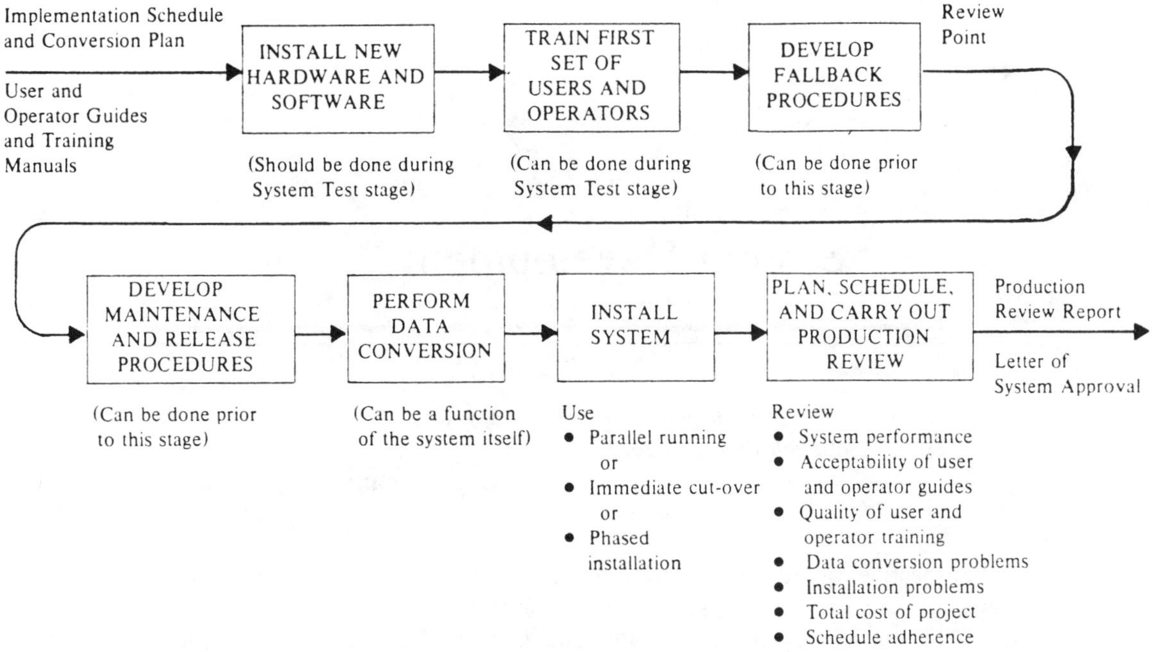

Figure 12-1. Major activities of the Implementation and Production stage.

12.4 Summary

At this point, the new system is fully installed, the users are happy, and the DP development staff can get on with the next project. Of course, some DP professionals need to be assigned to maintain the system, but if all of the procedures described in Chapters 6 through 12 have been followed faithfully and intelligently, the maintenance activities should be satisfyingly straightforward, if not actually pleasurable. Always remember, however, that simply following the approved life cycle stages, step-by-step, without the application of sound technical and management judgment and without imagination produces as bad a result as if the life cycle procedures had been ignored. Good rules and procedures need not stifle creativity; they can help turn creativity into productivity.

13

System Development People

The trouble with people is not that they don't know but that they know so much that ain't so.

— Henry Wheeler Shaw

Irrespective of all of the state-of-the-art methodologies, techniques, and tools brought to bear upon the system development life cycle, the single most important resource of any DP organization is its people. It is often easy to lose sight of the fact that without the people who developed them, none of today's labor-saving, business-expanding, mind-blowing DP systems would be possible. Somebody's imagination, hard work, drudgery, and just plain persistence made each of these systems happen.

Additionally, in relation to the cost-performance ratio of the DP hardware and software available today, the cost of DP's human resources is increasing at an exponential rate. Yet, despite all of the productivity-enhancing tools and techniques now provided to the DP professionals,, the individual DP person's productivity on average has not increased significantly over the last decade; worse, according to many observers, personal productivity has decreased. Obviously, something other than merely improved tools and techniques are needed. What is required is improvement in the way in which human resources in the DP industry are deployed, organized, and motivated.

In this chapter, I first briefly characterize the early data processing professionals and describe the management structures that have evolved to direct their activities. I then offer, based on my own experience, a practical organization that combines the team, functional, and matrix-types of management structures. I also suggest how both DP professionals, as well as their organizations, must change in order to meet the increased demands for productivity of the future, and how they can effectively use one resource in particular: outside consultants.*

---

*In this chapter, I assume that the people involved with the project, both within the project team and outside of it, are committed to the project's objectives. This of course is not always true. I do not cover how interpersonal and intra-organizational politics can affect a project, but Robert Block's *The Politics of Projects* [3] provides excellent insights into this potentially disruptive aspect of project management.

13.1 Evolution of DP management structures

In order to understand both the current demands and future requirements for the DP profession, let us briefly examine the history of the DP professional. During the heady, early days of data processing, the programmers were often engineers, mathematicians, and statisticians who had a pressing, practical need to use the computer. Much as the early automobile drivers lovingly tended their machines until they knew every part intimately, the first programmers became expert computer engineers. In both cases, of course, the symbiosis between man and machine was necessary because the machine was unpredictable and extremely unreliable.

Paper tape, punched with holes representing binary 1's and 0's, was a common form of input for early computing machines. It was not unheard of for programmers to repair old holes or punch new ones in the paper tape in order to effect changes in their programs. Such was the programmers' dedication and such was their "art" in the good old days.

Gradually, as the use of the computer expanded from the engineering, scientific, and research arenas into the business world, the programmers evolved into a cadre of technically oriented types who, unlike their practical-minded forebears, just *loved* playing with bits. Their indecent obsession was given respectability by being awarded the name of "bit manipulation." These programmers tended to be biased toward research and they regarded their skills as sacred, not to be shared with the non-DP "infidels." Assembly programming languages were, of course, the *only* way to write programs, and IBM's operating systems (OS, DOS, and TOS) epitomized user-friendliness. It was inconceivable to them that a better combination than OS, JCL, and BAL would ever be required. After all, the omnipotent superprogrammer who thought in BAL and who dreamed of dumps would always be around to act as high priest and to interpret for the almighty 360. Fortunately, DP management realized that although these dedicated programmers with ferrite cores for brains were essential, some organizational structure was required to control and monitor their activities. Five such structures are described below.

13.1.1 Functional management structure

Some of the earliest organizational structures attempted by DP management were loosely based on the perceived types of disciplines required in data processing. In these structures were separate "pools" of specific talents. The number of pools within an organization depended upon how many discrete skills were recognized by management. A typical such functionally organized DP group might have the structure depicted in Figure 13-1.

Not all organizations would have the same sections in their DP department. Some would have fewer, perhaps combining the designers and coders and including the testing personnel in the maintenance section. Other organizations would make the subdivisions even more refined by completely separating all of the functions, producing many sections.

The delineation between designers, coders, testers, and so on, occasionally resulted in disputes about which group should carry out certain tasks. Additionally, because of these misunderstandings about responsibilities, critical tasks were accidentally omitted. Hence, all concerned with these functional hierarchies realized that something more was needed — specifically some project-related structure to align the DP organization closer to its short- and long-term assignments and to ensure that all project-related tasks were assigned and completed.

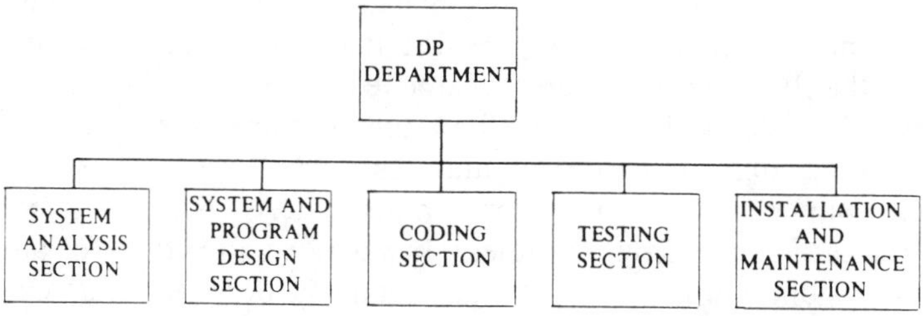

Figure 13-1. Functional management structure.

13.1.2 Project-related management structure

In the project-related management structure, each major project is set up as a primary subdivision of the DP department, and within each project organization is a substructure of disciplines required to complete that project. A "project," in this context, is the set of activities and resources required to specify, design, code, and implement a system or to maintain and support an already installed system. Clearly, for a development type of project, the organizational structure is transitory and lasts only as long as the project itself. Figure 13-2 illustrates this type of organizational structure.

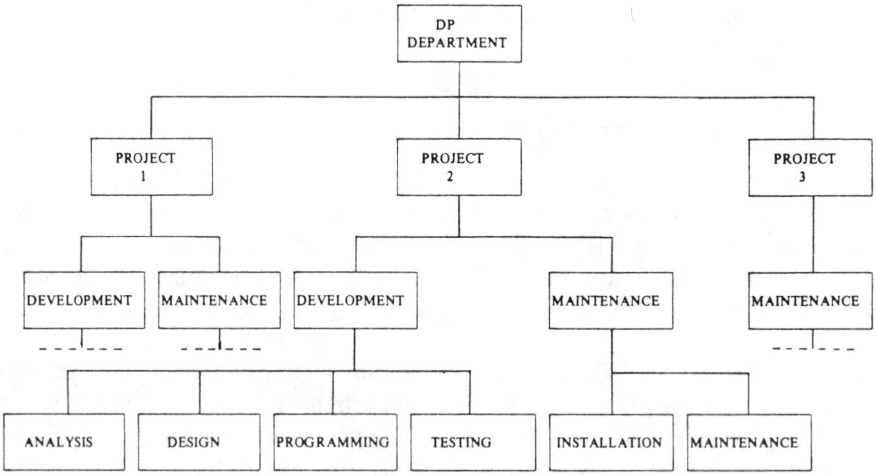

Figure 13-2. Project-related management structure.

This project-related organization is effective in developing systems, but its success depends upon a large amount of overlap and redundancy in functions. In many cases, for example, the development and maintenance organizations are defined to be separate; as a result, several identical functions, such as programming and testing, are staffed twice, one per organization.

As DP organizations experienced the respective problems and successes of functional and project-related structures, they realized that a hybrid type of management structure organization was needed to combine the best features of the two structures. That hybrid structure came to be called matrix management.

13.1.3 Matrix management structure

The matrix management style borrows the concept of discipline pools but superimposes the individual project structures upon them. Each project draws from the pool when a specific talent is required; when the need is over, the individual analyst, designer, or programmer returns to the pool to be reassigned to a new project. Figure 13-3 shows a simple version of a matrix type of organization.

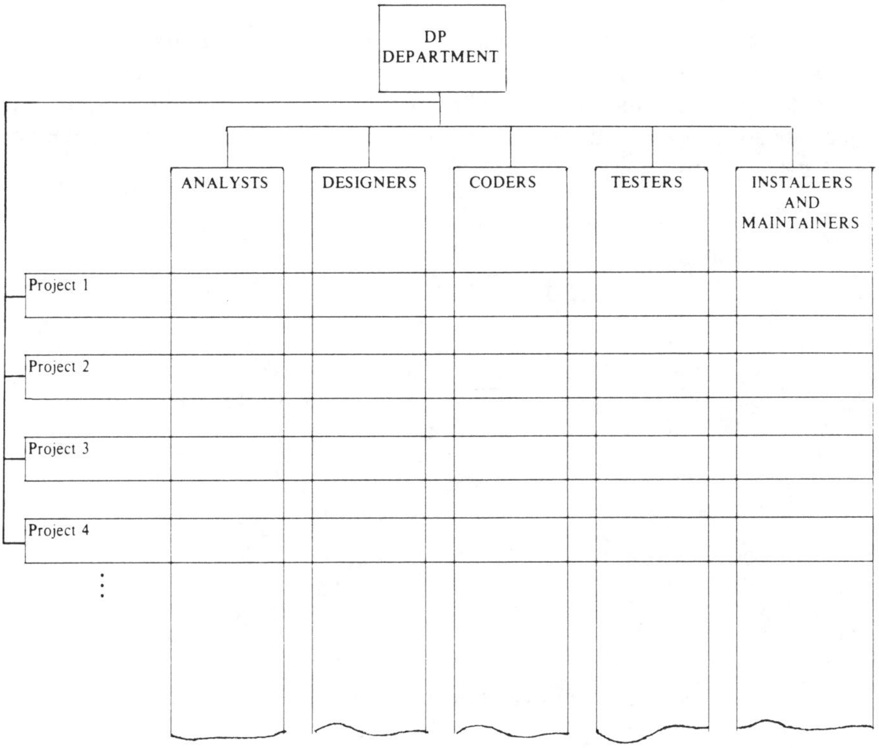

Figure 13-3. Matrix management structure.

The matrix management structure allows for more than one reporting relationship for each DP professional. Each person reports permanently to a functionally oriented manager such as the testing manager, and also reports on a temporary basis to a project manager when assigned to a particular project. Functional and project managers both report to the DP department manager.

Matrix management is popular in service organizations such as data processing, as well as in many consulting and subcontracting organizations, with the client usually providing the project managers. The matrix-oriented structure is more effective than the simple functional style of management, since it efficiently utilizes the available resources but retains a permanent structure to ensure career paths for the DP professionals. Even though an individual may be assigned to several different projects over a period of time, his functional management remains permanent. Therefore, with matrix management, the functional managers must be responsible for salary administration, performance appraisals, training assignments, and all other personnel-related functions.

The matrix shown in Figure 13-3 is, of course, two-dimensional. Some matrix management structures are set up as three- or even four-dimensional matrices, as when users and corporate management also try to control DP resources. In this case, each individual reports to three or four different managers. Not only are such matrices difficult to represent on a two-dimensional page, they are almost impossible for everyone to handle. Matrix management with more than two directions of reporting is *definitely* not recommended.

13.1.4 Chief programmer teams

As introduced in Chapter 2, the chief programmer team was first used successfully in the famous New York Times project, "fathered" by IBM's Terry Baker [1], just as the structured revolution started gaining momentum. This concept reflects the two-dimensional matrix management structure, but each project team is strictly defined in a hierarchical structure, as shown in Figure 13-4.

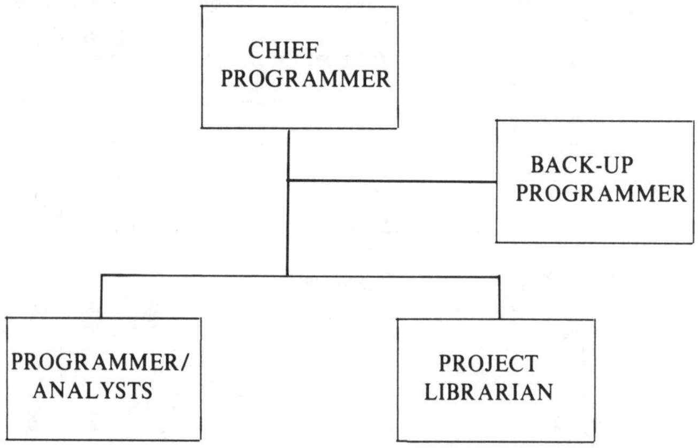

Figure 13-4. The chief programmer team structure.

A chief programmer team is likened to a surgical team in which each member has separate but equally critical skills and responsibilities. Even in such a democratic organization, however, there must be a chain of command to ensure consistent direction of effort and common objectives. Hence, every surgical team always has a head surgeon and an assistant for any particular surgical operation. Similarly, in the chief programmer team, the chief programmer has the lead role and the backup programmer is the second-in-command. A third member — the project librarian — plays a supporting role. These key roles have specific responsibilities.

The *chief programmer* is the leader, or technical manager, of the team. All other members of the team report directly him. The team he manages is usually assigned to develop a system during the System Design stage, and he is responsible for critical design decisions and for some critical programming activities. In addition, he coordinates the team's activities and oversees the quality of the end products of the System Design and Program Design and Development stages. Composition of the team inevitably changes as the project moves from system design through programming and testing, but the chief programmer remains the same through implementation. Clearly, the chief programmer is an experienced DP professional with considerable technical knowledge and with proved managerial ability.

At first glance, all team members enjoy equal status. But, as in George Orwell's *Animal Farm,* "some . . . are more equal than others." The *backup programmer* is always more equal than the rest of the team inasmuch as he can take over the chief programmer's tasks and responsibilities at any time. In terms of experience and ability, the backup programmer is the chief programmer's equal but, for the purpose of the project, he reports and defers to the chief programmer. As a direct assistant to the chief programmer, the backup programmer is usually regarded as the mentor of the other programming team members. He often performs critical and difficult development activities, such as the design of critical modules. The chief programmer and the backup programmer work closely together; in many small teams, they are the only technical members.

The *project librarian* is responsible for all the documentation that is produced as a DP system is being developed. This documentation is increasingly being generated and stored by means of an automated word processing system. Irrespective of the media or system used, the project librarian keeps it up-to-date and accurate and accessible to authorized personnel at all times. In addition, he maintains the machine-readable parts of the system being developed: the program source modules, JCL listings, load modules, test data, and other data that form the system. All controls used to maintain the separation and integrity of different levels of the system libraries and all project-related clerical and administrative tasks are his responsibility. Many software packages are available today to automate many of the librarian's functions. (The required structure of these packages and of a manual equivalent is described in detail in Chapter 15.)

The project librarian is often a transitory position, filled by someone who is on the way to becoming a full-fledged programmer. Some knowledge of the use of DP systems is required, although explicit programming and analysis skills are not usually needed.

The remaining members of the chief programmer team, the *programmer/analysts,* join the basic three-person team as required to carry out the detailed technical tasks involved in program and system development. Often, the powerful trio of chief programmer, backup programmer, and project librarian can complete all of the life cycle tasks from system design to implementation. Normally, however, some additional programmer/analysts are required, although a limit of seven or eight persons for the complete chief programmer team is recommended as being practical. A team larger than eight members means that the chief programmer probably spends more time as a manager than a technical practitioner, and the real purpose of the chief programmer team is usurped.

Chief programmer teams have proved effective in optimizing the people resources on development projects and in significantly improving productivity [1]. The team structure was set up not only to utilize high-quality technical people efficiently, but also to provide a vehicle for applying the then new structured techniques, including top-down design, structured programming, and code inspections. The team environment encourages all members to use common techniques in order to facilitate communication between themselves. This in itself improves productivity. One technique that is eminently suited for the chief programmer team environment is that of structured walkthroughs. A walkthrough is essentially a peer review of a product during the life cycle. Walkthroughs, described in Chapter 14, are conducted by and for the team prior to any formal end-stage reviews. As such, they constitute a kind of super desk-check of the products and are extremely effective in improving the quality of those products.

Another beneficial effect of the chief programmer team organization is that on-the-job training is maximized. The programmer/analysts on the team, through constant guidance by the chief and backup programmers, rapidly attain at least some of the expertise of those exalted professionals. The walkthrough technique in particular provides important educational benefits, since all team members can review and learn from their co-workers' efforts.

Unfortunately, this type of organization does demand a chief programmer for each team, and good chief and backup programmers are hard to find. Also, the most impressive results of using chief programmer teams seem to have been achieved when each member of the team was himself capable of being a chief programmer. This seems to prove the adage, If you get good people, you'll get good results!

Therefore, most organizations that choose to use the chief programmer team concept accept the lack of qualified chief programmers to lead each team, and so appoint (not annoint) normal mortals as project leaders of small teams, while the organization's few superstars each serve as technical consultant to several teams. In this way, the organizational benefits of the team structure are retained and the available technical expertise is optimized. Also, the project leaders can concentrate on *managing* the teams, a skill that is often sadly lacking in DP organizations.

13.1.5 Egoless teams

Soon after structured programming became well-known, it acquired the name in some circles of "egoless" programming. The reason for this name was the belief that coding a program according to a rigid set of rules is minimally influenced by the ego or the errant personality of the wild-eyed programmer.

This idea was incorporated with the organizational techniques in vogue at the time, and the strange concept of "egoless teams" was born. In such a team, there is no appointed leader or manager; instead, the natural leader rises when the need itself arises. Of course, this probably means a different leader arises for each technical phase: one leader for analysis, another for design, yet another for programming, and so on.

Unfortunately, in very few cases did the egoless teams prove to be effective because a natural leader almost never appeared. Generally, the team members lacked direction and motivation and drifted aimlessly until a clear leader, usually from outside the team, was formally appointed. An appointed leader or chief seems always to be necessary, however talented the individual team members happen to be.

13.1.6 A practical team organization

In a DP organization that is set up to serve other organizations within a corporation, a project-oriented, matrix style of management is often adopted (see Figure 13-5). The DP group itself is divided into functional departments, each of which gives data processing support to a specific part of the business. For example, one DP department may support the personnel and payroll functions and another the manufacturing functions, so that there are as many DP departments as there are discrete, supportable functions in the corporation. Each DP department is then itself organized in a classic matrix style, with pools of analysts, designers, coders, testers, installers, and maintainers. The pools provide teams of these professionals as required for individual projects, which can be development projects or maintenance projects or both.

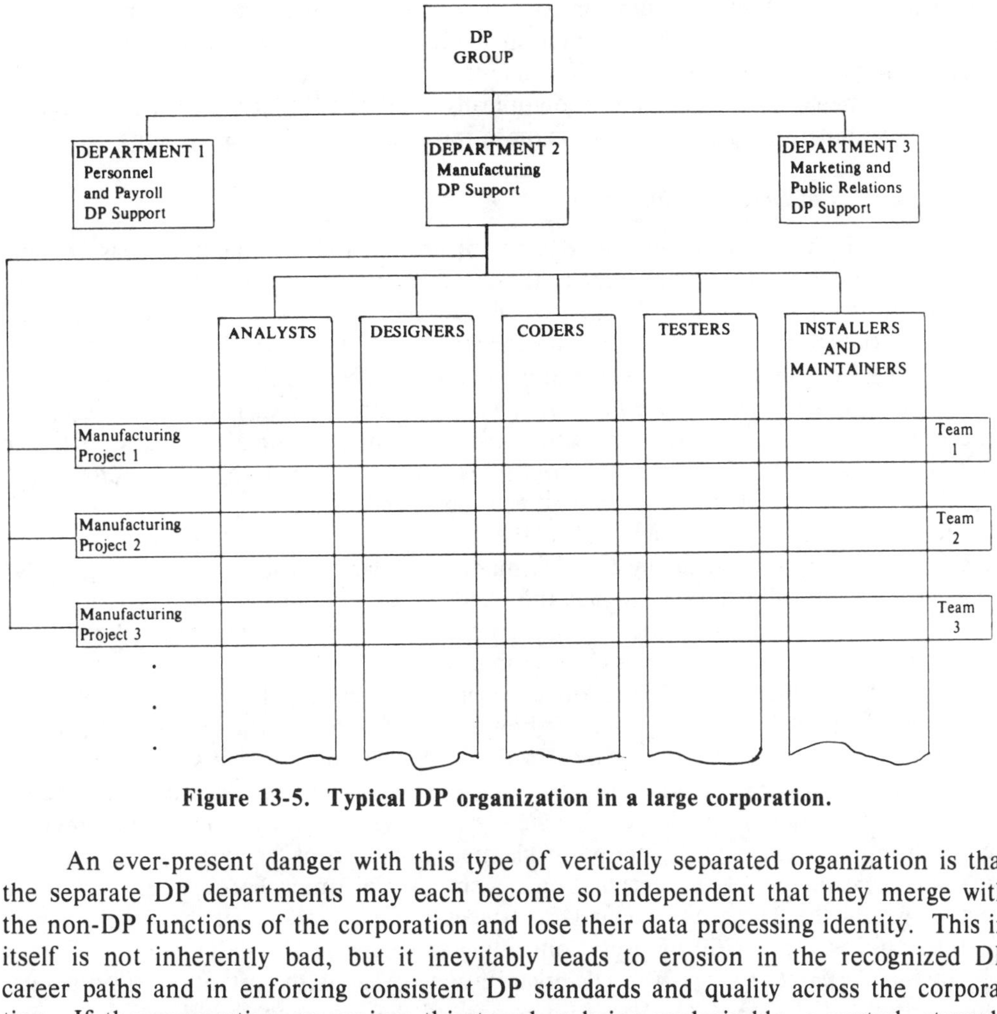

Figure 13-5. Typical DP organization in a large corporation.

An ever-present danger with this type of vertically separated organization is that the separate DP departments may each become so independent that they merge with the non-DP functions of the corporation and lose their data processing identity. This in itself is not inherently bad, but it inevitably leads to erosion in the recognized DP career paths and in enforcing consistent DP standards and quality across the corporation. If the corporation recognizes this trend as being undesirable, a central, strongly supported DP department must be created to counteract the trend. The DP department must be responsible for developing and enforcing standards and procedures, and for such activities as strategic planning, data administration, and data security. Unfortunately, top DP management often recognizes the need for this central facility only after its absence has resulted in a disaster.

13.2 Future requirements

However, it is not enough for the DP organization to manage properly its own personnel. The successful DP organization of the future must change its function within the larger organization it serves. Moreover, as DP techniques are used more and more by all parts of the business world, the DP professional must become more involved with that world in order to understand its changing needs. Specifically, he needs to understand how DP organizations must evolve, including his own role within that organization, in order to serve the corporation's future information needs. One resource that is often used and abused is outside consultants, who can offer DP organizations the flexibility to meet their user needs economically — if they understand the associated problems and potential pitfalls. I discuss these topics in the following sections.

13.2.1 Evolution of DP organizations

Richard L. Nolan, in a perceptive series of articles and presentations, has defined six stages through which all DP organizations must evolve in order to become "perfect" DP groups [34]. Nolan's theory itself is still evolving, but the six basic stages are Initiation, Contagion, Control, Integration, Architecture, and Maturity.

In the *Initiation* stage, the corporation uses data processing as a business tool for the first time and the DP group, perhaps fewer than ten in total, is composed entirely of technically oriented people — technicians, programmers, and operators. At this point in the organization's life, only one business function is typically being automated, and that function often is financial in nature, such as accounting or payroll.

If the Initiation stage is successful, the corporation may want to automate more functions, probably several at once. This marks the start of the *Contagion* stage. DP technicians still rule the DP roost, but the need for project management is grudgingly conceded. Until a standard system development life cycle is adopted for all projects, the DP organization remains in the Contagion stage.

In order to enter stage 3, the *Control* stage, the organization must commit to a project management methodology, either home-grown, purchased, or both, and it must allow the end user to be heavily involved with the development of the systems.

The *Integration* stage is characterized by the development of common DP systems throughout the corporation. Instead of simply growing to meet current requirements, the DP group now undergoes a period of planned growth in order to meet the business plans and expectations of the corporation, as strategic planning becomes an important function within the DP group. The DP services themselves start to be decentralized into the end-user areas with the users controlling some of the DP activities.

In the *Architecture* stage, the DP organization demands the attention of corporate management and the head of DP becomes part of the top executive decision making group in the corporation. However, this manager still is regarded as a junior member of this elite group, more as an advisor than a true decision maker.

In the final stage, *Maturity,* data processing is an equal partner with all other major business functions, such as marketing, manufacturing, and accounting. The DP director has a major voice in running the corporation and is able to ensure that his department meets the corporate information processing needs today and in the future.

All DP organizations must move sequentially through these stages of evolution; none can be omitted. However, some DP groups may remain in an early stage permanently. Very few DP groups have reached stage 6, Maturity, and most are in stages 3 or 4. Some never leave stage 2 because users are not admitted into the system development process, and a project development methodology is never installed or even investigated.

13.2.2 Changing needs for the DP professional

With the evolution of DP organizations comes the evolution of the DP profession itself. Nolan's stages of evolution show a clear trend away from the elite, separate technological type of DP organization and toward a business-oriented, planned, and controlled environment. This trend is mirrored in the changing disciplines that the DP professional needs to know, such as planning, budgeting, accounting, contracting, and so on. The DP professional is finding that it is no longer sufficient merely to be an expert in the technical aspects of data processing. The corporate needs for information processing must have the same level of priority in the DP professional's thinking as do the intricacies of the next software release. In addition, the DP project manager has to be aware of motivational techniques, demotivating trends, and project management methods, and he must possess all of the other knowledge, skills, and experience that compose the complete business DP professional.

There are primarily two requirements of DP professionals: continuing education and working closely with users. To ensure that DP professionals are trained in the disciplines and methods needed to become expert business people and managers as well as expert technologists, DP management *must* commit strongly to a continuing education policy using internal and external training resources. In particular, DP professionals need, in addition to their specific DP-related skills, regular training in at least all of the following: project management and control, estimating, people management, interpersonal communication, and the specific business of the corporation. Also, DP professionals must personally take on the responsibility for educating themselves by reading trade journals and textbooks regularly, and by active involvement in professional organizations such as the Association for Computing Machinery (ACM) and the Data Processing Management Association (DPMA). Only in this way can they hope to keep up-to-date on the latest software engineering tools and techniques. For example, since the new, user-friendly programming tools are breaking down the barriers between the jobs of designers and programmers, today's successful application programmer is an analyst and designer as well as coder. Above all, he is able to communicate with the non-DP personnel in order to function effectively in all these roles.

I have stressed that it is essential for the users and the DP staff to work together harmoniously so that the development of the new system can succeed. The modern application development techniques discussed throughout this book are happily forcing an increasing and continuous dialogue between the users and DP. In some cases, functions that were previously regarded as being DP-only or user-only activities are becoming increasingly less so; consequently, user and DP functions are being slowly, but inexorably, merged. In this type of environment, transfers of staff between DP and user organizations become attractive and productive. One of the more interesting types of transfer is that of a senior DP professional, who is involved in the design, development, and testing of a new system, and who transfers to the user organization upon the installation of that system. This person then becomes a full-time user-DP liaison expert for that particular user organization. The term "customer service representative" is being used often in the popular DP press for this type of function. This position is obviously useful to the organization, and it also helps to broaden the experience and the knowledge of the senior DP professional and greatly enhances his standing within the corporation.

Of course, there is no reason why a senior user cannot also fill this role and perhaps transfer to the data processing organization as a full-time member of the DP team. In this way, he could study and absorb the DP culture and also help the other team members by reviewing technical material from the users' viewpoint. I emphasize, however, that this customer service representative is *not* intended to be a maintenance programmer, although his existence usually makes the task of system maintenance much easier.*

13.2.3 Effective use of consultants

Finally, the successful DP professional and his organization of the future realize the value of using consultants in specific, well-defined situations. Often, consultants are used to provide information when local DP expertise from within the corporation is not available. Of course, the external consultant's services can easily be dispensed with at the end of a contract, and little or no overhead costs are associated with the price of a consultant. So, if the consultant's fees are not astronomical, use of consultants for specific, well-defined tasks can save the corporation money. In fact, decomposing system development activities into a series of discrete life cycle stages provides an impetus for using outside consultants. For example, a consultant can readily perform the Feasibility Study; and if the Project Review Board decides at the end of the study that the project is not viable, the consultant's contract can be terminated.

There are many reputable and excellent DP consultants within the industry, but even the best of them should not be called in every time an information-gathering exercise is required and in-house experts are either too busy or apparently unqualified to handle it. Sometimes, as any consultant who has handled such an activity knows, all that is needed to get the information is simply to interview the appropriate employee. A senior person within the corporation could probably carry out such an assignment, and, as an internal consultant, he could probably produce the report sooner and cheaper. The only real problem then would be to convince upper management that the report, in fact, had been written by an expensive outside consultant to ensure that it received sufficient attention.

There are three major problems in using outside consultants. First, the consultant often has no detailed knowledge of the corporation's organizational structure or of its culture. This knowledge must be acquired, or totally erroneous recommendations may be made based upon the information gathered. Acquiring the knowledge takes time and, as everyone knows, time is money.

The second major problem is that all knowledge gained by the consultant during the consulting assignment is largely lost to the corporation when the assignment is over, unless the work is extremely well documented or unless the consultant remains permanently with the corporation. Unfortunately, documentation of such a high quality is rarely produced and, the consultant rarely stays with the corporation.

The third problem is if too many plum assignments are given to outside consultants, the permanent staff of the corporation becomes resentful. This resentment transforms into a lack of cooperation when the consultant's recommendations are implemented.

---

*Japanese corporations have been using this type of cross-fertilization for decades to enhance their staff members' abilities and their companies' operations in all types of industries. See Peter F. Drucker's *Managing in Turbulent Times* [56] for more information.

Nevertheless, despite these major problems, outside consultants must be used in some situations. To help determine when they should be used, I recommend that at least one of the following conditions be true:

- when no relevant internal expertise is available and when the expertise itself will not be needed again in the corporation
- when no member of the organization expresses any interest in the assignment, or when carrying out the assignment internally would be de-motivating to those involved
- when the recommended outside consultant has an acceptable and demonstrable track record in similar projects or assignments in similar organizations
- when the organization's president or the chairman of the board or their direct representatives dictates the use of an outside consultant; this rule is particularly applicable when the name of the consultant or the consulting company is provided with the directive (some battles are not worth the fight)

My personal view of when to use outside consultants can be simply expressed as follows: The permanent, internal staff should be developed to fill the need whenever possible.

13.3 Summary

The day of the isolated, ivory tower DP professional is over, for major DP project development teams are here to stay. System analysts, program and system designers, and programmers must all become team players, since as we've seen in this chapter the matrix team concept provides the most efficient way of utilizing the organization's DP talents. Another fact of life for DP professionals is the acceptance of several masters, with DP management, users, and corporate management all making direct demands on the DP professionals' time. The environment is complex, evolving, and dynamic; embracing several disciplines simultaneously is now a way of life.

DP professionals can no longer afford to be simply technical experts. Like the dinosaur, they must evolve or die. They need to be aware of how their profession fits into the business being served. Extensive and continuously updated training must be available to keep them skilled not only in data processing techniques and methodologies, but also in management, interpersonal relationships, the business of the corporation, and many other disciplines. As mandated by DP management, *all* DP staff should attend a minimum set of these training courses. Users of DP services are no longer willing to put up with DP staff members who cannot and will not understand the users' priorities and whose communication skills are inadequate. Good communication and understanding between users and DP personnel save time and money on all projects and consequently increase the overall productivity of the DP department.

In any large DP organization that has reached the middle stages of Nolan's evolution, there are some crucial, strategic business and technical decisions to be made. The

DP professional must be fully equipped, through training and varied experience, to be fully involved in this decision making. DP management must make the commitment to invest in the training and the varied assignments to make this happen. The result will be a pool of experienced and accomplished DP professionals whose broad base of related knowledge will significantly increase the productivity of the DP organization.

14

Walkthroughs

Old ideas give way slowly; for they are more than abstract logical forms and categories. They are habits, predispositions, deeply ingrained attitudes of aversion and preference.

— John Dewey

Inevitably, since a DP product is the result of a team effort, some technique is required to ensure that the team members are all pulling together in the same correct direction. An objective team review or appraisal of each others' products and of the product as a whole on a regular basis is the kind of technique required. But, programmers being what they are, they tend to resist such group activities. This chapter suggests a technique called a walkthrough that helps to coordinate the many disparate skills and personalities in the typical project team along with my suggestions to overcome programmers' and others' resistance to the technique.

Throughout the system development life cycle, there is a need to monitor the activities of each stage. Consequently, a formal review of each stage's end product is held in order to obtain acceptance of that product and agreement to move into the next stage. Prior to the formal reviews, an informal technical review is conducted, several times if necessary, for each of the discrete, identifiable subparts of the stage's end product. This informal review can be a walkthrough.

As the system development life cycle progresses, problems are discovered and solutions generated. It would be tragic if the knowledge created by these problems and solutions were lost because of a lack of a method to disseminate the relevant information. The team appraisal, or walkthrough, provides a way to preserve this knowledge.

14.1 Definition

The walkthrough technique provides an efficient and effective means to perform the regular technical monitoring and appraisal of the project and simultaneously offer a project-oriented educational medium for the project team members. What is a walkthrough? My dictionary defines it as

> **walkthrough,** *n.* a perfunctory performance of a play or acting part . . . a television rehearsal without cameras.

This definition comes near to describing what the data processing profession means by a walkthrough.* More explicitly, a walkthrough is a process in which a product, or a partial product, of a data processing system development activity is examined, component by component, for compatibility with its specification and for errors. Of course, under this definition, the original Requirements Definition and the System Specification documents are subjects for a walkthrough.

According to much of the available literature, the use of the walkthrough technique is restricted to only the coding stage of development. In that case, it is a code inspection, the technique made famous by IBM's Michael Fagan [15], as explained in Section 14.9. The walkthrough is in fact a comprehensive technique that can be used in all stages of system development to improve product quality, people productivity, and even morale. Many different products can be walked through, as each stage in the life cycle produces one or more end products. A narrative system specification, program documentation, and a test plan all are typical stage end products. Additionally, the walkthrough becomes a perfect medium for educating the project members about the project itself and its progress, as discussed in Section 14.8.

In order to carry out the walkthrough, participants must obtain some documentation of the product to be reviewed. It could be in the form of a design document, structure chart, program listing, system test plan, or any other documents produced during the system development life cycle. The reason that documentation is required for walkthroughs is that it is the only way that reviewers can determine that the system is being developed on schedule and according to its specification. Documentation is the system's window to the world — without it, both users and management must rely entirely on the assessment of the analysts and programmers of the completeness and accuracy of the system. The phrase "ninety-percent coded" is not a very helpful description of progress even if it's true — particularly if the remaining ten percent requires as much effort as the first ninety percent.

14.2 Procedure

In order for the walkthrough to be most beneficial, it is carried out in stages. Three stages are necessary in the walkthrough: the review, the actual walkthrough, and the follow-up.

14.2.1 Review stage

The intent of the review stage is to acquaint (ideally not for the first time) all attendees with the product to be walked through in order to save time at the walkthrough itself. A copy of all relevant documentation is verified as complete and distributed to each prospective attendee by the moderator (see Section 14.3). Information about the scheduled date, time, and place of the walkthrough is also distributed, along with any

*The word "structured" has often been added as a prefix to give marketability to the phrase and to gain attention for the technique itself.

relevant in-house standards and a checklist to prompt a complete and correct analysis of the product. Each attendee is given time to review the product documentation and, using the checklist provided, to generate a series of questions, suggested improvements, apparent errors, and so forth. (See Section 14.4 for guidelines on how far in advance of the walkthrough this stage should be.)

During the review stage, the moderator determines the number of attendees to be present at the actual walkthrough. As a general rule, the number should be kept as low as possible and within the guidelines outlined in Section 14.3.

14.2.2 Walkthrough stage

In the walkthrough, the proposed product is actually reviewed in detail by the walkthrough attendees. A pre-selected presenter, either the product's author or a member of the team that developed the product, describes the product, referring to the documentation and explaining the reasoning behind the design and implementation of the product. At the appropriate time in the presentation, attendees mention any comments, criticisms, suggestions for improvement, or anything else they find. Using his judgment, the moderator of the walkthrough controls the meeting to ensure that it does not grind to a halt because of too much unnecessary detail or because of irrelevant suggestions or discussions.

The actual solutions or resolutions of the issues raised must wait until later, but recommendations as to where and how and who can help to start generating the solutions are appropriate at the walkthrough stage. Approximate target schedules for specific resolutions and solutions can be decided at this time, since many of the appropriate people needed to set schedules are usually present at the walkthrough. The complete list of suggestions, comments, criticism, and possible resolution schedules is known as the walkthrough action list, and it is recorded by someone designated as the recorder or secretary. (How the information is recorded is unimportant; for example, a word-processor could be used.) The list is given to the product's author at the end of the walkthrough for subsequent resolution.

The walkthrough stage should last no longer than one hour for walking through technical products, such as program listings, program designs, and test plans. Larger, more complex products may require more time (see Section 14.4).

14.2.3 Follow-up stage

It is one thing to identify required changes in a product, and it is quite another to ensure that these changes are implemented. Therefore, the third and final stage of the walkthrough procedure, the follow-up stage, is an essential one. It not only ensures the implementation of changes, but also ensures that all involved with the product are clearly informed of the implementation.

In this stage, the assigned author of the product makes the suggested changes, corrections, or improvements using the action list as a guide. All resolutions, whether they are solutions, recommendations, or even rejections, are fully documented and a copy distributed to the original walkthrough attendees. In most cases, this distribution is sufficient to ensure that all involved are informed of the amended product. However, sometimes the number of changes required to one product necessitates scheduling another walkthrough. This number varies from environment to environment and from product to product, but typically it reaches the critical level when changes amount to twenty-five percent of the product's whole. For example, if twenty-five percent or more of a program's lines of code is changed, it is essentially a new program and the walkthrough should be repeated.

The above three-stage procedure may be too formal and complex for organizations that do not accept or do not need very formal procedures, as well as for many small organizations in which several walkthrough tasks are carried out by one individual. Also, some of the documentary procedures, such as making checklists and standards, could be eliminated to reduce formalities. Additionally, the complete procedure could be compressed by merging the walkthrough and some of the follow-up, and by de-formalizing the process into more of a peer-group discussion. There may be an existing project management system or change management system that the walkthrough procedure must interface with. For example, if the organization is using a formal life cycle methodology such as Spectrum, review procedures are already built in to the methodology, and the walkthrough process must be made compatible with these procedures. The exact method of conducting reviews is not all important, but the concept certainly is.

14.3 Attendees

The people involved in the walkthrough technique are critically important. Each participant must have a reason for being involved with the walkthrough and must clearly understand his role. Therefore, it is necessary to decide upon a standard set of roles and responsibilities for the walkthrough process and to assign them to specific persons for every walkthrough carried out during the system life cycle.

The actual number of attendees at each walkthrough should be kept to a minimum (up to ten or twelve), but the following responsibilities are assigned each time:

- *Moderator:* a senior member of the project team to act as facilitator, chairman, moderator, and decision maker at the walkthrough; he also distributes the documentation prior to the walkthrough; he has management or project leader experience and is a respected member of the organization, but is not a manager *directly* involved with the project.

- *Presenter:* the author or developer of the product that is to be walked through. If the product is developed by a team, the author is selected from the team for the walkthrough.

- *Recorder:* the person who records all of the criticisms, errors, and suggested changes to the product, as well as the tentative schedule for implementing the changes, if available. (If the chief programmer team organization is being used, the project librarian is ideal for this role during the technical activities of system design, program design and development, and system testing.)

- *Team members:* the rest of the project team involved in developing the system or subsystem of which the current walked-through product is a part.

- *User representative:* the user working with the project team or, if one doesn't exist, the user designated to participate in the walkthrough to provide valuable insight and approval of any significant changes to the product.

- *Interested outsiders:* members of external organizations, who would benefit from attending the walkthrough; they include DP operations staff, developers of related systems, maintainers of related systems, quality assurance or systems assurance staff, DP audit staff, database and data administrators, and strategic planners.

This list of attendees is comprehensive and should cover all possible situations. Each case, however, must be assessed in terms of the true need for individual attendees, since the overall objective is to keep the numbers low enough to maximize the effectiveness of the walkthrough. A limit of ten to twelve attendees seems to be effective.

Who attends the walkthrough in each case also depends upon the product itself and the life cycle stage in progress at the time. Table 14-1, which assumes the project-oriented matrix type of organization, summarizes the likely specific assignments.

Table 14-1
Walkthrough Attendees: Stage by Stage

ROLE \ STAGE	REQUIREMENTS DEFINITION	SYSTEM SPECIFICATION	SYSTEM DESIGN	PROGRAM DESIGN & DEVELOPMENT	SYSTEM TEST	IMPLEMENTATION & PRODUCTION
MODERATOR	Senior User	Senior User	Senior DP System Analyst	Chief Programmer (Project Leader)	Chief Programmer	Senior User
PRESENTER	Business System Analyst	Business System Analyst	DP System Analyst or Designer	Program Designer	Testers	Business System Analyst
RECORDER	Another Business System Analyst	Another Business System Analyst	Project Librarian	Project Librarian	Project Librarian	Another Business System Analyst
TEAM MEMBERS	More Business System Analysts	Business & DP System Analysts & User Representatives	DP System Analysts & Designers	Programmers & System Analysts	Programmers & DP System Analysts	Business & DP System Analysts, Programmers, Testers
USER REPRESENTATIVE	DP System Analyst & User Business System Analyst	User Representative	Business System Analysts	Business System Analysts	Senior User, Business System Analysts	User Representative
OUTSIDERS	DP Operations, Quality Assurance, DP Audit, Data Administration, Strategic Planning	DP Operations, Quality Assurance, DP Audit, Data Administration, Strategic Planning	DP Operations, Quality Assurance, DP Audit, Data Administration, Database Administration	Quality Assurance, Database Administration, DP Audit	Quality Assurance, DP Audit, DP Operations	DP Operations, Quality Assurance DP Audit
PRODUCT TO BE WALKED THROUGH	Requirements Definition Document & Cost-Benefit Analysis	System Specification Document & Cost-Benefit Analysis	System Design Document System Test Plan Database Design Installation Test Plan	Program Design & Code, Program Test Results Data Design	System Test Results	Implementation Results Production Review Report

DP managers directly involved with the project should not attend the walkthrough. Since the walkthrough is a technique to improve the product, similar to data flow diagrams and any other development tools, it should not be used as a management device to assess the performance of individual staff members. Unfortunately, DP managers are very interested in the results of the walkthroughs, so it may be difficult, if not impossible, to keep them away. If, however, DP managers promptly receive the information they want on the schedule and the walkthrough actions, this should ensure that the walkthroughs themselves remain purely a technical tool for the project team and avoid taking on possible personal appraisal overtones.

14.4 Timing

The timing of each stage of the walkthrough is directly related to the specific product being walked through. Of course, the larger and more complex the product, the longer the review time, the longer the walkthrough time, and the more laborious the follow-up activities that are required. Also, with more complex end products, a second walkthrough is more likely to be needed than with simpler products. For example, a simple program design could be walked through in the following timeframe:

Day 1:	*Review* — notification of the schedule and distribution of the product's documentation to all potential attendees
Day 5:	*Walkthrough* — completion of the review in no more than one hour
Days 6 to 15:	*Follow-up* — completion of all follow-up activities, including rescheduling of the walkthrough if necessary

For such a simple product, the complete walkthrough process could be finished in just ten days. Each attendee would be involved for a few hours at most, and the author or developer of the product may be involved for up to four additional workdays. Yet, the improvement in the product could be dramatic.

A larger and more complex product, such as a totally new and comprehensive, large system specification, will require a longer timeframe, as follows:

Day 1:	*Review* — notification of the schedule and distribution of the product's documentation to all potential attendees
Days 15 and 16:	*Walkthrough* — completion of the reviews in several meetings of one hour or so over a period of two days
Days 17 to 45:	*Follow-up* — completion of the follow-up activities and the second walkthrough planned and scheduled if necessary

The type, size, and complexity of the product affects not only the walkthrough's timing, but also the type of attendee. Stage end products, such as system specifications or installation test plans, require walkthrough attendees from several different organizational entities outside of the data processing function (see Table 14-1). Merely organizing the schedules of the attendees from these disparate functions can take a significant amount of time.

Because of the wide variation in the timing required, a time allowance for the walkthrough process for each stage's partial and completed products must be built into the overall life cycle schedules and estimates. Table 14-2 demonstrates how the time requirements can vary from stage to stage.

Table 14-2
Walkthrough Timing: Stage by Stage

LIFE CYCLE STAGE	REQUIREMENTS DEFINITION	SYSTEM SPECIFICATION	SYSTEM DESIGN	PROGRAM DESIGN & DEVELOPMENT	SYSTEM TEST	IMPLEMENTATION & PRODUCTION
Typical Product of Life Cycle Stage	Requirements Definition Document	System Specification Document	System Design Document	Program Design	System Test Results	Production Review Document
Days Required to Review the Product						
Review	14	14	30	4	14	30
Walkthrough	1	2	2	1	1	2
Follow-up	45	29	30	5	15	30
Total Elapsed Days	60	45	62	10	30	62

14.5 Documentation

As with most of the structured techniques, the walkthrough uses and produces documentation. Depending upon the degree of discipline and formality acceptable to the DP staff, the walkthrough documentation used may be as complete as in the following description, or it may be only a small subset thereof. The comprehensive set of documentation described here can be used as a model that the project manager can modify to fit his specific environment.

At the start of the review stage, the moderator sees that every potential walkthrough attendee receives the following documentation:

- a copy of the product to be reviewed — a listing, set of design diagrams, or specifications, for example
- the location, schedule, and general agenda of the walkthrough
- a set of written objectives for the walkthrough
- the list of potential attendees and their expected roles
- a checklist of questions specific to the type of product being walked through

The walkthrough documentation should be standardized as much as possible to avoid reinventing the wheel with each project. For example, a pre-printed blank schedule could be provided, as shown in Figure 14-1. In the lower section entitled "Walkthrough Objectives," a standard statement would serve to remind the attendees of the walkthrough's purpose — to improve the product in question, *not* to destroy it or to unfairly criticize it or its creator. The schedule form in Figure 14-1 meets the need for three of the required pieces of walkthrough documentation: schedule, location, and agenda; walkthrough objectives; and list of potential attendees.

ABC, Inc. – DP Department

WALKTHROUGH SCHEDULE

PRODUCT NAME ____________ DATE ______

PRODUCT TYPE ____________ TIME ______

LOCATION ______

ATTENDEES

NAME	ORGANIZATION	ROLE
		– MODERATOR
		– RECORDER
		– PRESENTER
		– USER

WALKTHROUGH OBJECTIVES

Figure 14-1. A standardized walkthrough schedule form.

The product checklist is a standardized list of relevant questions intended to guide the walkthrough attendees in obtaining complete information about the product. For any one specific type of product — say, for all program code listings — there would be one specific, standardized checklist. In a structured PL/I environment, the questions might include these:

- Are all DOWHILE constructs coded in the standard manner?
- Are there any nonstandard constructs?
- Are there any blocks of unconnected code?

- Is the program documentation self-explanatory?
- Does the program code meet the physical formatting standards?
- Are there any unnecessary GOTOs?

During the walkthrough itself, an additional piece of documentation is generated, the action list, as described earlier. This list is used to resolve all required actions in the follow-up stage. At the end of the follow-up stage, the amended product documentation is distributed to the walkthrough attendees and, if another walkthrough is required, the process starts again. Figure 14-2 illustrates how the walkthrough documentation is used in practice.

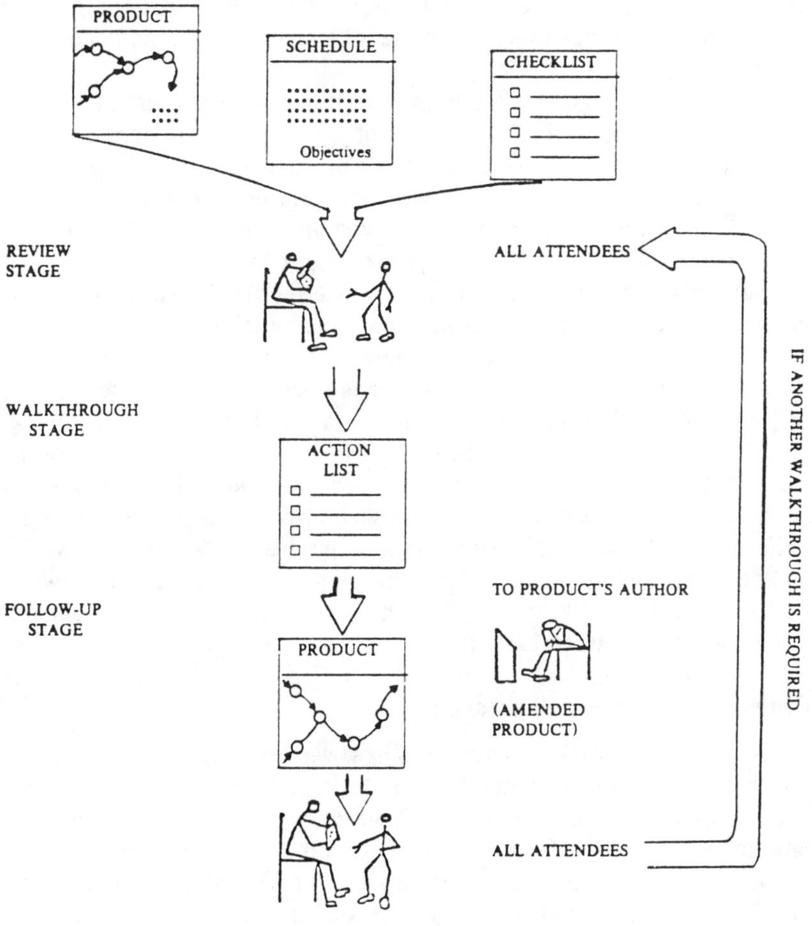

Figure 14-2. Flow of walkthrough documentation.

14.6 Psychology of the walkthrough

In successful walkthroughs, a mood of constructive criticism and of working together is maintained so as to promote a positive attitude of improving the team's product, *not* of rewriting so-and-so's dumb program. The witch-hunt mentality must be avoided. In some environments, the walkthrough procedure can easily and implicitly encourage personal criticism, and it can rapidly degenerate into an unfriendly "roast" of the product and of its author. It can expand into a forum for investigating all of the perceived ills of the DP organization. The moderator must be strong enough to prevent this from happening by disallowing any subjective, personal, or irrelevant criticism as soon as it is voiced.

The walkthrough technique enhances teamwork because it helps enforce standards in a nonthreatening way. It also offers educational benefits in that the team members, as well as nonmembers can observe how the team's stars perform and actually review in detail the stars' output.

An important psychological variable in determining the success of walkthroughs is who occupies the key roles. Clearly, the task of walkthrough moderator is not an easy one. Many of the failures of walkthroughs have occurred because this one role has not been given sufficient consideration. Often, a moderator is chosen from outside the project so that the benefits of being an uninvolved and therefore objective manager can be utilized. He must be able to keep the walkthrough on course and to maintain the proper improvements-to-the-product attitude. An effective initial approach is to insist that the project leader or manager, rather than the outsider, conduct the first walkthrough for a particular product. For example, a walkthrough of the overall system design or prototype for which the project leader is responsible could be carried out with the project team, both as an educational and as a working event. Adopting this approach would help to establish the authority of the project leader in a nonthreatening manner and would ensure that each team member starts with the same level of understanding of the project's objectives. This approach also would both encourage the team members who might otherwise be reticent about public display of their work and provide a moderating example for the natural thespians on the team. This would be the first and probably the last walkthrough that the project manager would actively participate in for the reasons discussed earlier.

14.7 Implementation of the walkthrough

The walkthrough is not like a turn-key software package or a new programming language and cannot be simply plugged in and switched on. A technique such as this, which inevitably involves human egos and sensitivities, is installed delicately and slowly with the caution that one would use to place by hand a sleeping tarantula among a nest of equally soporific rattlesnakes: very, very, carefully! In order to implement the walkthrough technique, it is essential to start with a single project, preferably one that is in one of the early stages of the life cycle, perhaps in the Feasibility Study, Requirements Definition, or System Design stage. After a suitable project has been selected, the complete project team, including both users and management, is then introduced to the technique by means of an in-depth, detailed presentation. The presentation can last from two hours to a complete day, depending upon the audience's level of previous experience or current knowledge of walkthroughs, the degree of acceptance of new methods, and the expertise of the presenter.

The first presenter of the walkthrough technique in any organization is a good marketer, since there is always a certain amount of resistance to any new or different technique. This resistance can sometimes only be effectively overcome by charm, persistence, salesmanship, expertise, a whole lot of patience, and some luck; but it can be overcome. The presenter is a strong believer in the technique, is a current or ex-DP development practitioner, and has already used walkthroughs in a real environment. The presenter acts as a consultant for the pilot project team and is available in the future to assist other projects in using the technique. In order to ease the introduction of walkthroughs into the organization, a set of standardized walkthrough documentation should be used, based on the set described earlier.

14.8 Benefits

Improved quality of the products and improved debugging of the systems in the early, relatively inexpensive stages of the life cycle are the two most obvious benefits of the walkthrough technique. However, there are other equally important benefits.

As discussed earlier, if the DP group is utilizing the chief programmer team organization, walkthroughs tend to raise the level of expertise of all team members to that of its most effective member, because reviewing the work of the best worker sends the rest of the team back to school on this example. Even the lowliest and least experienced team members can learn from this exercise.

During the system development life cycle activities, the pressure of meeting schedules and deadlines often blinds team members and management alike to the critical need for education of the team in the details of the evolving system. The individual team members can become so narrowly focused on their own specific area of responsibility that they lose sight of the big picture that is so important in maintaining the correct perspective. Walkthroughs provide effective product- and project-oriented lessons for every project team member, as well as for the other attendees. In fact, some walkthroughs are deliberately scheduled with primarily the educational objective in mind.

Another benefit of the walkthrough technique is that in order for it to work effectively, some design and documentation standards must exist. These standards provide the project team members and other walkthrough attendees with at least a common basis of understanding of the product. For example, if there is a standardized format and contents list for the System Design document, the review of that document is simplified because specific types of information are always in the same place. The more widespread and accepted the standards are, the more easily the walkthroughs will be successfully accomplished. In addition, the walkthroughs themselves will greatly assist in the general acceptance of the standards. Of course, the standards must be practical and usable or the missionary work carried out by the walkthrough disciples will be all for naught, and the walkthrough technique itself will become discredited.

Today, most data processing organizations have at least some standards or guidelines in place. The best of these standards encourage conformity and consistency in documentation, data naming conventions, design techniques, and coding rules. Unfortunately, standards are not easy to enforce in a high-technology profession such as data processing. Not only are standards difficult to implement, but it is hazardous duty to try monitoring the level of adherence to them. (Even to have been employed in a standards department in some organizations can hinder or stop one's career advances.) The image of the industrial engineering monitor, with clipboard and stopwatch in hand, still looms large as an industrial "bogeyman." The use of the walkthrough process, however, allows for painless and participatory monitoring of standards. Additionally, it is much easier to insist upon the use of common standards when each project team member has been shown how the standards should be applied. Walking through a program listing that is coded according to the best structured programming standards is more effective in convincing a programming team of the quality of those standards than are ten textbooks on the subject written by ten structured gurus.

14.9 Code inspections

Fagan, in the *IBM Systems Journal* [15], described a formal version of the walkthrough that he named a code inspection. Fagan's inspections follow generally the same process described here, the major differences being the number of discrete stages defined in the process (five instead of three), the detailed instructions on how to inspect the product, and the apparent concentration on the more technical stages of the life cycle. For those organizations prepared to commit the additional investment required to implement Fagan's precise and formal monitoring tool, the payback in higher quality and reduced errors in the final product can be significant. There is no doubt that the extreme formality of Fagan's inspections could be extended beyond using them only for system designs, program code, and test plans. However, the degree of training and subsequent monitoring required to apply them to earlier products of the life cycle may well be prohibitive.

14.10 Summary

Out of the plethora of panaceas, methodologies, and techniques of the structured revolution, the walkthrough seems now to be the least expensive, the most accepted, and one of the most effective techniques for improving product quality and programmer productivity. Certainly, it is more effective in the structured development environment, where life cycle stages, structured design and programming, and project teams are a way of life, than it is in the BS era organization.

Nevertheless, the technique is very powerful and effective even in unstructured environments and can be instrumental in moving such environments out of the dark ages into the modern system development era. The degree of formality can be tailored to fit the organization's culture; no special software, forms, or training are required; and the implementation can and should be carried out almost unnoticed. The walkthrough also has an important secondary use as an educational tool and as a gentle enforcer of standards.

15

The Project Library

Consider what you have in the smallest chosen library. A company of the wisest and wittiest men that could be picked out of all civilized countries in a thousand years have set in the best order the results of their learning and wisdom. The men themselves were hid and inaccessible, solitary, impatient of interruption, fenced by etiquette; but the thought which they did not uncover to their bosom friend is here written out in transparent words to us, the strangers of another age.

— Ralph Waldo Emerson

15.1 History

All libraries use the recording media of the time. The first libraries used stone tablets, then scrolls made of animal skins, and later papyrus appeared. The earliest mechanical printing, instead of individually hand-formed characters, appeared in China on rolls and scrolls of crude paper over one thousand years ago. It was five hundred or more years after that when printed books first appeared in Europe. The year 1456 saw Gutenberg's printed Bible in Germany, and in 1477 the Englishman William Caxton printed *The Dictes or Sayengis of the Philosophres.* The next year, Caxton printed the famous *Canterbury Tales* by Chaucer. The printing press heralded a new age when many copies of a book or document could be produced and, in theory, libraries of knowledge could be set up for all people to share. Hitherto, libraries had been utilized by only a very small, elite group of privileged scholars.

So, for five hundred years, libraries consisted mainly of collections of books, both private and public. The advent of the computer, however, has changed all that. Libraries now also contain electronically coded information, which is stored on machine-readable media, not human-readable pages. This stored information is accessible to people, however, and it can be displayed temporarily on the ubiquitous video screen or printed out on paper for more permanent retention. Computerized information is still only a very small percentage of the information in general-purpose libraries; other non-printed media such as phonograph records, audio and video tapes, video disks, and microfilm also are available for storage of information.

In the small, special-purpose private libraries in use within business, research laboratories, and military installations, however, the highly varied types of access and large number of users are not present, and so the digitized, computer-accessible electronic media are becoming the standard methods of storing information. For storing the information about a new data processing system, obviously the corresponding project library would be a computerized information store. But we human beings are still not completely comfortable with all-electronic information, so even data processing project libraries contain some paper information that we can touch, feel, and see. This may be only a temporary phase.

15.2 Definition and principles

As I have stated many times already, the end product of each stage of the system development life cycle constitutes documentation of one form or another. Over the complete life cycle of a major product, this means that a great deal of documentation is produced. Whether the documentation is manually or electronically stored, significant efforts are required originally to generate the documentation and then subsequently to keep it current and accurate as the associated system evolves. Accuracy and currency are two very good reasons for a central documentation storage and controlling area, called the project library.

What is a project library?* It is a combination of human-readable and machine-readable information about the progress of the system development project and the system being developed by the project. All of the life cycle stage end products are part of the library, as are the programs, data files, databases, data dictionaries, procedures, and processes that constitute the developing system. Hence, at any point in the life cycle, all known information about that system should be contained in the corresponding project library. Clearly, if a complete system data dictionary is being used, as recommended earlier, it will be part of the project library and will contain a reference to all other parts of the library.

Unfortunately, programmers and other DP professionals in general do not enjoy creating documentation. Worse, even those few who do enjoy documenting are often bad at it. Bad documentation, in terms of inaccuracy, ambiguity, and omission, is sometimes worse than no documentation at all. Sad to say, ignoring a problem does not make it disappear, contrary to that widely held opinion. Therefore, even though no one wants or can be found to do it, the documentation of a developing system must be done and it must be done accurately and consistently by the members of the project team. To many DP professionals, this task seems more daunting than all of the twelve labors of Hercules. Of course, the word-processing techniques available today can help minimize much of the drudgery in creating and maintaining the system's documentation.

Not only must the documentation of the system have all of the previously mentioned qualities of accuracy, consistency, and unambiguity, but it also must meet documentation standards defined by the DP and user organizations. Additionally, there must be a clear separation between what is regarded as development or test documentation and the production versions. Similarly, the system, as it resides on the computer

---

*I shall use the term project library, though it is variously known as the project support library, the program production library, or the development support library.

or computers and on the storage media of disks, tapes, solid-state storage, and others, must have at least two parts: one inviolable, heavily protected production part; and an equivalent, development part upon which all updates, corrections, and enhancements are first tested. This need for the control and separation of the development and production systems with their related documentation is what first prompted the concept of the project library in the mid-1960s.

Today, as more and more critical business functions are being automated often with extremely sensitive data, the need for strict control and reliable security of the systems becomes vital. Yet, at the same time, DP professionals must be allowed to work closely with test versions of these systems and their data in order to fix and enhance the systems without being obstructed and frustrated by many levels of bureaucratically inspired security. But, if the boundaries between the test systems and the live production versions are not closely controlled, the very characteristics that make the systems easy to maintain and enhance can also provide the careless and the unscrupulous with easy, unauthorized access to sensitive data and classified procedures. Again, the project library can minimize the confusion between production and test systems and ensure their security from unauthorized access.

The project library is a tool that can stand alone and be used effectively in any type of programming environment or organization. However, the library is more valuable and more manageable in projects that make full use of structured design and coding, a stage-by-stage development methodology, and a team concept of project organization. The reason is that the structured techniques, by creating separate, controllable modules in a logical manner and in a logical sequence, facilitate the creation of meaningful and manageable data structures and levels in the library. Hence, the techniques make it easier to structure the library, to provide security, to control releases, and to provide rigorous back-up and recovery procedures. In effect, the project library concept is one of the basic philosophies necessary to support the broad use of the complete spectrum of the structured techniques.

In summary then, the basic principles and goals of the project library are these:

- All documentation related to the project is stored and referenced in one central location.
- All code and related programming products are the public property of the project and the organization, but they all are rigorously controlled in terms of meeting established standards and of preventing unauthorized access at every stage or level of the product's development and at all stages of the system development life cycle.
- Clerical and routine work is carried out centrally and consistently and is isolated from technical work as much as possible so that technical personnel are relieved of routine tasks.

With this introduction to the project library, we now need to consider first the role of the library's caretaker, followed by a look at its detailed contents and its structure.

15.3 Role of the project librarian

The library is maintained, surprisingly enough, by a project librarian, who is the sole interface between the programmers and most of the project library, as described in Section 15.5. The librarian's primary responsibility is to maintain complete and up-to-date representations of all code, programs, and test data for the project team, and to keep a current status of the project's progress for management. His duties are these:

- to maintain strict control over all project programming and documentation assets
- to relieve technical project personnel from purely clerical duties (including activities such as documentation, updates, project status reporting, proofreading of project narrative descriptions, data generation, and data entry)
- to protect the production environment

The project librarian is an integral member of the project team. In a project library that includes complete and rigorously defined procedures, the librarian is not primarily a technician, although some formal DP-oriented training or experience is required. A familiarity with DP operations, particularly data entry and operational scheduling, is desirable and can be obtained through training courses in DP operations.

More important perhaps than having basic technical skills is having the correct personality traits. In order for the librarian to fit into the project development team and obtain the full confidence of all its members, he must be orderly, with disciplined thought and work habits; be meticulous about detail; be persistent in following through to assure documentation is updated as changes are made; be calm, not easily flustered or distracted; be able to work with technical people and to readily understand their jargon, often under pressure; and have lots of patience and a sense of humor, probably the most important personality requirement.

In some projects, the librarian is requested to perform standard secretarial duties, such as typing letters and reports and placing telephone calls. When secretarial work is included, the librarian is often called a programming secretary. This is definitely not a recommended variation, as the identification of the librarian with the team product rapidly becomes tenuous in this situation.

If the chief programmer team type of organization is being used, the project librarian naturally becomes the custodian of the project library. Otherwise, a librarian needs to be specifically assigned to this role. It may be difficult to convince some project managers that they should give up a programmer's spot on the project's resource plan to a semiclerical person. But remember the basic system development facts of life: Programmers can spend up to fifty percent of their time doing project-related clerical work. Such work not only takes away time more effectively spent on programming, but also interrupts their technical work, causing a loss of concentration and effectiveness or even causing errors to be made.

Programmers may contest the idea of a project library and of public programming assets, claiming that they are capable of maintaining all programming documentation satisfactorily. In such cases, it may be wise to suggest that not all programmers are equally careful about maintaining documentation. Whether through persuasion or management direction, programmers must be convinced of the necessity of centralized control of all project documents.

15.4 Library contents

The project library consists of a set of machine-readable and human-readable data that, combined under the direction of a project librarian, allows the filing, retrieval, and maintenance of all of the code and associated documentation generated during system specification, design, coding, testing, and implementation. This set of data includes all intermediate code and documentation, in addition to the final product that is delivered to the operational users.

The machine-readable part of the library contains source code, object code, test data, control data, operational data, and so forth. These items are usually controlled by various support or utility programs, which can be manipulated by the librarian normally through the use of catalogued procedures provided as part of the library's software. These procedures can perform such functions as project record keeping, copying and moving of programs and modules, automatic indention of source listings, syntax checking, library statistics, reformatting, and many other routine activities. Such support software is sometimes available through routines incorporated in the resident operating system software.

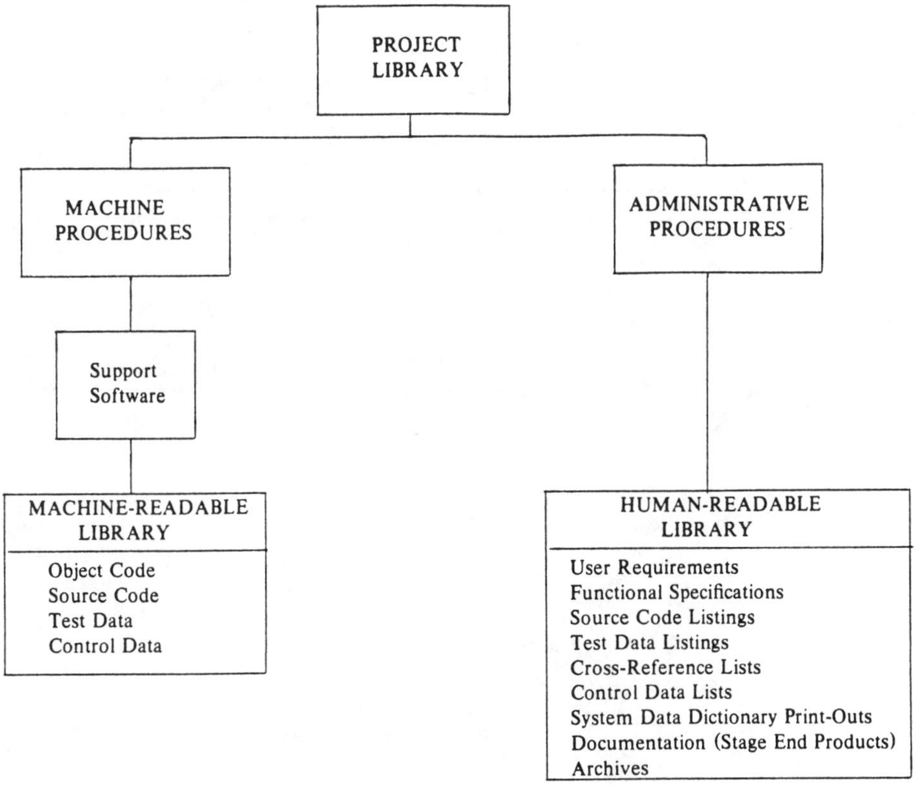

Figure 15-1. Contents of the project library.

The human-readable part of the library consists of user requirements, functional specifications, system and program design documents, program documentation, and operating procedures; it is kept in binders, in notebooks, on microfilm, or on electronic media in a word-processing system. The project librarian maintains this part of the library according to a complete set of administrative procedures that should be a DP organizational standard. Generally, the human-readable part of the library also contains lists of cross-references to different parts of the system; a directory of all contents of the library (a system data dictionary); and an archive of all superceded or corrected code and documentation, or at least a reference to where the archives are kept. An overview of the contents of the project library is given in Figure 15-1.

15.5 Library levels

The library serves several different functions, some of which can be represented by different levels. The levels are designed to help manage the system development process in a controlled manner and to prevent unauthorized updates to the production system once it is installed. Two important functions involve security and auditing requirements, and specific assignment of responsibility for the various levels is the first step toward developing security procedures for the system's data. Normally, four levels are sufficient, and some small projects use fewer than four. The library shown in Figure 15-2 has four levels, each of which is discussed in the subsections that follow.

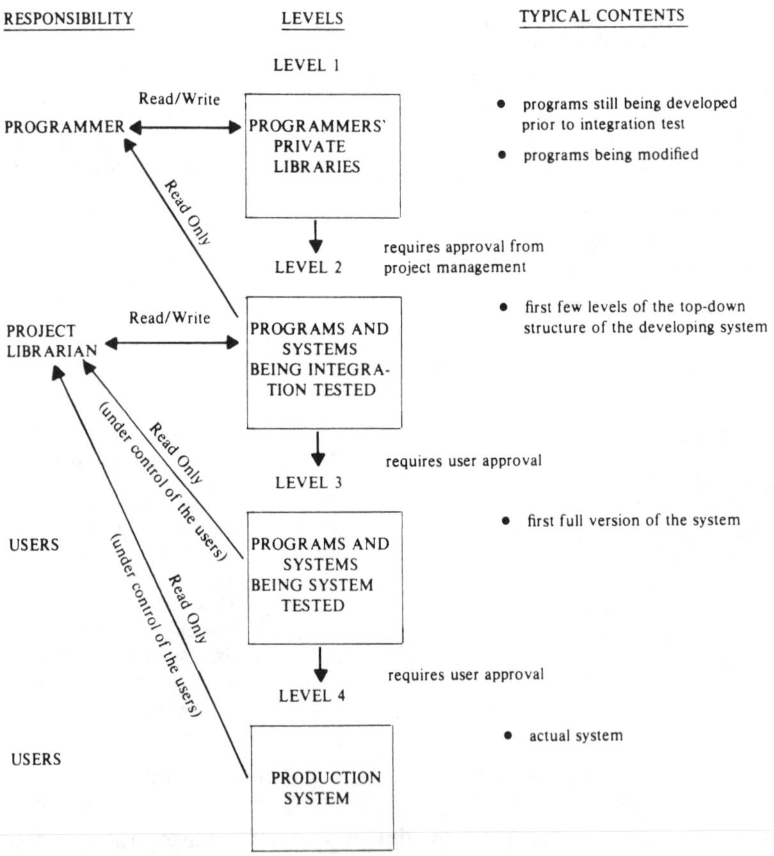

Figure 15-2. Levels of the project library.

15.5.1 Level 1 — Programmers' private libraries

Level 1 of the library contains all of the programs and modules that the individual programmers are developing, testing, maintaining, or enhancing at any given time within the definition of the project. Source code and load modules, test data, procedures, and even some documentation are contained at this level. A typical manifestation of this library level is private time sharing option (TSO) disk packs that only individual programmers generally have access to. Each programmer has unlimited access only to his portion of level 1. The project librarian generally has read-only access to this part of the library and can transfer programs to level 2 from level 1 only when approved by project management.

15.5.2 Level 2 — Programs and systems being integration tested

Parts of the system being stored at level 2 of the library have been completed by the programmers responsible, approved by project management, and are ready to be tested in an integrated fashion to ensure that they actually do work together. This is the point in a structured environment at which the top-down, hierarchical structure of the system starts to take shape.

The project librarian is usually given the specific responsibility to control the building of this level. Programmers have read-only access to level 2 and can invoke this only through the librarian when their programs fail their related integration test and need to be modified. The modified programs will then be copied back to level 2 to be retested. When integration testing is satisfactorily completed, the user makes the decision to transfer the system from level 2 to level 3, usually with assistance from the project librarian.

15.5.3 Level 3 — Programs and systems being system tested

Level 3 contains the full version of the system that is to be tested and eventually handed over to the user as the production system. If problems are discovered during system testing, the librarian is requested by the user and the DP development manager to copy or read the relevant parts of the system back to level 2 or even level 1 for modifications and retesting. When the system testing at level 3 is satisfactorily completed, the users authorize the copying of the system from level 3 to level 4.

15.5.4 Level 4 — Production system

The final, fully tested production version of the system is stored at level 4. At this time, all "test-only" facilities and data are removed from the system. Changes to the production system can be authorized only by the users of the system, and even then the parts of the system to be modified must go back at least to level 2 of the library before moving through level 3 back into production at level 4.

This multilevel concept is best implemented through one of the many automated library packages that are available today; my recommendations for two commercial systems appear in Section 15.8. In an emergency, the user may need to authorize an override of the system to get a quick fix into production. In this case, the correct procedures should be carried out retroactively to ensure that all changes are recorded, potential side effects resolved, and all necessary documentation updates carried out. The user is responsible for ensuring that this retroactive action occurs; and in doing so, he normally enlists the aid of the DP development manager and the project librarian.

The traditional view of the project library, as described by a series of papers and documents in the late 1960s and early 1970s, was one of the library and the librarian operating at the center of a network of controls and procedures. All compilations, test runs, changes to code, and documentation had to be coordinated through the librarian. In the predominantly on-line, interactive program development environment of the 1980s, this traditional view of the library is impractical and, if implemented, would only obstruct the progress of the project.

By contrast, the process of utilizing the various levels of the library allows the development programmers full flexibility in using the interactive facilities of their environment. Only when the programs are being built into a structure that can be integration tested does the control of the librarian need to be employed.

15.6 Benefits

The primary benefits of a successful project library are those that reflect its basic goals:

- tighter control over project programming and documentation assets
- minimized clerical workload for programmers and other technical project staff
- protection of the production system from unauthorized access

Even more, secondary advantages stemming from these basic benefits include

- improved communications made possible by accurate, up-to-date code and documentation available under controlled conditions to all project personnel, including management (increased visibility of project status for management)
- minimized risk of error caused by working with obsolete versions
- reduced time lost looking for the latest version of the system
- elimination of problems created by the departure (temporary or permanent) of a team member
- encouragement of egoless programming, with all of the associated benefits but without some of the undesirable, anarchic traits experienced by some practitioners
- greater availability of development measurement statistics
- increased reliability of the final product
- enhanced recovery in the case of system failures or other special problems, including loss of data
- enforcement of documentation standards because updating documentation is easier and because project management can oversee the complete set of documentation

Once installed, the project library must be used as a working tool throughout every stage of the project's life cycle and not just saved for use during the system test and implementation. Only in this way can the maximum benefit of the project library be realized.

15.7 Practical considerations

How then should the concepts of the project library and the project librarian be implemented? What problems are encountered when an apparently nontechnical function is introduced into the project team? And, how are changes to code in the library controlled? In the following paragraphs, I offer some tips gleaned from my experience.

15.7.1 Ratio of programmers to librarians

One basic implementation consideration is how many team members are required to support or to keep busy a full-time project librarian. Although a great deal depends upon such factors as the team members' level of programming skills, the programmer productivity achieved, and the complexity of the programming project, the general guideline is that between five and ten project team members can support (or be supported by) one full-time librarian.

In some cases, more than one project team could share one librarian. In other cases, the librarian's free time could be filled by secretarial duties, but this is not recommended, as stated in Section 15.3 above. It might be better from a team morale point of view to accept the slack time.

When secretarial duties are included as a standard part of the librarian's job, they should be defined clearly to the librarian in advance and made a part of the job description. Otherwise, the librarian may feel that he is being demeaned when asked to perform secretarial chores. In this case, there is a temptation to label the position programming secretary or something similar. This can create wage or salary problems, since it may be difficult to justify to personnel management a salary sufficiently above that of purely clerical wages to attract the right level of person. In some locations, of course, senior secretarial salaries may be higher than those that could be justified by the title of project librarian. Careful examination of the local job markets and of company wage and salary policies is advised. An alternative job title could be "Project Administrator."

15.7.2 Security and control

Ordinarily, rigorously defined and enforced procedures minimize the dangers of inadvertent changes to code or the loss of code or other data at critical stages. Special automatic or manual procedures can be installed that lock out unauthorized changes and avoid the cumulative effect of changes on dependent code, modules, or data. In effect, code and documentation at various stages can be kept within inviolable compartments, which can be accessed only by authorized personnel.

These compartments can exist at several different levels, as described earlier. Only after appropriate tests and updates are completed at each level and with proper authorization can the modified components be integrated with the rest of the system.

In addition, extensive cross-checks can be installed to reveal all of the components and data sets affected by any change to a particular module. Thus, a check can be made on all of the components dependent on, or related to, a particular module to ensure they are free from accidental changes in their current form before release into the production environment. The system data dictionary is an invaluable concept in achieving this level of control and cross-checking.

15.8 Automated library systems

There are many proprietary automated library systems on the market of various levels of sophistication and value. Many if not all of them were originally designed to solve specific problems and, as a result, different library systems are appropriate to different environments. Therefore, when choosing an automated library system, make sure that it enhances your specific library function and does not merely complicate it!

The following are some of the factors to be clearly defined before the decision regarding an automated library can be made:

- Is one already being used somewhere in the organization?
- Is it being used in a development or in a maintenance environment?
- Are the responsibilities of the librarian mainly technical? mainly administrative?
- What are the characteristics of the project's expected software, hardware, and operating system?
- What is the size of the project(s)? How many people are involved and for how long?
- Will one project or many projects use the library?
- What is the culture of the organization (that is, what is the attitude toward new methods)?

To answer the above questions, project members must decide upon the framework of the library and perhaps complete some of the preliminary system design before choosing the specific library system to be used. This should occur during the System Specification and System Design stages. For example, consider that you need to choose a library system for a combined maintenance and development environment that uses IMS on IBM mainframes with an expected large number of variable-sized projects. In this environment, the automated library system would obviously need to be compatible with IBM's operating system and with IMS; it would need to have a flexible structure in order to accommodate both large and small projects and maintenance activities; and its capacity would need to be large enough to cope with the large number of projects. The important consideration in choosing a system is that the required library structure defines the necessary automated system, and not the reverse.

Many of the major hardware and software manufacturers produce automatic library systems. One example is the on-line CICS source program maintenance system from IBM. Two library systems that are independent of the major hardware manufacturers are Panvalet [47] (from Pansophic Systems, Inc.) and Librarian [46] (from ADR, Inc.). Both systems subscribe to the library philosophy described in this chapter with password-type controls to ensure the security of modules and data above a certain defined level of development.

15.9 Summary

The project library is a key concept in the whole spectrum of the structured methodologies. It helps tie together many of the modern techniques of system development, but it also can be used as a stand-alone technique in any DP environment to improve programmer productivity. Specifically, the project library offers the production and maintenance of accurate and up-to-date documentation and the control of the integration of completed programs into a developing system.

16

The Evolving System Development Life Cycle

There is certain relief in change, even though it be from bad to worse; as I have found in travelling in a stage-coach, that it is often a comfort to shift one's position and to be bruised in a new place.

— Washington Irving

The system development life cycle as described in Chapters 6 through 12 is often referred to as the traditional life cycle. Unfortunately, it does not really live up to the definition of traditional, because the sequence of stages from Feasibility Study through Implementation is not yet regarded as second nature by the members of most DP development organizations. In fact, they may not have even heard of the life cycle, and may treat the development of a new system in the same way as Attila's Huns treated a potential new conquest — charge and overwhelm it with numbers! Clearly, changes are needed even to what is regarded as the traditional life cycle in order for more organizations to adopt its use and in order for them to adapt the life cycle to their own environment. In this chapter, I discuss five software development concepts that enhance the life cycle's effectiveness: the concepts of iteration, prototyping, nonprocedural languages, application generators, and application software packages. But first, let's examine the reasons for DP organizations' resistance to the traditional life cycle.

16.1 Resistance to new ideas

Most life cycle methodologies seem, unfortunately, to be characterized by massive volumes of procedures and formats that do little but gather dust on some project manager's bookshelf. This is because the misconception has arisen that in order to use such a methodology, an all or nothing policy must be adopted: Either all of the methodology's rules, procedures, and tasks must be used, or none of them. Obviously, using all of the contents of seven or eight bulky volumes for each project would be prohibitively intimidating and impractical. Therefore, in order to remain reasonably sane and efficient, the project manager often ignores the SDLC's volumes completely, leaves them on the shelf, and unwittingly invents the latest structured technique — structured bookends.

Project managers and DP professionals alike are justified in resisting an SDLC if it is presented to them simply as an exhaustive set of forms and rules to be slavishly adhered to. Instead, the SDLC should be regarded as a set of comprehensive guidelines that must be modified to fit individual organizations and individual projects. Each project can utilize a different set of those guidelines, and most DP organizations can usefully decide on a standard subset of life cycle activities that are applicable to their own environment.

Of course, the important concept within any life cycle methodology is that embodied in the various stage task lists discussed in Chapter 5. In fact, after the first reading of Chapters 6 through 12, you should realize that the most important parts required to develop a home-grown SDLC are the flow diagrams of each of the stage's activities.

Nevertheless, a sequential, logical progression through the stages is often an anathema to the seat-of-the-pants style of designer or developer. Why is this? Use of the life cycle stages forces the production of documentation at each stage. Additionally, heavy involvement by the user is encouraged. Both of these characteristics are resisted strongly by the typical old-style programmer who detests producing documentation and who often regards the user as a nuisance.

So, the fact remains that the so-called traditional system development life cycle is not traditional at all because it is not widely accepted by DP organizations. Meanwhile, innovative concepts in software development are transforming the sequential, stage-by-stage life cycle, rendering it obsolete and affecting its acceptance by DP organizations. The following sections describe some of the most important concepts.

16.2 Iteration

Among the exciting developments that add to the SDLC's effectiveness is a concept I've mentioned before. Iteration is allowed in structured design, for instance, within the life cycle stages so that the complete design, development, and implementation of some parts of the system are done before others. Let me illustrate this concept with the abstract example shown in Figure 16-1. As each level of the hierarchical structure is designed and coded, the system as it is being developed can be tested. Therefore, design, coding, and testing of level 1 may be complete, while only the design activities of levels 2, 3, and so on, have been carried out. Since the testing of level 1 may identify needed changes, some of the design work for level 1 may have to be repeated and level 1 may need to be tested again. This iterative process may occur at every level and several times at each of those levels of the system structure as it is developed.

What does this iteration mean to the sequential life cycle? It means that the seven stages are not visited only once each, but rather each stage can be entered several times if the top-down philosophy is used from the outset. The iterative path through the life cycle is shown in Figure 16-2.

The process of iteration is not exclusive to the use of the structured techniques. Whatever techniques are used to design and develop a system, there will be a need to redo some parts of the development cycle because of changes in requirements and errors found in testing. The difference is that this latter type of iteration is unplanned and unwanted, unlike the planned iteration mandated by the structured techniques.

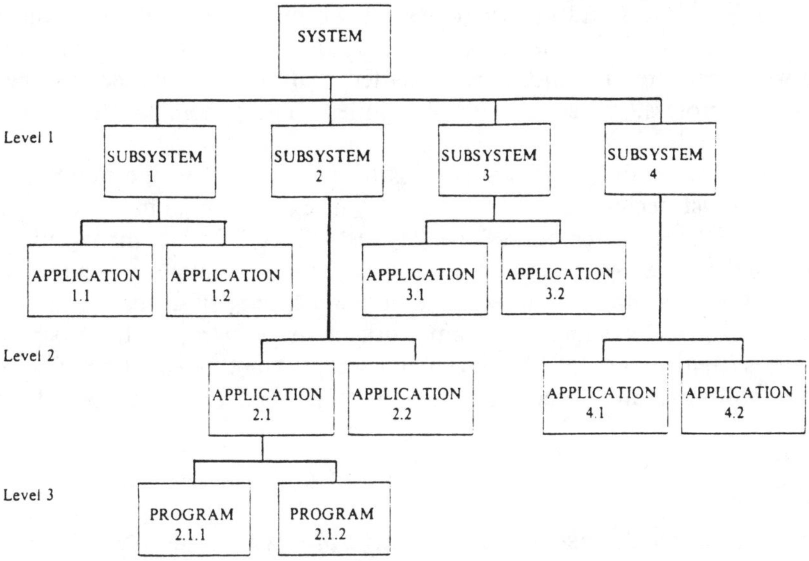

Figure 16-1. Hierarchical levels of a system.

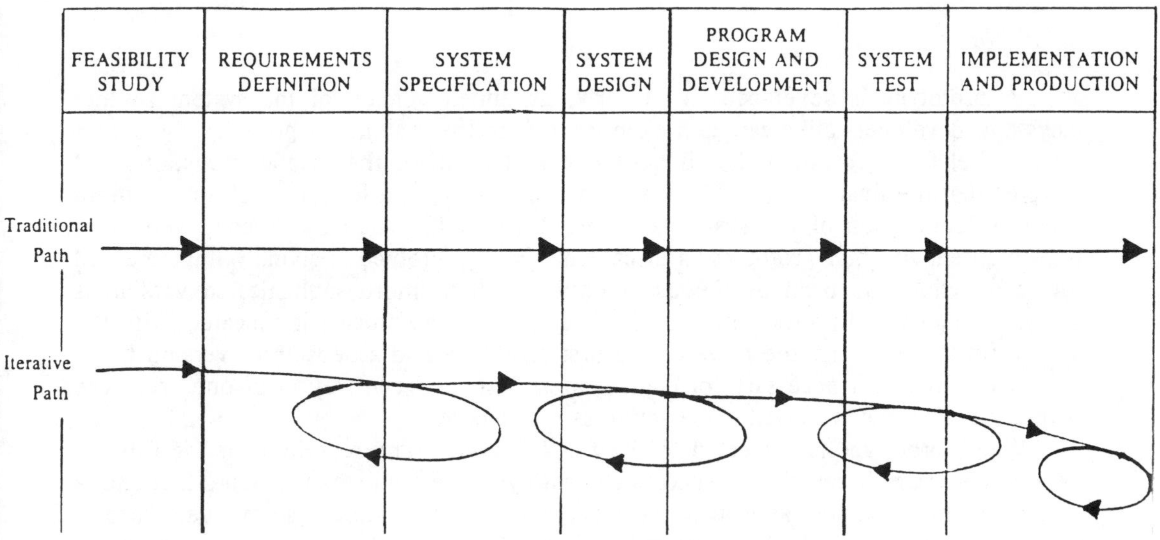

Figure 16-2. Traditional and iterative paths through the system development life cycle.

Although many project development teams accept the iterative approach, their managers may not formally accept it. Looping through the life cycle, although effective, is not without its problems, since management can no longer easily decide when a stage begins or ends. Also, management must determine what skills are required in order for personnel to be able to dive into and out of different stages. In the iterative approach, it is no longer a simple matter to identify the professional skills required in each stage, because many different activities may be occurring in parallel during any one stage. The trend in recent years has been to merge the disciplines of programming and system analysis, as discussed in Chapter 13. With the iterative life cycle, this trend will accelerate, and more user-oriented analysis skills will need to be integrated into the DP professional's portfolio of abilities. The generalist may make a comeback.

Along with determining what sort of skills are required in the iterative life cycle, managers also must decide what version of the design or program or whatever should be signed off of whenever the end of the stage is defined. Project management, for example, may define the System Design stage as being complete when enough design work has been carried out to enable the coding and testing of at least a first version of the system, a skeletal or superficial framework of the system, or the first one or two levels of the system hierarchy. Management accepts, in this situation, that additional design effort will probably be required once the initial version has been coded and tested.

16.3 Prototyping

Prototyping is an extension of the iterative processes made possible by the structured development methodologies. A *prototype* is defined as an original version or model on which a completed software system is formed. There are at least two approaches to prototyping in DP system development: separate prototyping and prototyping by progressive development.

16.3.1 Separate prototyping

A prototype is developed as an early, unrefined version of the system so that users and developers alike can gain experience with the system. It provides users with a basic feel for the system, but it does not contain all of the detailed functions and features that the final system will have. Simultaneously, in a longer timeframe, a more sophisticated version of the system is being developed. When this second version is implemented, the first prototype is discarded. Each prototype is actually implemented into production and used by the users until the next, more sophisticated version is ready. If the second prototype is not detailed enough, the process is repeated, with the second prototype taking the place of the first prototype and a new, third version being developed. It is not necessary, of course, to wait for the completion of one prototype before the next one is started. The activities can overlap.

Every prototype is subjected to the full life cycle. The repetition of the full life cycle is necessary because each successive prototype is effectively a new product and is treated in the same way as a major enhancement to an existing system. Later prototypes progress through the life cycle much faster than the earlier ones, since there is no need to completely repeat all of the activities in all of the stages for each prototype. Most of the work done in developing the design for earlier prototypes can be utilized for the later, more complete versions of the system. Additionally, the latter parts of the last two stages, System Test and Implementation and Production, can be omitted for some of the prototypes.

Figure 16-3 shows the overlapping life cycle stages of the development of three separate prototypes. The Feasibility Study and the Requirements Definition stages of the first prototype are completed before the second prototype is started. Similarly, the third prototype (the finished product, in this case) is not started until the System Specification stage of the second prototype is in progress. Therefore, at time A, the Program Design and Development of prototype 1, the System Specification of prototype 2, and the Feasibility Study of the finished product are all being carried out simultaneously.

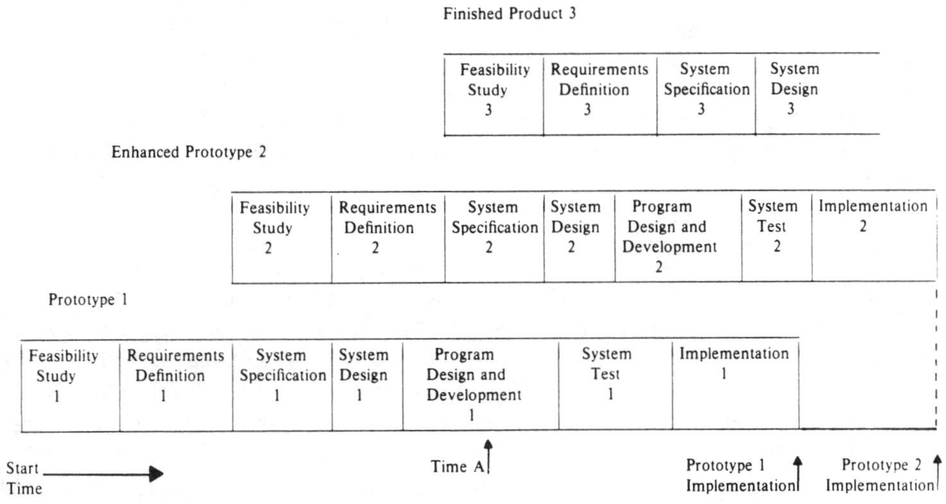

Figure 16-3. Three parallel lines of separate development of prototypes.

16.3.2 Prototyping by progressive development

The second major approach to prototyping is not really a great change from the first approach. Instead of earlier prototypes being discarded, in this approach the prototypes themselves are used as the basis for further development and refinement, iteratively, until the final, satisfactory product is implemented. So, in this type of prototyping, not just the work alone or knowledge gained by developing earlier prototypes is used, but each prototype itself is modified to form the next prototype.

The same overlapping stages of development occurs, as shown in Figure 16-3, but there is a conscious effort to use the end products of the earlier prototypes' life cycle stages. This progressive development type of prototyping is not very different from the iterative development resulting from the use of the structured development techniques, except that as successive prototypes are developed, the life cycle stages and activities become more compressed and reduced. Less and less of the full life cycle is necessary as the development and implementation of the final prototype approaches.

The main difference in practice between the two major approaches to prototyping is that, in the first approach, each separate prototype is often implemented with quite different software and different programming languages. For instance, the first, primitive prototype may be developed using a user-friendly language such as BASIC or RAMIS on a minicomputer or personal computer. When the user has gained enough experience with this prototype to refine the original specification, if necessary, the later prototypes may need the power of COBOL or FORTRAN in an MVS/TSO environment, for example, for full development. Of course, with the rapid development of user-friendly languages and sophisticated, powerful personal computers, the different techniques used to develop separate prototypes will inevitably disappear and the separate prototyping approach will automatically change to prototyping by progressive development.

A significant distinguishing factor of both prototyping techniques is that early versions of the system are developed completely so that the user can start working with the system and, in some cases, actually begin using it in a limited fashion. This is in contrast to the traditional practice of making the users wait until the System Test stage before they can get hands-on experience. With prototyping, the user is involved throughout the life cycle. In this way, the DP development organization can be confident of implementing the system that users really want. Because the users have early experience with the system prior to implementation, often another beneficial result of prototyping is fewer user-requested changes during the system's production lifetime.

16.4 Nonprocedural languages

The most commonly used programming languages during the 1960s and 1970s were those referred to as "procedural" languages. Put very simply, these languages are heavily formatted and need to be written within a fairly rigid logical and physical structure. Assembly languages such as IBM's BAL are the most procedural. COBOL, PL/I, FORTRAN, and even PASCAL, BASIC, and ADA, although more free-form, are also procedural languages.

Since the start of the 1980s, there has been a strong user-directed move toward the increased use of nonprocedural, more natural programming languages that allow a human language-type of dialogue between the programmer and the computer. With the distribution of inexpensive computing power to the end users, this trend toward nonprocedural, user-friendly languages will continue.

If the users can effectively develop programs and systems using these nonprocedural languages, a large part of the Program Design and Development stage of the life cycle can be eliminated, and perhaps the System Design stage can also be shortened. Certainly, the tasks of the users, system designers, and programmers will become somewhat merged and the distinctions between their functions will become decidedly blurred. Currently, there are few truly nonprocedural languages available, but such products as RAMIS, MARK IV, MARK V, CULPRIT, and DYL 280 are providing many non-DP users with the power of the computer without having to call on the services of the DP development organization, other than for initial training.

16.5 Application generators

Application generators, still in their infancy in the early 1980s, are software systems that generate code for programs and systems from a formatted list of specifications. The most effective of these application generators allow the developer to produce the program code via a conversational, interactive session at a terminal. In such a session, the system requests the developer to enter such basic information as what type of program is required (file update, report generator, transaction processor, and so on). As more information is entered, the questions become more sophisticated and detailed until the generator has received all of the necessary information about the program or system to be developed. At that time, a first, fully coded version of the program, perhaps the prototype, is automatically generated from an internal library of routines.

Because these routines have already been thoroughly tested, clearly such tools can eliminate not only much of the Program Design and Development activities, but also much of the System Design and System Test stages. Moreover, the programs produced by the generator are consistent and accurate. With an application generator, a moderately complex COBOL program of 1,000 to 2,000 lines of code can be developed from its specifications and be ready for testing in just three to four hours, maybe less. There seems to be no theoretical limit to the size or complexity of the programs and systems that application generators can be used to create. However, currently only small- to medium-size programs of average complexity (up to 5,000 lines of COBOL) are within the capacity of these tools. For this reason, application generators offer improved productivity over conventional methods.

Two major types of application generators seem to be evolving. One type produces source code, usually in COBOL. The developers can then modify the code directly as in traditionally developed software. The second type requires that changes be made to the generated programs via the generator itself. Most users seem to prefer the first type, but this preference may shift to the second type as they become more comfortable with application generators.

In sum, application generators that produce consistently accurate code offer greatly improved programmer productivity over other methods. As their benefits are recognized, application generators will be employed more in the future by DP and user organizations within large corporations.

16.6 Application software packages

With the benefits that application generators offer, many software houses are already employing them to produce high-quality application software packages for their clients. These packages now being marketed are so good and are produced at such a low cost that it is becoming increasingly difficult for internal DP organizations to justify developing their own systems.

As I said above, use of those software packages effectively eliminates most of the required activities in the System Design, Program Design and Development, and System Test stages. Although all of the task lists for these life cycle stages would still be valid, many of the tasks themselves would become trivial if purchased software could meet all or most of the system requirements.

16.7 The new system development life cycle

With the new techniques and tools described earlier, the total effect on the traditional system development life cycle can be quite dramatic if they all are implemented in one organization. In practice, a mixture of the techniques would probably be used, although not all at one time. Figure 16-4 demonstrates how the use of these concepts can affect the seven-stage life cycle and conceivably reduce it to four stages.

As shown in the figure, the Feasibility Study and the Requirements Definition stages require little change. Application generators, nonprocedural languages, and purchased software packages can be employed by the users during Requirements Definition to produce an automated definition of the system. These new system development techniques are not only encouraging the full-time involvement of the users with the complete life cycle, but the user and DP functions in many cases are becoming inextricably merged. With the users beginning to effectively develop their own systems and to use nonprocedural languages and application generators when purchased software will not do the job, the differences between the user requirements and the System Specification document become minimized. Therefore, the System Specification stage can be eliminated as a separate activity and combined with the Requirements Definition stage, and the need for the System Specification document also disappears.

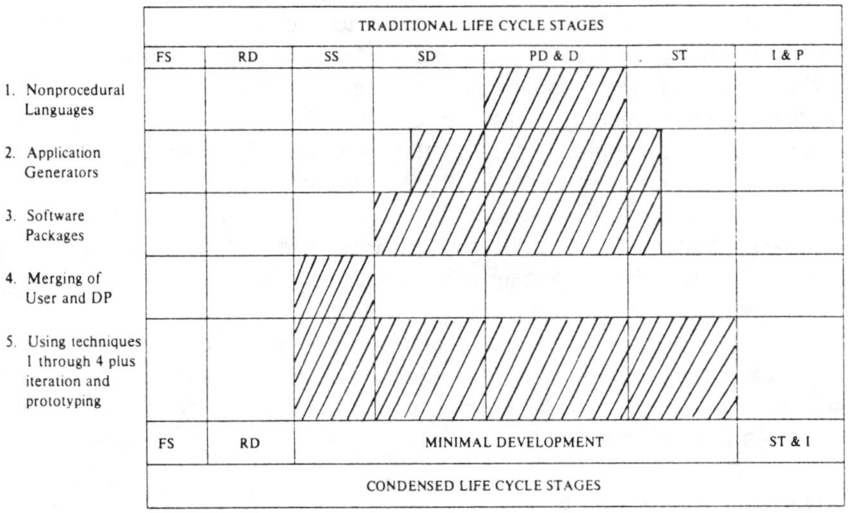

Figure 16-4. A condensed system development life cycle.

By the end of this new Requirements Definition stage, the first prototype of the system may well be available. Therefore, some system design and some program design and development is completed during this new stage.

Following the Requirements Definition stage, a single development stage involving further design, coding, and testing but with generally reduced activity is needed to refine the system into its final form ready for system testing and implementation. The amount of effort required in this development stage is highly variable. If a purchased software package proves to be sufficient to meet all of the system's requirements, the development time will be zero. If no suitable package can be purchased, both users and DP developers will need to perform some application development using nonprocedural languages and application generators.

Irrespective of the techniques and methodologies used to generate the system, acceptance testing is always needed, for the end users would be foolish to rely on the assurances of the software manufacturers or even their own colleagues that the system does not need testing. Acceptance testing takes the form of a system test, as described in Chapter 11.

Even with this greatly reduced development life cycle, the original set of activities for all seven traditional stages must still be examined to determine their validity in the new situation. Clearly, many of the tasks and activities will no longer be necessary for the developer to carry out explicitly, not because they are no longer required, but because they will have been effectively achieved by the purchased software or by the system software in the application generator packages. Therefore, the new development techniques will reduce the time required for the life cycle through automation and efficient implementation of the tasks.

Iteration and prototyping will still be used within the condensed life cycle, particularly when application generators are used. These particular tools lend themselves easily to the production of versions of progressively greater sophistication.

The trend toward the automation of the detailed programming activities and the increasingly heavy involvement of the users alarms many programmers and system analysts. These modern-day Luddites must recognize that change is constant. There is really no need for alarm; as the computer's power becomes more and more inexpensively available, the amount of new application development required will increase faster than new DP professionals can be employed and trained to carry out that development. Additionally, there will be an increasing need for specialized DP experts to support and maintain the software systems that provide the user-friendly computing facilities.

16.8 Summary

As we've seen, the traditional system development life cycle will be significantly affected by the current trends in system development methodologies. The overall effect will be to shorten the cycle into fewer, more user-oriented stages, with the encouragement of iteration and prototyping within the life cycle. The use of automated aids and packaged software will eliminate much of the detailed programming and coding activities practiced in the traditional life cycle. Tasks and end products identified in the standard seven-stage life cycle will still need to be considered, but many of them will have been automated, allowing the users to become intimately involved with the design and development of their systems. Finally, the data processing profession will move closer to its ultimate role: providing efficient service to assist business in meeting its information processing goals.

17
The Future

Predicting the future is a strange and elusive art. Many well-respected historical figures would have been considerably less well respected if their followers had had the benefit of hindsight to judge their statements.

For instance, Julius Frontinus, leading military engineer to the Roman Emperor Vespasian in the first century A.D., was heard to say, "I will ignore all ideas for new works and engines of war, the invention of which has reached its limits and for whose improvement I see no further hope." Poor Julius would be quite dismayed, I fear, by the sight of a modern warship or supersonic fighter-bomber, not to mention a space-borne multitargeted thermonuclear ballistic missile.

Shortsighted predictions are not limited to ancient times, however. Lord Kelvin, a prominent physicist whose name was given to the Kelvin temperature scale, stated publicly at the end of the nineteenth century, "Radio has no future. . . . X-rays will prove to be a hoax. . . . Heavier-than-air flying machines are impossible."

The twentieth century has had its moments also. In the late 1950s, just a few short years before Yuri Gagarin's historic, single-orbit journey, the president of Britain's Royal Astronomical Society stated that man would never travel into space because the environment is "too hostile."

After all these great men have failed so dismally in their predictions, I am somewhat nervous about my own. Perhaps Winston Churchill's advice, given in Cairo in 1943, is the best available on guessing the future: "I always avoid prophesying beforehand, because it is a much better policy to prophesy after the event has already taken place."

Of course, men do not necessarily take the advice of others, so I will press on. The DP profession in the 1980s is at a transitional point. There is far too much new development to do and not enough time and resources to do it.

In this book, I recommend a set of available techniques and tools that DP project managers can use to improve the productivity of their staff and the quality of the software products for which they are responsible. This recommended set, however, assumes that the traditional system development life cycle, or a derivative of it, is used to control the development activities. Even with the optimum use of all of the techniques and tools mentioned in the previous chapters, the productivity of the DP developers will probably be increased by no more than a hundred percent. Most of my experience with these tools indicates a productivity increase of considerably less than a hundred percent. Unfortunately, an increase in productivity on the order of a thousand percent is required to even significantly reduce the current backlog of new system development. In order to make some impression on the rapidly increasing new demands for DP systems, a dramatic revolution in how these systems are developed is required.

17.1 The role of education

How can the DP industry start to develop better and more maintenance-free systems? One answer must be through education and training that emphasize consistent design practices, good documentation, full user involvement in system development, and thorough testing before implementation. There are three main sources of education for data processing professionals: first, schools, colleges, and universities; second, professional training schools for data processing; and third, internal company training courses.

The first educational path normally results in the student's obtaining a degree in computer science. The graduate learns all there is to know about language compilers, esoteric hashing algorithms, and the Backus-Naur notation for programming languages, and he learns the most elegant way to add all the elements in an n-dimensional matrix — all great stuff, but probably not too useful in helping to get the new COBOL payroll system installed successfully five days before year's end.

I remember once demonstrating the Jackson design methodology, showing how the method can allow a relative novice in program design to easily design a simple reports program in minutes. One obviously young, earnest, and recent graduate of a computer science program asked, "But what about the eight Queens problem? Can this method solve that?" I replied with what I considered an equally relevant question, "What did you have for lunch?"

Computer science curricula just do not seem to be geared toward teaching someone how to fit into a program development team and, as part of that team, how to meet schedules and to program several mundane routines per month accurately, efficiently, and with monotonous regularity. (Of course, it would be hard to justify a four-year, full-time university course to do just that!)

In a field that is changing as rapidly as data processing, a four-year curriculum can probably never hope to be less than four years out of date in terms of information about software and hardware, design methodologies, management techniques, and so on. Also, many of the professors, bless their hearts, may never have worked in a production environment in which producing the perfect solution six months after the deadline is as bad as producing nothing at all. It may well be that the computer science graduates are not the right candidates for our system development teams. Perhaps asking these bright young people to code COBOL applications is an insult to them and to their qualifications. Or, perhaps the job of programmer or system analyst has been glamorized too much in the trade press so that the entry-level data processor feels let down when he fully realizes what the job really means. For whatever reasons, colleges and universities do not seem to supply quite the education needed for the job of programmer or system analyst. A university degree should prepare the student for much more than just a single profession. It should be a training ground for adult life, of which one single programming position is, I hope, only a small part.

Then there are the professional DP schools that fill the classified pages of some popular science magazines with their exhortations, "Take the first step to a better life! Become a computer programmer." These, too, perform a service, but is it a service that we need? To be sure, some professional programmer schools and operator training organizations turn out competent, well-trained, and effective graduates. But too often, these schools produce graduates who have been given a very rudimentary introduction to data processing, who are being pushed through the courses at an alarming, production-line pace, and who know only one specific localized DP environment. In their defense, these schools are reacting to a strong market demand that is steadily increasing; but I feel uncomfortable about the product of a school that advertises for its students on a matchbook cover.

The third major source of training for data processing people is the internal programs of many large data processing organizations. Some of these are excellent, especially those that involve trainers and instructors who are regularly rotated through the application development areas to refresh their practical experience. Major advantages of these in-house programs are that they can be geared to the specific environment of the organizations; they can generally use more state-of-the-art hardware and software than either the universities or the professional schools; and they can be updated quickly and easily with new techniques, methodologies, and standards as they are developed by the organization itself.

However, all of these desirable qualities must be taken advantage of in order for the internal training programs to be an improvement over the other types of training. Any lack of attention to the program results in a stagnation of the course content and a gradual erosion of the relevance of the training to the organization that it is trying to serve.

Some improvements to data processing education should be made in the following areas. Universities and colleges must recognize at least two specific and different needs: The need to produce computing gurus to develop and support new operating system and programming languages is already being met with the existing computer science curricula. The second need, that of more practical data processing training, must be met by the universities, colleges, and professional schools all working together. This is starting to happen with the development of model curricula for data processing by such organizations as the Association for Computing Machinery (ACM) and the Data Processing Management Association (DPMA) in cooperation with some universities. These curricula must concentrate on application program design, popular commercial programming languages, and the use of commercial environmental aids such as IBM's Time Sharing Option (TSO). Development of new curricula must be accelerated to meet the demand; otherwise, the overflow will continue to be under-trained, poorly trained, and a constant danger to their organizations and the integrity of their profession. This activity deserves serious funding and support by industry. The funding should be initially directed in the form of grants and scholarships to those organizations involved in developing practical data processing training curricula.

Commercial data processing organizations must devote the resources to develop, maintain, and keep current their internal training programs. The internal development or hiring of good data processing practitioners who can also communicate efficiently with their colleagues (a rare breed) is an investment that will pay off many times over.

Data processing professionals should spend at least ten percent of their time in training because of the constant, rapid developments in the profession. Most data processing organizations could triple or even quadruple their training budgets and not even come close to that ten percent figure. (I have heard that some DP organizations have no training budget at all — this is probably only a vicious rumor, spread by disgruntled DP professionals!)

Why all this talk about education? Education and training are how we impart all of the standards, techniques, and methods to the practitioners of our profession. Up to now, the education has been haphazard at best, downright destructive at worst. Certainly, the nature of data processing education that our system analysts, designers, and programmers have received has had a direct result on the types of system that we have installed: DP systems of inconsistent quality and standards.

To illustrate my point, I'll relate a story. There is an old man who runs a small lumber yard in the forests of the State of Washington. The small yard is part of a vast, nationwide, lumber-producing enterprise, but the old man just cuts down trees and saws them into logs. He's been cutting and handling logs the same way for forty years. One day, two executives from the big city nearby check the records and decide that the old man's productivity is too low. They drive, to the small lumber yard in their gleaming, four-wheel drive pick-up truck and quietly watch the old man at work. After a while, the executives climb out of the truck and tell the old man, "You could produce many more logs in a day if you used a chain saw instead of that old hand saw. We're going to get you a chain saw." The old man agrees and carries on with his sawing.

The executives drive to the nearest hardware store, return to the yard, and present a new chain saw to the old man in his log cabin. It's dark now and he has finished work for the day. He says, "Thank you very much" to the executives and promises to use the chain saw the very next day.

A month passes and the two executives check the records again. "You know," says one of them, "that old man's productivity hasn't improved a bit with that chain saw – in fact, it's gotten worse. I think we'd better go see him." So once again, the sleek pick-up truck roars into the small lumber yard. The old man is resting, sitting on a log. The executives express their concern and the old man agrees, "That newfangled saw didn't help very much."

One of the executives says, "Well, perhaps you're not using it quite right. I'll show you how." The old man smiles. The executive picks up the saw and pulls the starter; the saw roars, "Brrrrrrr, brrrrrrrr, brrr!" The old man jumps to his feet in fright. "What's that noise?" he asks.

We cannot simply provide the tools; we must ensure that we train the people in the proper use of the tools.

17.2 New systems, new roles

Not only must we train DP professionals to produce higher-quality systems faster, but new types of systems must be created to meet new demands for information. For example, there is an increasing need for management information systems (MIS) and executive information systems (EIS). These decision support systems provide the business executive with rapid access to information databases. Using very high-level, nonprocedural languages, they enable the executive to produce ad hoc reports, manipulate data, extrapolate trends, develop budgets, and produce multicolor graphic representations of business information – all at a terminal on the executive's desk. These systems allow the business manager to make better decisions faster, based on more accurate and timely data than ever before.

There will always be a need for the large, transaction-based processing systems, but these will be built by utilizing existing software packages. The detailed requirements for these systems may well be determined by the user and the DP professional working together with a user-friendly decision support system to produce a quick-and-dirty, reduced-function prototype of the required system, as described in Chapter 16.

This basic model will then be used to guide the purchase of the correct package or packages to implement the full system. In many situations, the prototype will actually be adequate for the purpose and no more development or implementation will need to be carried out.

Eventually, the users themselves will be able to develop most of their own systems, calling on the DP development department only when a new situation arises. This embodies the concept of the "Information Center," in which members of the DP department advise users of the DP facilities that are available and tutor the users on their operation. The Information Center also supports the DP facilities and updates them with new, suitable packages and techniques as they become available. The facilities themselves consist of nonprocedural, high-level languages, database management systems, preprogrammed basic reporting systems, and many business-oriented software packages for budgeting, planning, project management, statistical analysis, office automation, and so forth. Additionally, in most environments, the use of personal desk-top microcomputers is encouraged.

The software package industry of the 1980s and 1990s will continue to grow at an increasing rate as more and more DP organizations realize that purchasing software packages may be the only way to reduce the staggering size of their application development backlogs. Application generators will mature in the late 1980s; and although many business organizations will utilize these tools to develop their own business system, the software houses will find they can use them to build customized versions of their products at such a low cost that most non-DP business organizations will cease to develop their own system.

Those organizations that still find it necessary to build all or part of their own systems will use many of the techniques mentioned in Chapter 16 and in Appendices A and B, and the system development life cycle will be similar to the extremely foreshortened set of four stages suggested in Chapter 16. Software engineering, or the planned, structured building of software, will at last become a reality in those organizations.

No coding as we know it today will be carried out. Application generators and prototyping techniques will be used fully, and the required documentation will be produced automatically as part of the automated development process. Systems that today require six months and five programmer/analysts to move from system design to implementation will require perhaps two weeks and one business system analyst to carry out the equivalent task in 1995 or perhaps sooner!

Therefore, the future of the DP group lies partly in developing those few systems that require their esoteric services but more in supporting the user-friendly decision support and executive information systems described earlier. Supporting the Information Center concept will be a major function of the data processing group.

Another major DP responsibility in a well-organized corporation will be the coordination of the software package evaluation and implementation activities. In any situation where the demand is high and product expertise is low, a certain number of unscrupulous businessmen will emerge. The DP professionals, with their keen awareness of the potential shortcomings and limitations of the purchased software must be responsible for protecting the unwary user from overzealous software salespersons. DP professionals will also be responsible for ensuring continuous support and maintenance of the purchased software. In this brave new world, the DP organization will be regarded more as a major service to the corporation, similar to personnel or payroll. Finally, DP will have reached maturity, the ultimate stage of Nolan's DP organizational life cycle, described in Chapter 13.

Prior to this state of nirvana being reached, and during the transitional period from today's environment to Nolan's maturity, the use of programming body shops will increase as the task of coding from the very clear structured program specifications becomes more and more routine. Eventually, of course, the application coding activity and the body shops will disappear, having been superceded by application generators, nonprocedural languages, and software packages.

Does all this mean the demise of the profession of programmer as we know it today? If the profession remains as it is today, the answer is yes. But change is a way of life for the DP professional. The role of the application development programmer will change, slowly but surely, into that of support programmer. He will become the system programmer for those software systems to serve as the tool by which the users will develop their own DP applications. There is and will be enough of this activity to keep all of today's application programmers busy and to provide healthy growth in the profession for the future. For those programmers who love to program in the traditional way, the software houses and the manufacturers of application generators, database management systems, future operating systems, and other user-friendly artifacts will have a permanent need for them.

Therefore, few breakthroughs are required to make the DP department the fully professional, effective part of business that it should be. All of the techniques, methodologies, tools, and technology are available today. What we as DP professionals must do is to break away from the traditions that seem to have so rapidly bound us. The opportunity is here to profoundly influence the future; all we have to do is to grasp this opportunity and make full use of it. As someone once said (and it wasn't Edsger Dijkstra), "We have nothing to lose but our chains."

APPENDICES

Be not dismayed nor be surprised
If what you do is criticized.
Mistakes are made, I'll not deny
But are only made by those who try.
— Anonymous

Appendix A
A Practical Set of Life Cycle Techniques

In this book, I present an overview of the techniques, methods, and methodologies available today to help the manager and DP system developers carry out their project-related tasks effectively, efficiently, and consistently. I also explain how the many structured techniques can be applied in the context of the system development life cycle. In order to learn any of these techniques effectively, the DP system developers need to invest significant time in a detailed investigation of the available literature and training courses. Additionally, whichever courses and techniques are chosen, some customization will likely be necessary by the particular organization receiving the training and using the techniques.

The first problem that the system developer recognizes in this investigation is the large number of available techniques. Clearly, one cannot utilize all of these new ideas during the development of a single system. Unfortunately, some large projects have tried just this approach, with the results ranging from no improvements and increased costs to total disaster. Project management needs a set of clear guidelines for indicating when and where to use each of these techniques and a set of reliable criteria for choosing between them. This book, particularly this appendix, provides a menu of techniques and some opinions as to their preferred usage.

The first technique to be chosen is one that provides a convenient framework to contain all of the other techniques. This first technique is, of course, the much-discussed system development life cycle. At the very least, a set of life cycle stages must be agreed upon with clearly defined stage end products by the DP system developers within the organization. To define where the techniques described in this chapter fit, I will use the seven life cycle stages discussed in Chapters 5 through 12 as a framework: Feasibility Study, Requirements Definition, System Specification, System Design, Program Design and Development, System Test, and Implementation and Production.

If some of the modern techniques such as application generators, prepackaged software, and user-written applications are chosen, the life cycle may be shortened considerably and fewer of the other techniques will be necessary.

Feasibility Study

The specific techniques selected for this stage of the life cycle depend largely upon the size of the study itself. As discussed in Chapter 6, the effort expended on the Feasibility Study can vary enormously. It may be as little as the time that it takes the Chief Executive Officer to say, "I want it!" or it may involve a team of five expensive consultants for six months or more. The more significant the effort, the more likely it is that specific techniques will be used. Since the Feasibility Study is such an organization-dependent entity, it is not easy to define generally usable techniques, but they should include payback schedule graphs and estimating techniques.

Requirements Definition

In this stage, when the user requirements of the proposed system are pinned down, a Ranking Matrix can help set the relative priorities of the individual requirements. Since the system data dictionary is begun in this stage, any available automated documentation technique can be used to create and store the Requirements Definition document.

For perhaps the first time, walkthroughs should be employed to review the user's requirements, with data flow diagrams providing a graphic view of the user's idea of the system.

Since the original project estimate is refined in this stage, the estimating techniques and the payback schedule graphs are again used. In fact, these two estimating-related techniques are applied in almost every stage of the life cycle, because the phase-limited commitment concept provides for reestimation of the next stage and of the remainder of the project at the end of each life cycle stage.

In summary, the life cycle techniques and methods employed during the Requirements Definition stage are payback schedule graphs, estimating techniques, Ranking Matrix, system data dictionary, automated documentation, walkthroughs, data flow diagrams, and team organization.

System Specification

In the System Specification stage, the user requirements are translated into data processing terms. The techniques needed are the same as those in the previous stage with perhaps a greater use of data flow diagrams and the system data dictionary. In some cases, structure charts and HIPO diagrams are used instead of data flow diagrams.

System Design

At this stage, the Ranking Matrix is used only if a series of alternative designs are proposed, and then it is used more as a Decision Matrix to determine the best design alternative. Additionally, the payback schedule graphs are used extensively as are the estimating techniques in order to determine the relative costs of each of the alternatives.

Other techniques of use in this stage are structure charts and structured English, as well as the functional decomposition type of structured design. If data structured design is to be used for program design, it will probably start to be used in this stage. A project library is also begun by this stage and all of its contents recorded in the system data dictionary.

The list of techniques for this stage is

- payback schedule graphs
- estimating techniques
- Ranking or Decision Matrix
- system data dictionary
- automated documentation
- walkthroughs
- data flow diagrams
- team organization
- structured design (functional decomposition)
- structure charts
- structured English
- data structured design techniques (in some cases)
- project library

Program Design and Development

The Program Design and Development stage is when the system is finally implemented in terms of programs, code, and procedures. Therefore, in addition to all of the above techniques, the chosen methods of structured programming and structured program design must be utilized. If data structured program design is chosen as the design standard, then it has already been used in the previous stage to a certain extent.

It is unlikely at this stage that data flow diagrams will be used or that estimating-related techniques are necessary. Therefore, the list of available techniques for the Program Design and Development stage is

- system data dictionary
- automated documentation
- walkthroughs
- team organization
- structure charts
- structured English
- project library
- structured design (functional decomposition)
- data structured program design
- structured programming

System Test

The complete system is tested by the user organization in this stage to ensure that it will meet all of the requirements and specifications agreed upon in the Requirements Definition stage. Since some changes will probably need to be made to the system as a result of this test, almost all of the previously mentioned techniques are needed to implement these changes.

The system test itself is carried out according to a detailed system test plan, which contains a comprehensive set of test conditions and test criteria. One technique that seems to be effective in determining an all-encompassing set of these criteria and conditions for any one system is cause-effect graphing. The specific activity of developing the system test plan is carried out long before the actual System Test stage.

The complete list of techniques to be used in the System Test stage is as follows:

- system data dictionary
- automated documentation
- walkthroughs
- data flow diagrams
- team organization
- project library
- structure charts
- structured English
- structured design (functional decomposition)
- data structured program design
- structured programming
- cause-effect graphing

Implementation and Production

In this final stage, the project library is initially one of the most important techniques in controlling the installation of the new system. Inevitably, as the new system stabilizes, changes will be requested as a result of errors, new requirements, and desired enhancements to the system. Sometimes, there will be so many change requests outstanding that some ranking must be carried out, and the Ranking Matrix is useful for this purpose. Additionally, if many changes are grouped together to form a release, this release can be viewed as a "mini-project" and its schedule and required resources must be estimated.

The Implementation and Production stage of the new system requires most of the techniques already mentioned:

- estimating techniques
- Ranking Matrix
- system data dictionary
- automated documentation
- walkthroughs
- data flow diagrams
- team organization
- project library
- structure charts
- structured English
- data structured design
- structured programming
- cause-effect graphing

As you can see, the techniques listed above are not only for system development, but also for operation and maintenance of the system following its installation. The post-implementation period of a system's life is normally called maintenance, and this activity can utilize all of the structured techniques. The key is the way in which the maintenance activity is organized. Multiple changes to the system *must* be ranked and grouped together in sets to form significant and meaningful projects.

Figure A1-1 illustrates where in the system development life cycle all of the above techniques can be used. The broken-line parts of the bars in the chart indicate that a technique is not essential in the corresponding part of the life cycle but it is likely to be used or its results utilized.

Chapter 3 takes a close look at the System Design and Program Design and Development stages and recommends a practical implementation of the various structured design techniques. That detailed recommendation should be taken in conjunction with the general, life cycle encompassing recommendations provided here. Of course, the system development life cycle methodology that is chosen is critical, since it will define the stages of the life cycle and the framework into which the project activities will fit.

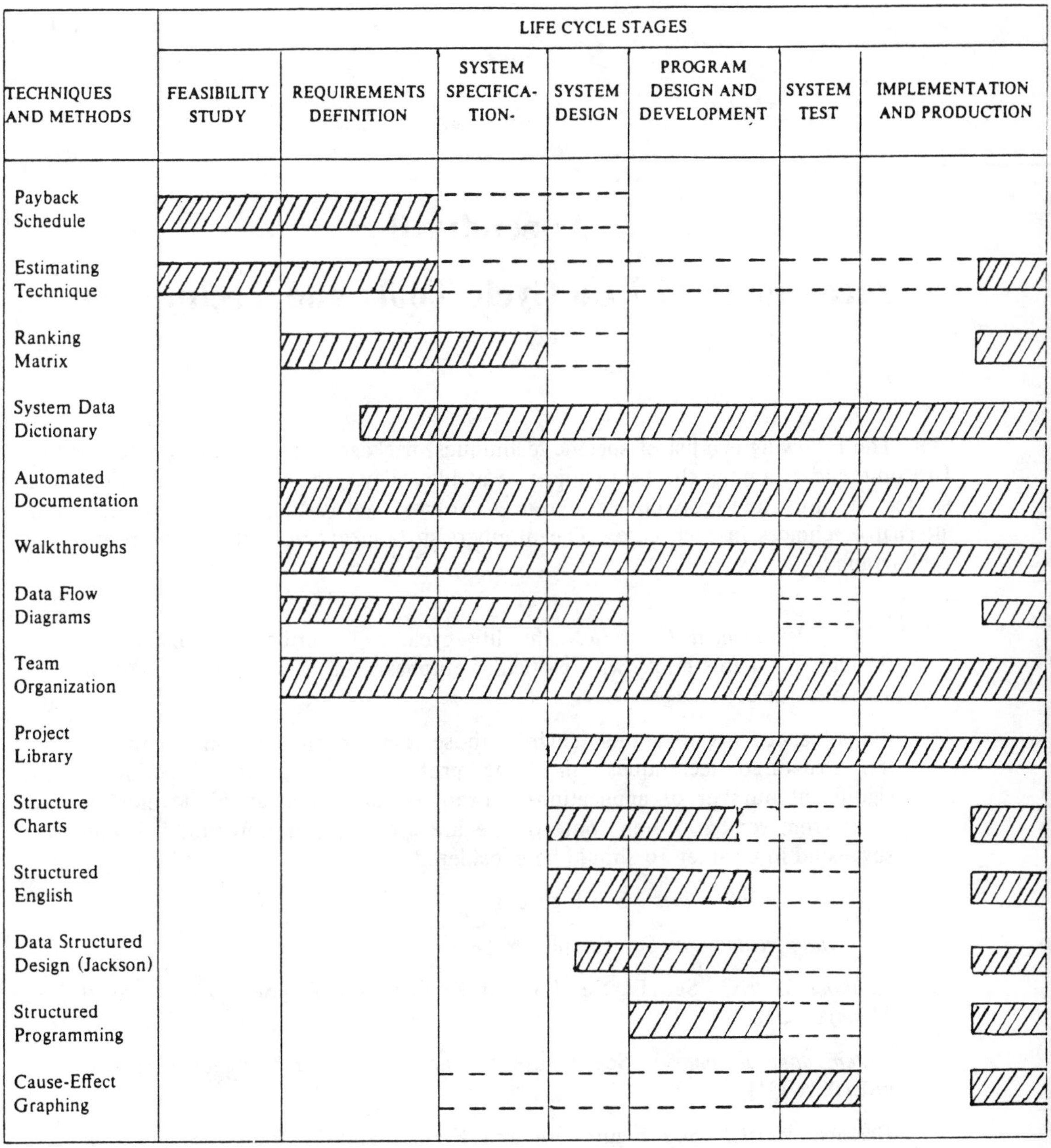
LIFE CYCLE STAGES
TECHNIQUES AND METHODS
FEASIBILITY STUDY
REQUIREMENTS DEFINITION
SYSTEM SPECIFICA-TION-
SYSTEM DESIGN
PROGRAM DESIGN AND DEVELOPMENT
SYSTEM TEST
IMPLEMENTATION AND PRODUCTION
Payback Schedule
Estimating Technique
Ranking Matrix
System Data Dictionary
Automated Documentation
Walkthroughs
Data Flow Diagrams
Team Organization
Project Library
Structure Charts
Structured English
Data Structured Design (Jackson)
Structured Programming
Cause-Effect Graphing

Figure A1-1. How the techniques fit into the life cycle.

Appendix B
Recommended Life Cycle Tools and Techniques

The following is a list of specific techniques, packages, products, and methods that I recommend as among the best choices available today. The reader can use these as a starter set, substitute individual preferences, or carry out further research to determine alternative choices in each case. The numbers in brackets refer to the sources in the Bibliography.

System development life cycle: the life cycle as described in Chapters 5 through 12 of this book, with particular emphasis on use of the flowchart of activities for each stage.

For advanced organizations (such as those that are already using many of the structured techniques, including prototyping, and are installing a significant number of application software packages instead of developing them from scratch), then some of the life cycle acceleration modifications suggested in Chapter 16 should be considered.

Payback schedule charts: See Figure 6-1.

Estimating techniques: See Chapter 6.

Ranking Matrix: See Figure 7-3 and Kepner and Tregoe's *The Rational Manager* [22].

System data dictionary: See Figure 8-2 and also Data Manager [45] and PSL/PSA [51].

Decision Matrix: See Figure 9-4 and Kepner and Tregoe's *The Rational Manager* [22].

Automated documentation: There are not many automated documentation tools available but the Stradis/Draw package [55] now being marketed by McDonnell Douglas Automation seems to be promising.

Data flow diagrams: For the Gane and Sarson methodology, see Chapter 3 and [11, 17, and 43].

Team organization: See the modified chief programmer team organization described in Chapter 13.

Project library: Pansophic Systems' Panvalet package [47] or ADR's Librarian [46].

Structure charts: For the Gane and Sarson methodology, see Chapter 3 and [17, 34, and 43].

Top-down development: See the recommended procedures in Chapter 10.

Structured English: For the Gane and Sarson methodology, see Chapter 3 and [17].

Data-structured program design: For the Jackson design methodology, see Chapter 3 [19].

Structured programming: See the recommended rules in Chapter 4.

Cause-effect graphing: See *The Art of Software Testing* by Myers [27].

Summary

There is probably no one complete or ideal set of techniques for all environments or even for all projects in one environment. However, the list of recommended techniques provided here is a basic set of tools from which the project manager can choose or that he can customize to fit specific needs.

The list is a practical set of basic techniques, and as such it can be used as a basis for a complete life cycle methodology. It can be modified to fit any environment and, if implemented carefully, can be instrumental in producing significantly improved software products.

However, a significant investment in time and resources must be devoted to the implementation, and the improved results may not be seen for two or three years from the start of the new methodology's use. Therefore, top management must be solidly committed to the implementation and use of these methodologies, and this commitment must be regularly made visible to all levels of the DP organization through the use of management presentations, newsletters, and policy decisions.

Nevertheless, these techniques are not altogether new, and some have been used with great success for more than a decade. Therefore, it would be foolish for members of an organization to draw back and say, "They won't work here!" After all, to paraphrase the quotation at the start of the Appendices, you'll never know unless you try.

Bibliography

The following is a list of books, documents, papers, and products that are referred to in the text.

1. *Baker, F.T. "Chief Programmer Team Management of Production Programming." *IBM Systems Journal,* Vol. 11, No. 1 (1972), pp. 56-73.
2. Bentley, C. *Computer Project Management.* Philadelphia: Heyden & Son, 1982.
3. Block, R. *The Politics of Projects.* New York: Yourdon Press, 1983.
4. Boehm, B.W. *Software Engineering Economics.* Englewood Cliffs, N.J.: Prentice-Hall, 1981.
5. Böhm, C. "On a Family of Turing Machines and the Related Programming Language." *ICC Bulletin,* Vol. 3 (July 1964), pp. 187-94.
6. Böhm, C., and G. Jacopini. "Nuove Techniche di Programmazione Semplificanti la Sintesi di Macchine Universali di Turing." *Rend. Acc. Naz. Lincei.,* Vol. 8, No. 32 (June 1962), pp. 913-22.
7. *_______. "Flow Diagrams, Turing Machines and Languages with Only Two Formation Rules." *Communications of the ACM,* Vol. 9, No. 5 (May 1966), pp. 366-71.
8. Cherry, G.W. *Pascal Programming Structures.* Reston, Va.: Reston Publishing, 1980.
9. Chumra, L.B., and H.F. Ledgard. *COBOL with Style: Programming Proverbs.* Rochelle Park, N.J.: Hayden Book Co., 1976.
10. Dahl, O.J., E.W. Dijkstra, and C.A.R. Hoare. *Structured Programming.* New York: Academic Press, 1972.
11. DeMarco, T. *Structured Analysis and System Specification.* New York: Yourdon Press, 1978.
12. *Dijkstra, E.W. "Programming Considered as a Human Activity." *Proceedings of the 1965 IFIP Congress.* Amsterdam, The Netherlands: North-Holland Publishing, 1965, pp. 213-17.
13. *_______. "Go To Statement Considered Harmful." *Communications of the ACM,* Vol. 11, No. 3 (March 1968), pp. 147-48.

14. ______. *A Discipline of Programming.* Englewood Cliffs, N.J.: Prentice-Hall, 1973.

15. †Fagan, M.E. "Design and Code Inspections to Reduce Errors in Program Development." *IBM Systems Journal,* Vol. 15, No. 3 (1976), pp. 182-211.

16. Freeman, P., and A.I. Wasserman. *Tutorial on Software Design Techniques.* IEEE Computer Society, IEEE Catalog No. 76CH1145-2C. New York: 1976.

17. Gane, C., and T. Sarson. *Structured Systems Analysis: Tools & Techniques.* Englewood Cliffs, N.J.: Prentice-Hall, 1979.

18. Gries, D.A. "An Illustration of Current Ideas on the Derivation of Correctness Proofs and Correct Programs." *IEEE Transactions on Software Engineering,* Vol. SE-2, No. 4 (December 1976), pp. 238-44.

19. Jackson, M.A. *Principles of Program Design.* London: Academic Press, 1975.

20. ______. *Systems Development.* Englewood Cliffs, N.J.: Prentice-Hall, 1983.

21. Jones, J.C. "Designing as a Creative Activity," *Beyond Structured Programming.* Maidenhead, U.K.: Infotech International, 1979.

22. Kepner, C.H., and B.B. Tregoe. *The Rational Manager.* New York: McGraw-Hill, 1965.

23. King, D. "Current Methodologies in Structured Design." *Computerworld,* Vol. XV, No. 41 (October 12, 1981), pp. 23-44.

24. ______. "What Is a Walkthrough?" *Telesystems Journal,* Vol. IX, No. 1 (January-February 1982), pp. 1-8.

25. Martin, J. *Computer Database Organization.* Englewood Cliffs, N.J.: Prentice-Hall, 1975.

26. †Mills, H.D. *Mathematical Foundations for Structured Programming.* IBM Corp. Report No. FSC 72-60. 1972.

27. Myers, G.J. *The Art of Software Testing.* New York: Wiley-Interscience, 1979.

28. Nassi, I., and B. Shneiderman. "Flowchart Techniques for Structured Programming," *ACM SIGPLAN Notices,* Vol. 8, No. 8 (August 1973), pp. 12-26.

29. Orr, K.T. *Structured Systems Development.* New York: Yourdon Press, 1977.

30. ______. *Structured Requirements Definition.* Topeka, Kan.: Ken Orr & Associates, 1981.

31. Page-Jones, M. *The Practical Guide to Structured Systems Design.* New York: Yourdon Press, 1980.

32. Ross, D.T. "Structured Analysis (SA) – A Language for Communicating Ideas." *IEEE Transactions on Software Engineering,* Vol. SE-3, No. 1 (January 1977), pp. 6-15.

33. *______, and K.E. Schoman. "Structured Analysis for Requirements Definition." *IEEE Transactions on Software Engineering,* Vol. SE-3, No. 1 (January 1977), pp. 6-15.

34. *Stage by Stage.* Lexington, Mass.: Nolan, Norton and Co.

A quarterly newsletter on issues of importance to the DP professional.

35. *Stevens, W., G. Myers, and L. Constantine. "Structured Design." *IBM Systems Journal,* Vol. 13, No. 2 (May 1974), pp. 115-39.

36. Warnier, J.-D. *Logical Construction of Programs,* 3rd ed., trans. B. Flanagan. New York: Van Nostrand Reinhold, 1976.

37. Welburn, T. *Structured COBOL — Fundamentals and Style.* Palo Alto, Calif.: Mayfield Publishing, 1981.

38. Yourdon, E. *Structured Walkthroughs,* 2nd ed. New York: Yourdon Press, 1978.

39. ______, ed. *Classics in Software Engineering.* New York: Yourdon Press, 1979.

This particular volume is a boon to all of those interested in the evolution of software engineering and structured programming. It contains copies of many of the original landmark papers, letters, and treatises on the subject that have since become classics. All of the references that are preceded by an asterisk appear in this volume.

40. ______. *Managing the Structured Techniques,* 2nd ed. New York: Yourdon Press, 1979.

41. ______. *Managing the System Life Cycle: A Software Development Methodology Overview.* New York: Yourdon Press, 1982.

42. ______, ed. *Writings of the Revolution.* New York: Yourdon Press, 1982.

A companion volume to [39] above. All references preceded by a dagger appear in this volume.

43. ______, and L.L. Constantine. *Structured Design: Fundamentals of a Discipline of Computer Program and Systems Design,* 2nd ed. New York: Yourdon Press, 1978.

Software design methodologies and associated products

44. ARIANE. System development methodology of Philips Corp.

45. Data Manager. Data dictionary system of MSP, Inc.

46. Librarian. Automated library package of ADR, Inc.

47. Panvalet. Automated library package of Pansophic Systems, Inc.

48. PRIDE-ASDM. System development methodology of M. Bryce and Associates, Inc.

49. Program Structured Techniques — PST. Program design technique of Exxon Corp.

50. PROMPT. Project management system of Simpact Systems Ltd.

51. PSL/PSA. Software package of the University of Michigan.

    An industry-sponsored software product for system specification, design, development, and documentation.

52. SADT. Structured analysis and design technique of SofTech, Inc.

53. SDM/70. System development methodology of Atlantic Management Systems, Inc.

54. SPECTRUM. System development methodology of Spectrum International, Inc.

55. Stradis/Draw. Software package of McDonnell Douglas Automation.

    An automated implementation of data flow diagrams and structure charts based on the Gane and Sarson method.

Additional recommended reading

The following books are ones that I've found instructional in informing me or in confirming my own philosophy regarding the process of software development. They may not be to everyone's liking, but they each have something to offer in the interpretation of structure and quality. In addition, they are a change from all those tomes whose titles start with "structured."

56. Drucker, P.F. *Managing in Turbulent Times.* New York: Harper and Row, 1980.

57. Herbert, F. *Dune.* East Rutherford, N.J.: Berkley Medallion Books, 1965.

58. Persig, R.M. *Zen and the Art of Motorcycle Maintenance.* New York: Bantam Books, 1974.

Index